WITH

UTSA LIBRARIES

DATE DUE

The Standard & Poor's Guide to
Building Wealth with Dividend Stocks

THE Standard & Poor's Guide to Building Wealth with Dividend Stocks

JOSEPH R. TIGUE

McGRAW-HILL

New York | Chicago | San Francisco | Lisbon
London | Madrid | Mexico City | Milan | New Delhi
San Juan | Seoul | Singapore | Sydney | Toronto

The *McGraw·Hill* Companies

2 3 4 5 6 7 8 9 0   DOC/DOC   0 9 8 7 6

ISBN 0-07-145782-8

This publication is designed to provide accurate and authoritative information in
regard to the subject matter covered. It is sold with the understanding that the
publisher is not engaged in rendering legal, accounting, or other professional
service. If legal advice or other expert assistance is required, the services of a
competent professional person should be sought.—*From a Declaration of Principles
Jointly Adopted by a Committee of the American Bar Association and a Committee of
Publishers and Associations*

McGraw-Hill books are available at special discounts to use as premiums and
sales promotions, or for use in corporate training programs. For more
information, please write to the Director of Special Sales, Professional
Publishing, McGraw-Hill, Two Penn Plaza, New York, NY 10121-2298. Or contact
your local bookstore.

This book is printed on recycled, acid-free paper containing a minimum of 50%
recycled de-inked paper.

Library of Congress Cataloging-in-Publication Data

Tigue, Joseph.
  The Standard & Poor's guide to building wealth with
dividend stocks / by Joseph R. Tigue.
    p. cm.
  ISBN 0-07-145782-8 (hardcover : alk. paper)
  1. Dividends—United States.   2. Stocks—United States.   3. Portfolio management—
United States.   I. Title.
  HG4028.D5T54 2006
  332.63'22—dc22
                                    2005023348

Contents

Acknowledgments

"No man is an island," as John Donne famously remarked, and that's certainly the case with this book. Without the aid and encouragement of so many colleagues, friends, and family, the author would still be staring at a blank computer screen and a blinking cursor.

My special thanks go out to a host of people at Standard & Poor's, my former stomping grounds for close to 25 years. Howard Silverblatt, S&P's chief massager of the company's impressive data bank, was the source for the many useful tables in this book. Chris Peng, statistician for S&P's flagship newsletter, *The Outlook*, gathered the data for the charts, which were drawn with a skilled hand by Susanna Lee. Joseph Lisanti, editor-in-chief of *The Outlook* acted as a good sounding board, as did Arnold Kaufman, former long-time editor of *The Outlook*.

Jim Dunn, a consultant for Standard & Poor's and former vice president and treasurer of GTE Corp. (now part of Verizon), critiqued the manuscript and came up with some solid, creative suggestions, which I incorporated into the book. Jim also spurred me on; it's the nature of most writers to put off until tomorrow what should be done today.

McGraw-Hill professional Book Group editor Stephen Isaacs did a first-rate job of keeping me focused. Also, thanks to George Gulla, vice president and member of the Standard & Poor's Press Committee, for his valuable input.

Last but not least (I'd better say that or else...), the four women in my life (wife Barbara and daughters Melissa, Elizabeth, and Barbara Susan) deserve my gratitude for putting up with me, not only when writing this book.

Foreword

After being temporarily out of investor favor in the overheated stock market of the late 1990s, dividends have come back with a vengeance. Whereas capital appreciation held the spotlight when the technology sector was king, dividends are now regarded as a key component of one's investment return.

Besides the "bird in the hand" aspect, dividends are popular as the aging baby boomers look to a steady income stream to help pay the bills in their retirement years. And of course, the fact that the tax on dividends is at the same lower 15 percent rate as capital gains has been an important impetus.

Though the favorable tax rate is slated to expire at the end of 2008, many observers (including the author of this book) believe that it will be made permanent or at least extended for a few more years. At this writing, it appears that Congress is leaning toward approval of a two-year extension. But even if the tax break disappears, dividends should still be a key component of your investment program.

In recent years, tomes on dividends have proliferated. What sets apart the book you are holding in your hands? One important distinction is the data and analysis supplied by Standard & Poor's, which is widely regarded as a premier provider of financial information and a prime source of objective stock market research. S&P's 500 stock index is considered *the* market benchmark by professional money managers. In addition, billions of dollars are tied to the S&P 500 via index mutual funds.

What also makes this book unique is its author, Joe Tigue. Joe has had more than 40 years of experience in the investment field, with a specialization in dividends. This is the third book he has authored, and for nearly 25 years, he researched, wrote, and edited feature articles for one of the oldest and most successful investment advisory publications, Standard & Poor's *The Outlook*. He also was the founding editor of *Standard & Poor's Directory of Dividend Reinvestment Plans* and penned a monthly dividend column on the Internet.

I believe Joe's insight and practical advice on how to invest in dividend-paying stocks in the most cost-efficient and advantageous way, as well as his specific recommendations, will help you to make dividends a successful part of your investment plan.

Sam Stovall
Chief Investment Strategist,
Standard & Poor's

The Standard & Poor's Guide to
Building Wealth with Dividend Stocks

Introduction

The considered and continuous verdict of the stock market is over-whelmingly in favor of liberal dividends as against niggardly ones. The common stock investor must take this judgment into account in the valuation of stock for purchase.

—Benjamin Graham and David Dodd, widely regarded as the founders of the valuation approach to security analysis and investing

During the "anyone can make a fortune in the stock market" days of the late 1990s, investors looked on dividend-paying stocks as dinosaurs. They figured: Why buy a stodgy blue chip when you could easily double your money in a biotech or startup Internet company?

A corporation that returned some of its earnings to stockholders in the form of a dividend was thought to be shortsighted. Why couldn't the company make better use of the money? Instead of paying dividends, why not make acquisitions so that profits could grow and stockholders benefit from a resultant higher share price?

That thinking vanished with the devastating market decline of 2000–2002. Those two years saw the S&P 500 index (regarded by professionals as a proxy for the stock market) plunge 49 percent, and the Nasdaq, where the tech high fliers were traded, skid 78 percent. The Nasdaq performance was the worst for any major U.S. market index since the 1930s.

When the market was falling off the edge, corporations began to change their tune. Rather than making acquisitions and/or buying back stock to reduce the number of shares outstanding to boost per-share profits, many companies shifted to initiating dividends or increasing them in order to keep stockholders from selling their positions. From January 1, 2003, through March 31, 2005, 36 companies started to pay dividends for the first time. Twenty-four of those companies also increased them at a later date (Figure 0-1).

In 2002, a two-year downtrend in dividends paid by companies in the S&P 500 was reversed. Dividends climbed 2.1 percent, versus a 3.3 percent drop in 2001 and a 2.5 percent slide in 2000, which represented the first back-to-back declines since 1970-71.

FIGURE 0-1 Recent Dividend Initiators

Cash payments based on ex-dividend dates from January 1 to December 31 of each year

COMPANY	TICKER	SECTOR	YEAR INITIATED	MONTH INITIATED	INCREASED AFTER INITIATION
Amer. Power Conversion	APCC	Industrials	2003	JUN	YES
American Standard	ASD	Industrials	2005	FEB	
Analog Devices	ADI	Information Technology	2003	NOV	YES
Applied Materials	AMAT	Information Technology	2005	MAR	
Best Buy	BBY	Consumer Discretionary	2003	OCT	YES
BJ Services	BJS	Energy	2004	JUL	
Cendant Corp	CD	Industrials	2004	FEB	YES
Citizens Communications	CZN	Telecommunications Services	2004	JUL	
Clear Channel Commun.	CCU	Consumer Discretionary	2003	JUL	YES
Costco Wholesale	COST	Consumer Staples	2004	APR	
Edison Int'l	EIX	Utilities	2003	DEC	YES
Federated Dept Stores	FD	Consumer Discretionary	2003	APR	YES
Freep't McMoRan Copper&Go.	FCX	Materials	2003	FEB	YES
Guidant Corp.	GDT	Health Care	2003	FEB	YES
Harrah's Entertainment	HET	Consumer Discretionary	2003	JUL	YES
Int'l Game Technology	IGT	Consumer Discretionary	2003	JUN	YES
Jones Apparel Group	JNY	Consumer Discretionary	2003	JUL	YES
KLA-Tencor Corp	KLAC	Information Technology	2005	FEB	
Louisiana-Pacific	LPX	Materials	2004	MAY	YES
Manor Care	HCR	Health Care	2003	JUL	YES
Maxim Integrated Prod.	MXIM	Information Technology	2003	FEB	YES
Microsoft Corp.	MSFT	Information Technology	2003	JAN	YES
Noble Corp.	NE	Energy	2005	FEB	
PG&E Corp.	PCG	Utilities	2005	FEB	
Phelps Dodge	PD	Materials	2004	JUN	
QUALCOMM Inc.	QCOM	Information Technology	2003	FEB	YES
Quest Diagnostics	DGX	Health Care	2003	OCT	YES
Reebok Int'l	RBK	Consumer Discretionary	2003	JUL	
Robert Half Int'l	RHI	Industrials	2004	APR	YES
SABRE HoldingsCl A	TSG	Information Technology	2003	APR	YES
Staples Inc.	SPLS	Consumer Discretionary	2004	MAR	YES
Tektronix Inc.	TEK	Information Technology	2003	SEP	YES
Viacom Inc. Cl B	VIA.B	Consumer Discretionary	2003	JUL	YES
Xcel Energy	XEL	Utilities	2003	JUN	YES
Xilinx Inc.	XLNX	Information Technology	2004	APR	
Yum Brands	YUM	Consumer Discretionary	2004	MAY	

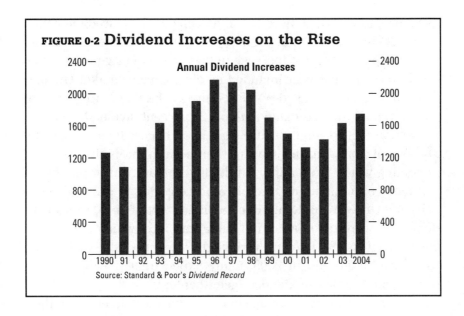

FIGURE 0-2 Dividend Increases on the Rise

Annual Dividend Increases

Source: Standard & Poor's *Dividend Record*

Dividends on the S&P 500 index in the two years following 2002 continued their uptrend, with increases in 2003 and 2004 of 4 and 15.3 percent, respectively. The gain in 2004 was the best since 1977. Also, of the more than 7,000 companies tracked by Standard & Poor's, 1,745 reported dividend increases in 2004, up 7.2 percent from 2003 and the third consecutive yearly rise (Figure 0-2).

The biggest dividend news in 2004 came from Microsoft. The giant software company paid out a special onetime dividend of $3 a share, which amounted to $32 billion and was the largest payout in corporate history. Microsoft also doubled its quarterly dividend to eight cents a share, putting an additional $3.5 billion in stockholders' pockets.

The generous payout helped pacify Microsoft shareholders, who, because of the company's slowing revenue growth and other problems, saw little or no appreciation in the stock after a knockout performance in the 1990s. At the same time, Microsoft was sitting with a cash hoard of $56 billion.

Other companies, though not on the same scale as Microsoft, also were more generous with dividends. In 2004, McDonald's, which had been out of favor with investors because of lagging sales and not using profits wisely, showed that it had changed its direction with a new CEO by upping its dividend by 70 percent, the behemoth fast food company's biggest increase in 25 years. Other generous dividend hikers in that year included medical-devices maker Guidant Corp. and Chicago-based power company, Exelon Corp., both of which treated their stockholders to a 25 percent dividend boost.

Several factors suggest that it's a good bet we'll see a growing number of corporations sharing their wealth via higher payouts in coming years. Most important is the dramatic cut in the tax on dividends to a maximum rate of 15 percent, due to passage of the Jobs and Growth Tax Relief Reconciliation Act of 2003. Previously, dividends were taxed at an individual tax rate, which could have been as high as 38.6 percent. Though the lower tax rate is scheduled to expire at the end of 2008, many expect that it will be made permanent or at least extended (see Chapter 2).

Another reason for companies to be more beneficent with their dividends is the heavy cash stashes in corporate coffers. At the end of 2004, companies in the S&P 500 were sitting with $600 billion of the long green (Figure 0-3). Investors have made it known that they

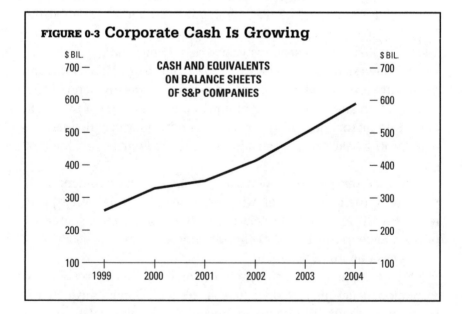

FIGURE 0-3 Corporate Cash Is Growing

CASH AND EQUIVALENTS
ON BALANCE SHEETS
OF S&P COMPANIES

prefer cash dividends to costly mergers and acquisitions, which often prove disastrous. At the same time, with the lower dividend tax rate, corporate honchos will be big beneficiaries from increases in payouts since they normally own large chunks of stock. For example, Microsoft chairman Bill Gates reaped $3.35 billion as a result of the company's special $3 dividend in 2004.

With investors now geared toward hard cash, dividends are becoming an important ingredient in initial public offerings (IPOs) and takeover deals. Valor Communications Group, which offers local and long distance telephone services in Arkansas, New Mexico, Oklahoma, and Texas, went public in 2005 and paid an annual dividend of $1.44 a share. Verizon's 2005 offer for MCI included a $4.50 dividend, while MCI's competing offer from Qwest Communications included $6 in dividends.

Managements are also aware that there will be a growing number of retirees hungry for income. The oldest baby boomers turned 59 in 2005 (there are 76 million boomers), and with pensions doing a disappearing act, they will look to dividend-paying stocks and mutual funds for steady income streams.

Finally, all investors will rely more on dividends over the next several years to fatten their returns. According to Standard & Poor's, stock prices may appreciate on average only about 6 percent annually in the near future, so the dividend component of total return will become crucial. (Total return is the price change of a stock or index plus the dividends.)

In this book we'll show you why dividends are key to a successful financial future and how to make them work for you to maximize your investment returns. The first part will guide you on what to look for in determining the better-situated dividend stocks; the second part includes write-ups of some of our favorites. In addition, in the appendices you'll find a listing of companies in the S&P 1500 index (which consists of the S&P 500, the S&P Mid Cap 400, and the S&P Small Cap 600) that have dividend reinvestment plans (DRIPs), as well as a table of these DRIP companies that have five-year dividend growth rates over 6 percent, and a list of the 100 largest S&P 500 companies.

By the way, we highly recommend joining DRIPs, particularly those that permit you to buy directly from the companies. Direct purchase plans offer an excellent low-cost, convenient way for long-term investors to build sizable portfolios over the years, while reaping the benefits of dollar cost averaging (see Chapter 6).

Our belief is that the simple strategies outlined in this book will work for you as well as they have for the author.

CHAPTER 1

Why Dividends Are a Key Factor in a Successful Investment Program

Investors learned a hard lesson when the stock market tanked in March 2000. Most of the action in the previous roaring bull market was in technology and biotech stocks that didn't pay a dividend. When these issues went down the tubes, stockholders were left with sudden, deep losses. Those who held shares of companies that paid dividends in the bear market fared much better. Not only did these investors have the dividend as a consolation prize, but the stocks performed better than the go-go nondividend payers.

Stocks in the S&P 500 index that paid dividends in 2000 climbed nearly 16 percent, while nondividend payers slipped more than 2 percent. On average, in the latest three bear market years, 2000–2002, the dividend payers in the index roughly broke even, while the nondividend stocks fell 35 percent. In 2004 dividend-paying stocks in the S&P 500 had a total return (appreciation plus dividends) of 18.2 percent, compared with 13.2 percent in 2003. From 2001 to 2004 dividend payers in the S&P 500 rose 40.5 percent, versus a 27.4 percent gain for nonpayers (Figure 1-1). Over a longer period—from 1975 to 2005—dividend payers in the S&P 500 racked up an annual increase of 10.2 percent, while nondividend-paying

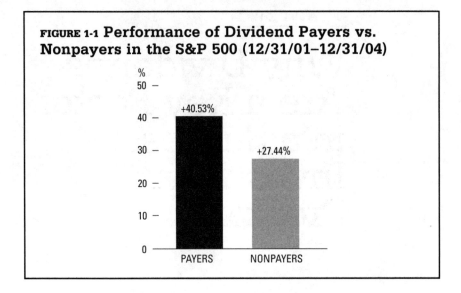

FIGURE 1-1 **Performance of Dividend Payers vs. Nonpayers in the S&P 500 (12/31/01–12/31/04)**

stocks in the index advanced at an annual rate of only 4.4 percent. In the past 75 years, there have been 10-year periods where dividends have provided the only return for the S&P 500.

So one reason to own dividend payers is the stability they provide. These stocks are far less volatile than the nonpayers. Over the past 25 years the returns from nondividend-paying stocks were some 50 percent more volatile than the returns from stocks that paid high dividends. In other words, dividend payers tend to be safer investments and offer a degree of comfort in a declining market, as well as good returns.

From 1980 through mid-2005 dividend payers outpaced nonpayers by 3 percentage points a year. The more favorable tax treatment of dividends, which we mentioned in the introduction and will go into in more detail in the next chapter, makes dividend payers even more attractive.

Why There's Less Volatility

Dividend payers fluctuate less because, when stock prices are falling, investors have a monetary incentive to hang on to them. They can still look forward to periodic payments, usually every three months, despite the lower value of the stock price. In a strongly rising market, shares of companies that pay dividends don't normally appreciate as much as the nondividend payers. Keep in mind, though, that many studies have shown solid dividend-paying stocks and mutual funds that emphasize dividends outperform their aggressive brethren over the long term. (See *The Standard & Poor's Guide to Long-Term Investing: 7 Keys to Building Wealth*, Joseph Tigue, McGraw-Hill.)

An example of the support a good dividend lends to a stock is Bank of America (ticker symbol: BAC). In 2003, when it was the number two bank in the United States, Bank of America announced that it would buy Fleet Boston Financial for $47 billion. Securities analysts believed the price was too high and downgraded BAC. The stock was then paying a hefty dividend of $3.20 a share and yielded 3.9 percent. The analysts' downgrade had little effect on the stock, which fell less than 10 percent, mainly because of the plump dividend.

The shares also were little affected when, before the merger was completed, Bank of America and Fleet Boston agreed to a $675 million resolution to allegations of improper mutual fund trading. The merger was consummated in 2004 for $48.8 billion, and the shares have done well since then. A two-for-one stock split occurred in August 2004, and the $1.80 dividend paid in early 2005 yielded 3.9 percent, the same yield at the time the merger was announced.

Dividends and Compounding Power

Another way to look at dividends is that over time they reduce the cost of your original purchase price. If you hold a dividend-paying stock for a certain number of years—particularly one that boosts its payout regularly—your dividends could eventually cover what you paid for the shares. This works because of the power of compounding. Or the way your investment increases as it earns a return on the initial money you invested and on the interest and dividends earned. The money grows exponentially. For instance, if you own a stock that pays a dividend of $1 a share and the payment increases at 10 percent annually, the dividend will double every seven years. So at the end of 28 years, the dividend will amount to $16 per share.

In terms of yield (the dividend divided by the price of the shares), consider this example: If ABC stock yields 1 percent when you buy it and the dividend doubles every five years, your yield would amount to 16 percent on your original investment in 20 years.

The bird in the hand aspect of dividend payers is a key reason for owning them. But in addition to getting a tangible return on your investment regardless of what the stock or the general market does, a combination of price appreciation and the dividend is a powerful force in the long run. Historically, dividends have accounted for 41 percent of the S&P 500's total return. In the 20 years through 2003, the S&P 500 climbed 370 percent, but with dividends reinvested, that number jumps to more than 880 percent (Figure 1-2).

Put another way: $1 invested in the S&P 500 in 1930 was worth $54 in 2004 without dividends reinvested. With dividends reinvested, however, the figure balloons to $1,189. We'll get into reinvesting dividends and the resultant compounding and dollar cost averaging benefits in Chapter 6.

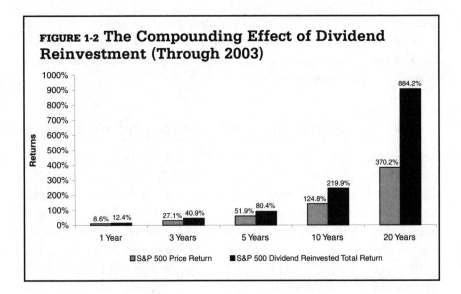

FIGURE 1-2 The Compounding Effect of Dividend Reinvestment (Through 2003)

Dividends Are Real

Another important advantage is that, unlike a company's earnings, dividends can't be manipulated. In recent years we've seen many instances of corporations cooking the books. The more notorious include WorldCom and Enron, both of which declared bankruptcy after years of fraudulent accounting.

Consider, for instance, Federal National Mortgage Co. (known as Fannie Mae), the largest mortgage lender in the United States and chartered by Congress to promote liquidity in the mortgage market. The company was forced by the Securities and Exchange Commission to restate its earnings from 2001 through mid-2004 by $9 billion because it violated accounting rules in order to smooth out its volatile earnings. (In early 2004, Fannie Mae announced that it would halve its first-quarter dividend in order to meet its regulator's minimum capital requirements. That marked its first dividend cut since 1981.) Fannie Mae's borrowers tend to prepay their mortgages when interest rates decline, as they refinance, and to slow prepayments considerably when rates increase. The other big mortgage lender—Federal Home Loan (Freddie Mac)—had experienced similar accounting problems a year earlier.

According to the U.S. General Accounting Office, 10 percent of all publicly traded companies restated their earnings at least once since 1997. In 2004, Huron Consulting Group estimated that the number of annual earnings restatements by publicly held companies surged to a high of 253, a 23 percent jump from 206 in 2003. Another 161 companies in 2004 restated their quarterly profit statements, versus 117 in 2003.

So, to repeat, profits can be manipulated, but dividends cannot. They are either paid or not paid, increased or not increased. There can be no sleight of hand.

It's hard to argue with Jeremy Siegel, the well-regarded Wharton School professor and author of the best-selling *Stocks for the Long Run*, who said: "I believe that more attention will be paid to dividends and current earnings and less to growth. There are increasing questions about the quality of earnings. By and large, companies that are paying dividends have to have earnings. They can't do that with smoke and mirrors."

Further, former Federal Reserve chairman Alan Greenspan commented: "Earnings are very difficult to estimate; cash dividends are not. Fifty years ago, people bought stocks for dividends; they did not buy them for earnings. And one of the problems that we did not have back then is earnings manipulations; they were not very important because nobody cared."

A company that has paid a dividend over a long period usually can boast of well-established products or services and steadily increasing revenues, profits, and cash flow. Continuance of the payout, moreover, reflects management's confidence that the corporation will remain healthy.

In their 1997 study, Professors Eugene F. Fama, of the University of Chicago Graduate School of Business, and Kenneth R. French, of the Tuck School of Business, Dartmouth College, maintain that dividends contain positive, otherwise unavailable information about a company's earnings. Boards of directors use dividend policy announcements to signal private information about their companies. The signal is credible if other firms whose future prospects are not as good cannot mimic the dividend policy actions of firms with better prospects. Another study found that companies about to experience permanent, large increases in cash flow raised their dividends before the cash flow increased.

A Brief History

Corporations in the United States began to have dividend policies in the second half of the eighteenth century. In 1781, the charter of the Bank of North American specified that the board pay generous dividends regularly out of profits. In 1790, the charter of Bank of the United States specified payment of semiannual dividends. Statutes and laws regulating dividends followed. In 1925, New York enacted a law that prevented payment of dividends from sources other than corporate profits. And in 1830, Massachusetts prohibited dividends if the firm was insolvent or could become insolvent if dividend payments were made.

In the second half of the nineteenth century, manufacturing companies usually paid 8 percent of their profits in dividends. The lack of other operating and financial information about corporations made investors look toward stable and growing dividends as a tool in valuing shares. Corporate managers recognized this, and by the early twentieth century corporations began to boost dividends on a regular basis.

For the past 75 years, dividends have been influenced by tax policies, market cycles, and the prevailing wisdom on payouts. Tax relief on dividends generally increased payouts. Following the crash of 1929, corporations paid as much as 80 percent of their earnings in dividends to restore faith in the markets. New Deal legislation in 1938 actually created a tax on undistributed profits, based on the premise that corporate hoarding of profits was one of the causes of the Great Depression.

After World War II, until the late 1960s, capital gains were taxed at 25 percent, while dividends were taxed at a much higher income tax rate. This led to a slow drop-off in payout ratios. From the late 1960s to mid-1970s, capital gains taxes rose to 39 percent, which led to an improvement in payout ratios (dividends as a percentage of earnings).

For a short period in the early 1970s, dividend payments were also restricted as part of a broad package of measures to curb inflation. Then, beginning at the end of the 1970s, a set of tax cuts drastically reduced capital gains taxes. Income taxes were also reduced, and in 1986 taxes on dividends and capital gains were made equal. This situation was soon reversed, and by the 1990s, dividends were again unfavorably taxed vis-à-vis capital gains, and the S&P 500 payout ratio dropped to all-time lows. In 2003, parity between taxes on dividends and capital gains was restored.

Until 1958, stock yields were greater than bond yields. Following a stock market rally in that year, stock yields dropped below bond yields for the first time, and that situation has continued to this day.

Some Characteristics of Dividends

They Say Something About a Company

Companies that pay dividends tend to be more thoughtful about where to invest their capital. A nondividend paying corporation, flush with cash, will be tempted to go on an acquisition binge. And studies have shown that two-thirds of acquisitions don't work out.

Business Week magazine found that of the mergers and acquisitions that occurred in 1990–95, 83 percent of the deals achieved, at best, marginal returns, while 50 percent recorded a loss.

Examples of corporate marriage mishaps abound. Some of the more notable are the acquisitions of Time Warner by AOL, Chrysler by Daimler Benz, Columbia Pictures by Coca-Cola, NCR by AT&T, Snapple by Quaker Oats, and, more recently, Compaq Computer by Hewlett-Packard. The last was such a fiasco that it led to the ousting of chief executive Carly Fiorina, who was considered the most powerful woman in corporate America.

They Can Usually Be Counted On

Once companies start to pay a dividend, they are reluctant to cut or omit it. Reducing the payment or doing away with it, particularly after a long history of rewarding shareholders with steady dividends, sends a decidedly negative signal to investors. An unfavorable dividend action usually means the company's financial picture is dimming and management has less confidence in the future. Even during the Great Depression of the 1930s and the heart-stopping market plunge of 2000–2002, relatively few companies cut their payments.

Good Income Stream

Retirees and others looking for a steady source of income would do well to assemble a portfolio of stocks similar to those in Figure 1-3. The 18 stocks are grouped according to the dates on which they usually pay quarterly dividends. There are three stocks in each of six payment time slots: (1) early in the first, fourth, seventh, and tenth month of the year; (2) in the middle of those months; (3) early in the

FIGURE 1-3 Steady Dividend Stream

	QUALITY RANKING	INDICATED DIVIDEND RATE ($)	NUMBER OF SHARES	QUARTERLY DIVIDEND RECEIVED
1️⃣ EARLY JAN., APRIL, JULY, OCT.				
Alltel/AT	A-	0.38	135	51
Altria Group/MO	A+	0.73	70	51
AmSouth Bancorp/ASO	A-	0.25	200	50
2️⃣ MID-JAN., APRIL, JULY, OCT.				
BCE Inc./BCE	B+	0.33	150	50
Sempra Energy/SRE	B+	0.29	175	51
Trizec Properties/TRZ	B-	0.20	250	50
3️⃣ EARLY FEB., MAY, AUG., NOV.				
National City Corp./NCC	A	0.35	145	51
RPM International/RPM	A-	0.15	335	50
Vornado Realty Trust/VNO	A-	0.76	70	53
4️⃣ MID-FEB., MAY, AUG., NOV.				
Hospitality Properties Trust/HPT	NR	0.72	70	50
Oneok/OKE	A-	0.25	200	50
Washington Mutual/WM	A	0.46	110	51
5️⃣ EARLY MARCH, JUNE, SEPT., DEC.				
Deluxe Corp./DLX	B+	0.40	125	50
Exelon Corp./EXC	B	0.40	125	50
Hudson United Bancorp/HU	B+	0.37	140	52
6️⃣ MID-MARCH, JUNE, SEPT., DEC.				
Bank of Hawaii/BOH	B+	0.33	155	51
Dominion Resources/D	B+	0.67	75	50
Wachovia Corp./WB	A-	0.46	110	51

second, fifth, eight, and eleventh months; (4) in the middle of those months; (5) early in the third, sixth, ninth, and twelfth months; (6) in the middle of those months.

By purchasing just six of these issues (one in each time slot) you would receive two dozen dividend checks annually, with income from these shares spaced fairly evenly (twice a month) through the year.

For example, to receive a semimonthly income of about $50, you could buy 75 shares of Altria Group, 200 shares of Sempra Energy, 155 shares of National City Corp., 70 shares of Hospitality Properties Trust, 135 shares of Deluxe Corp., and 165 shares of Bank of Hawaii. (The portfolio is for illustrative purposes only. The dividends likely have changed since publication of the portfolio in Standard & Poor's *Outlook* in February 4, 2004.

Stodgy Dividend Payer or Hot Growth Stock?

A good example of the effectiveness of a stock that pays a fairly high dividend versus one that pays a small one or doesn't pay one at all was clearly demonstrated in Jeremy Siegel's book *The Future for Investors*. The Wharton professor of finance compared Standard Oil of New Jersey and International Business Machines. He found that Standard Oil of New Jersey, which became Esso, then Exxon, and in 1998 ExxonMobil, outperformed IBM by 0.6 percent annually over a 53-year period (1950–2003) with dividends reinvested. That difference doesn't seem to amount to a hill of beans (to quote Rick in *Casablanca*), but compounded, the humdrum oil company beat the then tech leader by 32 percent.

While IBM's sales, profits, and even dividends rose faster than those of ExxonMobil, IBM's stock in 1950 yielded only about 2 percent, compared with ExxonMobil's 5 percent yield. ExxonMobil's lower valuation, higher dividends, and the opportunity to reinvest dividends in additional lower-priced high-yielding shares more than made up for the large difference in earnings growth.

Professor Siegel found that a portfolio consisting of the 100 top-yielding stocks in the S&P 500 beat the index by 3 percentage points annually and outpaced the lowest-yielding 100 S&P stocks by almost 5 points. The highest-yielding quintile was slightly more volatile than the "500" index, but the lowest-yielding stocks were the riskiest of all.

In a Nutshell

For an investment program to be truly successful, we believe that dividends must play an important role. Dividends account for a large part of the stock market's total return. And dividend payers are not only less volatile than nonpayers, but also tend to be of a higher quality. Finally, studies have shown that their long-term market performance is superior to stocks of companies that don't pay dividends.

Dividends, which are per-share cash payments to stockholders from a company's earnings, are declared by the board of directors. The board decides how often it will declare a dividend—usually every three months, although some dividends are paid annually or semiannually—and the two dates associated with the dividend. The first is the record date, which is the date the books of the corporation are closed; shareholders who are on record at the end of that day will receive a dividend. Since virtually all stock trades are settled in three business days, you must buy the shares at least three days before the record date in order to be the shareholder of record.

After the record date, the stock is traded ex-dividend (without the dividend). The price of the stock is reduced by the amount of the dividend that has been declared because the purchaser will not get the current dividend.

The second date is the distributions date—sometimes called the payable date. This is the date the dividend will actually be paid to shareholders. It may be a few days or several weeks after the record date.

Points to Remember

➤ Stocks that pay dividends are less volatile and carry less risk than nondividend payers; they hold up better in down stock markets.

➤ Over the long term, studies have shown that shares of dividend payers usually outperform those companies that don't pay dividends.

➤ Dividends historically have accounted for more than 40 percent of the stock market's total return.

➤ Dividend-paying stocks provide a steady income stream. (For an example of how you can set up a portfolio that gives you two dozen dividend checks annually, see Figure 1–3.)

➤ Over time, dividends could eventually cover what you paid for the shares.

➤ Unlike earnings, dividends can't be manipulated.

➤ Companies that have paid dividends over a long period usually boast of well-established, quality products or services and steadily increasing revenues, profits, and cash flow.

CHAPTER 2

The More Favorable Dividend Tax Rate

As we mentioned, dividends, which have accounted for a large part of total return through the years—more than 40 percent—became even more attractive with passage of the Jobs and Growth Tax Relief Reconciliation Act of 2003. This major tax cut package, the third largest in U.S. history, became a law in May 2003 and was made retroactive to January 1 of that year.

President Bush originally wanted to completely eliminate the dividend tax, citing its double taxation aspect; that is, corporations pay taxes on profits, out of which they pay dividends, and then individuals pay taxes on the dividends when they receive them. While the new tax law didn't change the taxes that corporations pay on earnings, it did drastically reduce shareholders' dividend tax rates. For those in the top four federal income tax brackets, the dividend tax was dropped to 15 percent. (Under the old law, if you had dividend income of $25,000 and were in the top tax bracket, of 38.6 percent, you would pay $9,650 in ordinary income taxes; under the new law, you pay only $3,750—a 61 percent saving, or $5,900.) The tax on dividends is now only 5 percent for shareholders in the 10 percent and 15 percent income tax brackets.

Some critics complained that the reduction in the dividend tax rate benefited only the rich. But in fact more than 45 percent of taxpayers who report dividend income earn less than $50,000 annually.

The Jobs and Growth Tax Relief Reconciliation Act also reduced the tax on long-term capital gains rates. Gains on the sale of securities held for more than one year for shareholders in the top four federal tax brackets fell to 15 percent from 20 percent. Those in the 10 percent and 15 percent brackets, formerly taxed at a 10 percent capital gains rate, are taxed at 5 percent. Short-term capital gains (gains realized under 12 months) continue to be taxed at the higher ordinary income rates.

As of this writing, the lower dividend and capital gain tax rates are scheduled to expire at the end of 2008, though it's expected that President Bush, with the support of a Republican majority in Congress, will be successful in making the cuts permanent or pushing back the date.

The reduced rates, as we've seen, have increased the demand for dividend-paying stocks and have triggered a growing number of companies to either initiate dividends or to boost them. We saw a similar reaction in 1981 when the capital gains tax was slashed from ordinary income rates as high as 50 percent to 20 percent for gains on stocks held more than a year. The move set the stage for a strong economic expansion and a roaring bull market. The S&P 500 index began its surge in August 1982, rocketing 1,426 percent to its peak in March 2000. (Figure 2-1 shows the annualized total return of the S&P 500 from December 31, 1969 through November 30, 2004). The Jobs and Growth Tax Relief Reconciliation Act, with its twin cuts in capital gains and dividend taxes, could well have a similar effect on the stock market.

Holding Periods

An important proviso in the 2003 tax law is the holding period. In order to benefit from the lower rate, you must hold a stock for more than 60 days during the 121-day period that begins 60 days before the ex-dividend date (the day that a stock trades without the dividend, which is the last date on which a shareholder of record is entitled to

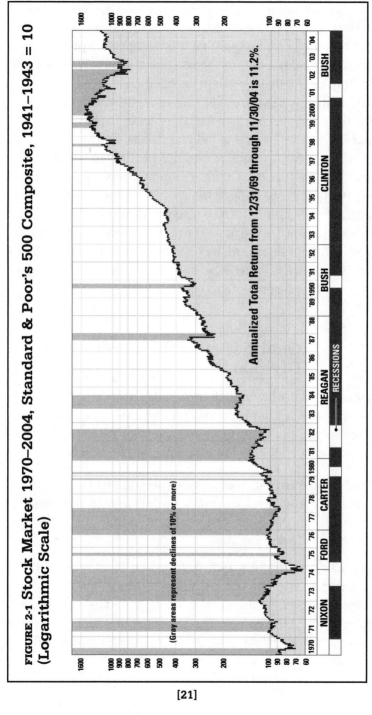

FIGURE 2-1 Stock Market 1970–2004, Standard & Poor's 500 Composite, 1941–1943 = 10 (Logarithmic Scale)

Annualized Total Return from 12/31/69 through 11/30/04 is 11.2%.

(Gray areas represent declines of 10% or more)

RECESSIONS

NIXON FORD CARTER REAGAN BUSH CLINTON BUSH

[21]

receive the upcoming dividend). In other words, you can buy a stock up to 60 days (but at least one day) before the ex-dividend date.

The holding period requirement is designed to prevent investors from using dividend-capture strategies that involve buying stocks just before the ex-dividend date in order to receive the dividend and then immediately sell the stock while benefiting from the tax breaks.

The dividends you receive from mutual funds have the same holding period requirement as individual stocks. Your mutual fund company will notify you concerning the portion of dividends that is eligible for the qualified tax treatment. However, you must still satisfy the holding period for the mutual fund shares you purchase.

Mutual fund companies will also notify you if your dividends are ordinary, which are taxed at your regular income tax rate and include interest from bonds and money market funds, or nonqualified dividends (which we'll discuss below), and whether capital gains are long-term—which benefit from the lower tax—or short-term—which do not.

Qualified and Nonqualified Dividends

Under the 2003 tax law, not all dividends are created equal. Qualified dividends, which take in nearly all common stock dividends, are eligible for the lower 15 percent rate after 60 days. Nonqualified dividends, which include the following, are not eligible:

Real estate investment trusts. Because REITs are tax exempt at the corporate level, their dividends generally won't qualify. Distributions in the form of long-term capital gains, though, will receive the 15 percent rate.

Certain preferred stock dividends. Most preferred stock is structured as debt to receive an interest expense deduction at the corporate level, so the dividend is regarded as interest and does not qualify. Many companies, however, are expected to restructure their preferred stock or issue new stock to qualify for the 15 percent rate.

Certain foreign stock dividends. Dividends from foreign stocks traded as American Depositary Receipts (ADRs) on a U.S. exchange will qualify. The 15 percent rate also applies to foreign companies based in U.S. territories, such as Puerto Rico or Guam, as well as to companies traded in a foreign country that has an established tax treaty with the United States. Other foreign stock dividends do not qualify for the lower tax rate.

Miscellaneous. Excluded from the new tax law are dividends paid and held by an employee stock plan (ESOP), and dividends paid on insurance policies and money market funds, as well as dividends paid by mutual savings banks and charities. Also, if you borrow to buy stocks on margin and your broker lends out your stock, you don't receive dividends but "payment in lieu of dividends," which is treated as ordinary income and is not eligible for the favorable tax treatment.

Taxable vs. Tax-Deferred Accounts

The change in the tax law suggests a change in strategy when it comes to investing in tax-deferred accounts, such as 401(k) plans and IRAs (Individual Retirement Accounts), and in taxable accounts. Under the old law, dividend-paying stocks were best held in tax-deferred retirement accounts because of the higher taxes imposed on dividends. Now, with the tax at only 15 percent, it may make more sense to hold dividend payers in a taxable account.

Mutual funds and individual stocks with unrealized losses should also be held in a taxable account. When you or the fund sell the losing stocks, you receive capital loss carry-forwards, which can offset future gains, essentially lowering taxable capital gains in your account. *You can't realize losses for tax purposes in a tax-deferred account.*

In addition, international stocks and funds should be held in a taxable account. That's because investors who pay foreign taxes can receive a tax credit, which is lost if the foreign equities are held in a tax-deferred account.

For tax-deferred accounts, the following investments are suitable:

Real estate investment trusts (REITs). As discussed, these issues do not qualify for the lower tax rate.

Bonds. The income from most bonds is federally taxed at ordinary income rates. Municipal bonds, however, don't belong in a tax-deferred account since they are already tax-free. Also, Treasury bonds are not subject to state or local taxes.

Treasury Inflation-Protected Securities (TIPS). Income from these securities is subject to ordinary income taxes, even though it is free from state or local taxes. Although you don't receive any inflation-adjusted additions to your principal (which is imputed interest) until you redeem the bond, all annual interest payments are considered ordinary income.

Mid- and small-cap stocks. These issues tend to have the highest long-term growth potential and are least likely to pay dividends.

Benefiting from Lower Tax Rates

Low costs are an essential ingredient in a successful investment program. If, before costs, the stock market returns 10 percent (the average annual total return of the S&P 500 stock index from 1929 to 2004 is 10.1 percent), and the cost of commissions, management fees, and taxes are about 2 percent, then investors earn 8 percent. Compounded over 50 years, 8 percent results in a $10,000 investment climbing to $469,000. But at 10 percent, $10,000 becomes $1,179,000, or more than two and a half times as much.

The lower tax rate on dividends is a big factor in boosting investment returns. For example, if you buy 1,000 shares of ABC Company, which pays an annual dividend of $0.88, and the company raises the payment by 11 percent each year for six years, you will have received $8,600 at the end of seven years. Under the old tax law if you were in the highest 38.6 percent bracket, you would pay $3,320; with the new 15 percent tax rate, your tax bill would be $1,290. That's a saving of $2,030. If you reinvest that saving, and the stock's dividend continued to grow at 11 percent annually over 10 years, compounding would work its magic. Your $2,030 saving would swell to more than $8,000.

Other Tax-Cut Benefits

As the National Center for Policy Analysis observed, the former high dividend tax rate discouraged saving and investment and also prompted corporations to assume more debt because interest on debt is deductible from corporate income for tax purposes. Rising debt levels hurt corporations during recessions, and in some cases result in bankruptcies. With the lower tax on dividends, companies have been encouraged to raise money by selling more shares, rather than by borrowing.

Since dividends represent part of a company's cost of capital, the reduced dividend tax has made it easier for a corporation to return money to investors, because the new law lowered the cost of doing business and the cost of funding new projects. When the cost of capital drops, managements are more inclined to hike their companies' investment in equipment and buildings. These investments typically lead to the creation of new jobs, and in the long run fuel strong economic growth.

Also, a study by Thomson Financial shows that the dollar volume of stock sold by corporate insiders falls off the more a company pays in dividends. The research found that managements of companies in the S&P 500 index whose stock had a 4 percent dividend yield sold only $763,041 worth of stock on average each quarter in a recent five-year period. On the other hand, insiders at corporations that paid no dividend cashed in an average $8.4 million. Even more telling, stocks of companies with heavy insider selling underperformed the New York Stock Exchange average by 11 percent in the six months after insider sales.

All in all, then, the dividend tax cut has widespread advantages to the investor, the corporation, and the economy. If the lower tax rate is made permanent, it no doubt will continue to exert its powerful force.

Points to Remember

> The Jobs and Growth Tax Relief Reconciliation Act of 2003 gave dividend-oriented investors a big break by reducing dividends to a maximum of 15 percent from the old ordinary income tax rates, which ran as high as 38.6 percent. The new law also cut the long-term capital gains rate from 20 percent to 15 percent.

> Though the new tax law is scheduled to expire at the end of 2008, chances are the cuts will be made permanent or at least extended by the Republican Congress.

> To get the benefit of the lower tax rate you must hold a stock or mutual fund for more than 60 days during the 121-day period that begins 60 days before the ex-dividend date.

> Only qualified dividends are eligible for the lower tax rate. But these include nearly all common stock dividends. Nonqualified dividends are those paid by real estate investment trusts (REITs) and certain preferred stock and foreign stock dividends.

> The 2003 tax law in most cases makes it more profitable to keep dividend-paying stocks in a taxable account, as well as international stocks and funds and stocks or funds that have unrealized losses. Real estate investment trusts (REITs), most bonds, Treasury Inflation-Protected Securities (TIPS), and small-cap stocks should be held in tax-deferred accounts, such as 401(k) plans and traditional Investment Retirement Accounts (IRAs).

> The lower tax rate reduces your investment costs, which can boost your long-term investment program dramatically, especially when you reinvest your dividends.

> Dividends represent part of a company's cost of capital. The lower tax rate made it easier for companies to return money to investors because it lowered the cost of doing business and funding new projects.

➤ A study by Thomson Financial shows that there is far less insider selling when the stock has a good dividend yield versus one that doesn't pay a dividend. Also, stocks of companies with heavy insider selling underperformed the New York Stock Exchange average by 11 percent in the six months after the insider sales.

➤ Bear in mind that tax law can change frequently. Keep on top of the latest tax developments and their implications.

CHAPTER 3

How to Find the Best Dividend Payers

The uninitiated investor seeking income from stocks often will start and end the search by looking for the highest-yielding issues. That is the worst way to come up with a list of candidates. Purchasing a stock with a rich yield without doing some research could well make you poor.

A yield that is considerably above average (remember, the yield is determined by dividing the dividend by the price of the stock) may mean that the stock price is depressed either because earnings have been disappointing or because the market is anticipating some adverse news that is about to be announced. The high yield thus could signal either a dividend cut or dividend omission down the road.

To help you determine if the yield of a stock you're interested in buying is out of whack with the other issues in its industry, you can go to several sources. Two of the best are *Standard & Poor's Analysts' Handbook Monthly Supplement,* which contains dividend yields of all industry groups, and *The Value Line Investment Survey,* both of which can be found in many public libraries. If you find that the average yield of stocks in the industry is considerably lower than that of the stock you are researching, look elsewhere, unless you're willing to take on above-average risk.

Important Ratios to Consider

Payout Ratio

The payout ratio—dividends expressed as a percentage of earnings—is an important indicator of a company's ability to sustain growth of the dividend. For example, if ABC Corp. is paying a dividend of $1 per share and its earnings are $3 a share, its payout ratio is 33 percent ($1 divided by $3).

You don't want the payout ratio to be too high, since you'd like to see the company invest in the growth of its business, as well as have sufficient room for further dividend increases. And, of course, the payout ratio should not exceed 100 percent. If it does, that means the company is handing out more in dividends than it earns and could well presage trouble. Stocks in some industries have normally high payout ratios, which we will talk about later.

Generally, stocks with a payout ratio below 50 percent have more room to increase their dividends. The payout ratio can also serve as a good gauge of growth stocks. Any issue that has more than doubled its dividend over a 10-year period and still has a payout ratio under 50 percent has shown strong earnings progress.

From the end of World War II through 2004, the payout ratio of the S&P 500 index averaged 51 percent (based on reported earnings), which means more than half the index's profits were paid in the form of dividends. Based on operating profits, which excludes onetime nonoperational charges such as gains or losses on sales of assets or onetime acquisition costs, the average payout ratio from 1968 to 2004 was over 40 percent (Figure 3-1).

In recent years, though, the payout ratio has shrunk to about 32 percent. In view of the favorable tax rate on dividends, companies' large cash positions, and management's awareness that more investors are looking for a tangible return on their money, it's likely that we'll see the average payout ratio for companies in the S&P 500 index return to the norm.

Dividend Coverage Ratio

This important ratio shows how safe the dividend is based on the cash flow being generated by a company. To calculate the dividend

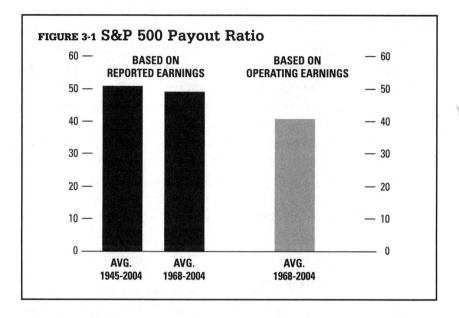

FIGURE 3-1 **S&P 500 Payout Ratio**

coverage ratio, divide cash flow per share by the dividend per share. The higher the dividend coverage from cash flow, the better.

A key point to keep in mind: If a stock's yield shows wild swings over a period of time, beware. That suggests yoyo stock price moves and unpredictable earnings. Also, if a corporation boosts its dividend at a faster pace than its profit growth, the dividend may soon have to be trimmed or eliminated.

Quick Ratio

The quick ratio can indicate if a company has enough liquidity to pay its dividend at the current level. To calculate this ratio, you take current assets (these are assets that are liquid, or easily turned into cash) minus inventories (assets that are not particularly liquid) and then divide that figure by current liabilities (short-term debts that have to be paid within a year). If a company has a quick ratio of at least 1.0, it suggests that it could cover all current liabilities with the liquid assets it has on hand. If the ratio is below 1.0, it's important to determine if the company is generating sufficient cash flow from operations to cover its normal expenses and any short-term debt obligations.

Short-Term Debt Coverage Ratio

The short-term debt coverage ratio can help determine if the company can easily pay its short-term debt obligations by using the cash being generated from operations. The ratio is calculated by dividing income from operations (which is found in the income statement) by current liabilities or short-term debt (listed on the balance sheet).

A short-term debt coverage ratio of 2.0 or greater means the company is generating more than twice the cash flow it needs from operations to pay off all of its short-term obligations. This ratio indicates that the dividend is fairly secure and that there is enough operating income to offset a lower liquidity position if that were indicated by the company's quick ratio.

Cash Flow

Cash flow is another useful tool to ascertain the safety of a company's dividend. It is a company's net income plus noncash items such as depreciation and amortization. If Company ABC has a net income of $3.2 million, we add to that its $100,000 of depreciation and amortization (which has no affect on cash flow) and divide by the 900,000 shares it has outstanding. We get a cash flow per share rate of $3.67.

Free cash flow is an even better measure. It is a company's cash flow minus its capital expenditures—in other words, what the company has left over after it has made the necessary investments back into the business.

An example of how a company can chalk up big profits but have little free cash flow is Home Depot in the 1990s. The giant do-it-yourself retailer reported strong earnings in that decade, but its free cash flow generation was paltry because the company used the available cash to construct new stores and expand into untapped markets.

A study by the College of Management at the Georgia Institute of Technology indicates that corporations are continuing to strengthen their finances. The study shows a growing number of companies are in a position to initiate or increase dividends, even if they also begin to reinvest in their business or make large acquisitions.

Cash flow from operations at the 86 nonfinancial companies that make up the S&P 100 increased more than 20 percent between 2000 and 2004, while free cash flow jumped almost 60 percent. The big improvement in free cash flows mostly came from reduced overhead, shedding less profitable assets, and increasing operating cash flow.

Statements of cash flow usually can be found toward the back of annual reports, after the balance sheet. Or as a shortcut, you can consult *Value Line Investment Survey* or *Standard & Poor's Stock Reports* (both available in libraries), which give a cash flow per share figure for hundreds of companies.

As a rule of thumb, cash flow should be at least three times the dividend payment. Financial companies, such as thrifts and banks, are the exception, since nearly all of their assets are cash.

S&P Quality Rankings

A good shortcut in deciding whether a dividend-paying stock is worth buying is to check the stock's Standard & Poor's Quality Ranking. S&P has provided Quality Rankings on common stocks since 1957. These Rankings are labeled A+ (highest), A (high), A– (above average), B+ (average), B (below average), B– (low), C (lowest), and D (in reorganization). They reflect the growth and stability of a company's earnings and dividends over at least the past 10 years. The Quality Rankings can be found in Standard & Poor's *Stock Guide*, *Stock Reports*, and *The Outlook*, all of which are available in the business section of most public libraries.

A study has shown that portfolios of stocks with high S&P Quality Rankings outperformed the S&P 500 index over a 17-year period and substantially outpaced portfolios of stocks with low Quality Rankings. The portfolios with the highest Quality Rank of A+ outperformed the S&P 500 by almost 2 percentage points. The study also found that risk—the volatility of investment returns—is lower in portfolios of stocks with companies carrying high Quality Rankings. The portfolios exhibited stable earnings growth, high returns on equity, wide profit margins, and low debt levels.

A+ Stocks an Exclusive Group

The number of stocks accorded Standard & Poor's top Quality Ranking fell to 87 in the first quarter of 2005, from 217 at the end of 1981 (Figure 3-2). That's only about 2 percent of the more than 4,000 stocks ranked in the Quality Rankings. Although the number of A+ stocks has remained below 100 since 1992, it's likely that the top category will see an increase in its ranks in coming years. That's because dividends are back in favor, and stocks that don't pay them can't attain the A+ height. Figure 3-3 lists the A+ stocks as of March 31, 2005.

In 2004 a closed-end exchange traded fund based on S&P's Quality Rankings became available. Called the S&P Quality Rankings Global Equity Managed Trust (American Stock Exchange symbol: BQY), its investment objective is to provide total return through a combination of current income and capital appreciation by investing primarily in stocks that it believes pay above-average dividends and have appreciation potential. BQY invests at least 80 percent of its total assets in stocks that carry an S&P Quality Rank of at least B+ at the time of investment. BQY's investment adviser is BlackRock Advisors (www.blackrock.com).

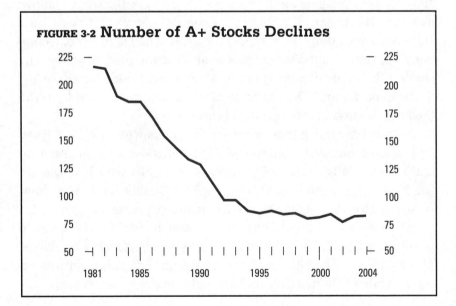

FIGURE 3-2 Number of A+ Stocks Declines

FIGURE 3-3 A+ Stocks

COMPANY	TICKER SYMBOL	SECTOR	COMPANY	TICKER SYMBOL	SECTOR
Alberto-Culver	ACV	Consumer Staples	Johnson & Johnson	JNJ	Health Care
Altria Group	MO	Consumer Staples	Johnson Controls	JCI	Consumer Discretionary
Ambac Financial Group	ABK	Financials	Kimco Realty	KIM	Financials
American Int'l Group	AIG	Financials	LSB Financial	LSBI	Financials
Anheuser-Busch Cos.	BUD	Consumer Staples	Lakeland Financial	LKFN	Financials
Applebee's Int'l	APPB	Consumer Discretionary	Loblaw Cos.	L	Consumer Staples
Automatic Data Proc.	ADP	Information Technology	Lowe's Cos.	LOW	Consumer Discretionary
Bank of Montreal	BMO	Financials	M&T Bank	MTB	Financials
Brown & Brown	BRO	Financials	MBNA Corp.	KRB	Financials
Capital One Financial	COF	Financials	M.D.C. Holdings	MDC	Consumer Discretionary
Cardinal Health	CAH	Health Care	McCormick & Co.	MKC	Consumer Staples
Carlisle Cos	CSL	Industrials	Merck & Co.	MRK	Health Care
Carnival Corp.	CCL	Consumer Discretionary	Metro Inc. Cl. A	MRU.SV	Consumer Staples
Cathay General Bancorp	CATY	Financials	MidSouth Bancorp	MSL	Financials
Centex Corp.	CTX	Consumer Discretionary	National Bankshares	NKSH	Financials
Cintas Corp.	CTAS	Industrials	Nat'l Penn Bancshares	NPBC	Financials
Citigroup Inc.	C	Financials	Nuveen Investments Cl. A	JNC	Financials
Coastal Financial Corp.	CFCP	Financials	Omnicom Group	OMC	Consumer Discretionary
Colgate-Palmolive	CL	Consumer Staples	Park National Corp.	PRK	Financials
Commerce Bancorp	CBH	Financials	Paychex Inc..	PAYX	Information Technology
Commerce Bancshares	CBSH	Financials	PepsiCo Inc.	PEP	Consumer Staples
Compass Bancshares	CBSS	Financials	Popular Inc.	BPOP	Financials
D.R.Horton	DHI	Consumer Discretionary	Power Corp. of Canada	POW.SV	Financials
Dollar General	DG	Consumer Discretionary	Power Financial	PWF	Financials
Donaldson Co.	DCI	Industrials	Ross Stores	ROST	Consumer Discretionary
Doral Financial	DRL	Financials	S&T Bancorp	STBA	Financials
Expeditors Int'l Wash.	EXPD	Industrials	S Y Bancorp	SYI	Financials
Family Dollar Stores	FDO	Consumer Discretionary	Sigma-Aldrich	SIAL	Materials
Federal Home Loan	FRE	Financials	Sterling Bancorp	STL	Financials
Fifth Third Bancorp	FITB	Financials	Suffolk Bancorp	SUBK	Financials
First Horizon Nat'l	FHN	Financials	SunTrust Banks	STI	Financials
Gallagher(Arthur J.)	AJG	Financials	Synovus Financial	SNV	Financials
General Electric	GE	Industrials	Sysco Corp.	SYY	Consumer Staples
Glacier Bancorp	GBCI	Financials	TJX Companies	TJX	Consumer Discretionary
Golden West Financial	GDW	Financials	Target Corp.	TGT	Consumer Discretionary
Great West Lifeco	GWO	Financials	Texas Regional Banc. Cl. A	TRBS	Financials
Harbor Florida Bancshares	HARB	Financials	Total System Svcs.	TSS	Information Technology
Harley-Davidson	HDI	Consumer Discretionary	Trustco Bank Corp. NY	TRST	Financials
Henry(Jack) & Assoc.	JKHY	Information Technology	United Technologies	UTX	Industrials
Home Depot	HD	Consumer Discretionary	Wal-Mart Stores	WMT	Consumer Staples
IGM Financial	IGI	Financials	Walgreen Co.	WAG	Consumer Staples
IBERIABANK Corp.	IBKC	Financials	Wilmington Trust Corp.	WL	Financials
Illinois Tool Works	ITW	Industrials	Wrigley, (Wm) Jr	WWY	Consumer Staples
Jefferson-Pilot	JP	Financials			

Price-Earnings Ratio

As with any type of stock you're considering buying, you should pay close attention to a dividend-paying issue's price-earnings ratio (P/E), which is the relationship of a company's share price to its per-share earnings. It is the most widely used tool for evaluating stocks. To calculate the P/E, divide the current stock price by the company's earnings per share.

The P/E is also referred to as the multiple, because it shows how much investors are willing to pay for each dollar of earnings. For example, if a stock sells at $40 and the company earned $2 a share, then the P/E is 20 ($40 divided by $2). You can either use trailing earnings—over the past 12 months—or analysts' estimates of current year profits. Professionals normally employ estimated earnings.

The P/E by itself is not enough to assess a stock. You also have to compare the stock's P/E to its historical P/E, as well as to the P/E of its peers and to the P/E of a market benchmark, such as the S&P 500 index.

While lower-than-average P/E multiples can indicate attractive buys, they don't always. Cyclical stocks—such as chemicals, papers, and steel—whose fortunes are closely tied to economic cycles, often sell at low P/Es when investors believe that their peak profits for a given cycle are near. Figure 3-4 shows a summary of the various ratios used in appraising a dividend-paying stock.

There Are Earnings and Then There Are Earnings

A word about earnings in general is in order here. As we've mentioned, earnings can be manipulated. Deceptive accounting practices were rampant in the late 1990s, with three of the worst abusers becoming infamous household names: Enron, Global Crossing, and WorldCom. Even such old-line companies as Lucent Technologies (an AT&T spinoff) and Xerox cooked the books. Lucent booked more than $600 million in revenues from sales to its distributors before the distributors actually sold the products, while Xerox inflated revenues by $3 billion from 1997 to 2000 and was compelled to restate earnings for those years.

The Sarbanes-Oxley Act of 2002, which toughened corporate governance and created a regulatory board to oversee the accounting industry, is helping to keep companies and auditors honest. But greed usually finds a way to be satisfied.

FIGURE 3-4 Measures for Dividend-Paying Stocks

Measure	Formula	What to Look for
Dividend yield	Dividend per share divided by stock price	Yield at least equal to that of the S&P 500 and not out of line with that of the S&P industry yield
Price-earnings ratio	Stock price divided by per-share earnings	P/E that is not excessive compared with company's historical P/E and with S&P industry P/E
Cash flow per share	Net income plus depreciation and amortization divided by number of shares outstanding	Should be at least three times dividend payment
Quick ratio	Current assets minus inventory divided by current liabilities	Should be at least 1.0
Payout ratio	Per-share dividends divided by per-share earnings	Should be higher than 50% but not exceed 100%
Dividend coverage ratio	Cash flow per share divided by dividends per share	Minimum should be 120%
Short-term debt coverage ratio	Operating income divided by short-term debt	Should be at least 2.0

S&P's Core Earnings

Because of the many questionable accounting practices, Standard & Poor's in 2002 came up with a new methodology for calculating companies' earnings to enable investors to make apples-to-apples profit comparisons. S&P's so-called core earnings excludes certain nonrecurring items such as gains or losses from asset sales, pension gains, litigation or insurance settlements, goodwill (the difference between the purchase price of an acquired company and its book value), and the reversal of prior-year changes and provisions.

Included in the core earnings as valid costs of doing business are employee stock options, restructuring, charges from ongoing operations, write-downs of depreciable or amortizable operating assets, purchased research and development, pension costs, merger/acquisition-related expenses, and unrealized gains/losses from hedging activities.

Standard & Poor's core earnings approach provides consistency and transparency to earnings analyses and makes it easier for investors to form comparisons between companies and over different time periods.

Figure 3-5 shows the differences between operating earnings (profits from operations, excluding special charges), as-reported earnings (what the company reports), and S&P's core earnings.

FIGURE 3-5 S&P Core Earnings vs. Operating and As-Reported Earnings

	S&P Core Earnings	Operating Earnings	As-Reported Earnings
Stock option expense	Included	Excluded	Excluded
Pension expense	Excludes pension fund gains and includes cost of services and interest	Included	Included
Goodwill	Excluded	Excluded	Excluded unless impaired
Restructuring charges and write-offs	Included	Excluded	Included
Purchased R&D	Included	Excluded	Included

Points to Remember

➤ In deciding which dividend-paying stocks to buy, looking at only the yield is a definite no-no.

➤ The payout ratio (dividends divided by per-share earnings) is a key indicator of a company's ability to sustain growth of its dividend.

➤ Cash flow (net income plus noncash items depreciation and amortization) is also an important gauge of the safety of a company's dividend, as is free cash flow (cash flow minus capital expenditures) and the quick ratio (current assets minus inventories divided by current liabilities).

➤ The dividend coverage ratio (cash flow per share divided by dividends per share) is another dividend safety measure.

➤ The short-term debt coverage ratio (income from operations divided by current liabilities or short-term debt) permits you to see if the company's short-term debt obligations can be paid by using the cash being generated from its operations.

➤ In evaluating a dividend-paying stock, you can take a shortcut by consulting Standard & Poor's Quality Rankings. These Rankings, which measure the growth and stability of a company's earnings and dividends over at least the past 10 years, range from the highest (A+) to the lowest (D). The Rankings can be found in Standard & Poor's *Stock Reports*, *Earnings Guide*, and *The Outlook*.

➤ Price-earnings ratios (price divided by per-share earnings) are an essential valuation tool for both dividend-paying and non-dividend-paying stocks. Compare the stock's P/E to its historical P/E, as well as to the P/E of its peers and to the P/E of a market benchmark, such as the S&P 500 index.

The yield of a stock is simply calculated by dividing the indicated annual dividend by the market price of the stock. What is the indicated annual dividend? Since the board of directors can decide to increase or decrease a company's payment at any time during the year, investment professionals take the latest quarterly per-share dividend and multiply that figure by 4 to come up with the indicated dividend, which is what you would expect to receive in the coming year. If the quarterly dividend is 50 cents, multiply that by 4 to get the indicated annual dividend of $2. If the price of the stock is $40, the yield is 5 percent ($2 divided by $40).

CHAPTER 4

Traditional Income Stocks

I ncome stocks usually don't have the same high appreciation potential as growth stocks. However, offsetting this fact is their stability, generally low-risk nature, income stream, and the likelihood of above-average total return over the long run.

Stocks of electric, gas, and water utilities, real estate investment trusts (REITs), banks, energy companies, and pharmaceutical firms historically have carried relatively high yields and are favorites with income-oriented investors. (Electric, gas, and water utilities and REITs typically have the highest yields, but banks, energy companies, and pharmaceutical firms, while carrying lower yields, boast histories of above-average dividend hikes over the longer term). Figure 4-1 lists S&P 500 sectors that contain the most dividend payers.

Electric and gas utilities, banks, and REITs are all sensitive to interest rates, and their shares normally come under pressure in a high interest rate environment. Rising interest rates cut into the profits of the utilities because they need a large amount of capital to run operations and thus borrow heavily. Banks suffer from high interest rates because of a narrowing of their net interest margins (the spread between the cost of funds and the rate charged for loans). Margins can be squeezed because of the lag between the time rates on deposits increase and the time various assets, including loans, are repriced.

Also, high interest rates reduce the value of a bank's fixed-rate (bond) portfolio. When interest rates climb, older bonds fall in price, so their yields move up to match the higher yield of new bonds.

FIGURE 4-1 **Inside the S&P 500: Focus on Dividends**

S&P 500 SECTOR	NUMBER OF COMPANIES IN SECTOR	NUMBER OF COMPANIES PAYING A DIVIDEND	AVERAGE YIELD OF DIVIDEND PAYERS (%)*
Consumer Discretionary	87	70	1.55
Consumer Staples	36	34	2.07
Energy	29	25	1.30
Financials	82	80	2.39
Health Care	55	31	1.16
Industrials	56	51	1.52
Information Technology	80	24	0.81
Materials	32	29	1.79
Telecommunication Services	10	8	4.05
Utilities	33	28	4.07
Total	500	380	1.93

* As of mid-2005.

Conversely, when interest rates fall, older bonds rise in value. As a result, when rates climb, banks have to reposition their portfolios to account for the reduced valuations and then they often incur charges against profits.

The earnings of REITs are affected by high interest rates because their borrowing costs for property purchases increase. At the same time, REIT stocks are regarded as bond substitutes, or yield plays. Since bonds trade primarily based on interest rate movements, REIT issues do also. When interest rates advance, REITs, like bonds, generally drop in value, and when rates decline, the stocks typically advance.

All of these groups, in fact, compete with fixed-income investments.

The sections below provide an overview of traditional income groups, along with key measures to look for in each industry to help you pick the right stocks.

Electric Utilities

Shares of electric utilities historically have been a top favorite for equity investors looking for income. The group pays out a large part of its earnings in dividends, and a good many of the companies' profits and cash flow are healthy enough to support modest dividend hikes.

Though selectivity is key in any industry, it is especially important with electric utilities. The electric power industry has been through a period of major changes. Historically, the regulated investor-owned utilities have had exclusive franchises to provide vertically integrated electric services (all aspects of the business) to retail customers, usually within a given state, in contiguous areas outside the state, or both.

However, the monopolistic, tightly regulated utilities created under trust-busting legislation more than 60 years ago are with us no longer. The Energy Policy Act of 1992 made the industry increasingly competitive, at the level of both production and sale of wholesale power. Instead of being local monopolies, utilities now have to compete for business.

In the years ahead, Standard & Poor's expects the industry to become more concentrated, with mergers resulting in only a few dominant companies. While the consolidation could conceivably produce a market environment that is notably less competitive than regulators initially intended in the 1992 act, it should still allow electricity buyers to choose the supplier from which they purchase power.

Utilities were helped in 2005 by passage of the new energy bill, which, among other features, repealed the Public Utilities Holding Company Act. That act, originally dating from the 1930s, prohibited certain utility mergers. The new energy bill gives the Federal Energy Regulatory Commission (FERC) more review oversight of utility mergers, which should have the effect of attracting much more investment into the sector.

Key Measures

To evaluate a utility's stock, you should examine the price-earnings ratio (P/E) and the dividend yield. Is the P/E greater or less than the expected sustainable growth rate of the company's earnings (called the PEG ratio)? How does the P/E compare with the industry average? Investors tend to pay a higher P/E and to accept a lower dividend yield if a company's profits are expected to rise rapidly.

For companies in the S&P Electric Utilities index, the shares normally trade between nine and 15 times historical earnings. The P/E of the Utilities index typically is at a discount to that of the S&P 500 index because of the slow-growth nature of utilities' regulated operations. Dividend yields normally fall within a range of 3 to 5 percent, usually significantly higher than the yield of the S&P 500.

Gas Utilities

Natural gas has enjoyed growing popularity mainly because of its environmental advantages versus coal and oil and the fact that very little is imported from overseas. The electric power sector, including both regulated utilities and unregulated independent power producers, is the fastest growing market for natural gas in the United States.

Key Measures

To decide if a particular gas utility is worth buying, consider the following measures:

Return on equity (ROE). This reveals how well a company invests its capital. It is calculated by dividing net income (less preferred dividend requirements) by average shareholders' equity. In recent years the average has been about 8 percent.

Return on assets (ROA). This shows how efficiently a company uses its assets. It is calculated by dividing utility operating income by total plant assets less accumulated depreciation. The average ROA has climbed in recent years to more than 7 percent.

Price-earnings ratio. As with other stocks, you should compare a gas utility's P/E ratio with that of its industry peers and with its own historical range. A useful related measure is the P/E to growth ratio (PEG). Is the stock's P/E, divided by the current or expected future earnings growth rate, higher, lower, or equal to the industry overall? How does it compare with the company's historical PEG ratio?

Payout ratio. The annual dividend divided by earnings per share, as we've discussed, is an important gauge of whether a dividend is secure. In the case of gas and electric utilities, the payout ratio often is around 90 percent. As many gas utilities began investing in unregulated activities, such as exploration and production, they sought to reduce their payout ratios by either immediately cutting the dividend or holding it steady as earnings rose over time. In cases where the dividend payout ratio is falling, investors must analyze the potential returns from growth-oriented unregulated investments compared with the value of the foregone dividend stream.

Utility Mutual Funds and ETFs

A good way to diversify your investment in utilities is via mutual funds. Three that have had returns of more than 12 percent annually over the three years that ended in March 2005 are Jennison Utility (phone: 800-225-1852), Evergreen Utility & Telecom (800-343-2898), and Eaton Vance Utilities (800-225-6265). Exchange traded funds (ETFs), which we will talk about in Chapter 7, are also an attractive way to invest in utilities. These include iShares Dow Jones U.S. Utilities (IDU), Utilities Select Sector SPDRs (XLU), and Vanguard Utilities Vipers (VPU)

Banks

The list of long-term dividend payers in Figure 4-2 includes many bank stocks. The industry as a whole has a solid record not only paying out reasonably sized dividends, but also of increasing them

FIGURE 4-2 Long-Term Dividend Payers

Company	Ticker Symbol	Quality Ranking	Dividend Paid Since	Company	Ticker Symbol	Quality Ranking	Dividend Paid Since	Company	Ticker Symbol	Quality Ranking	Dividend Paid Since
Bank of New York	BK	A-	1785	McCormick & Co..	MKC	A+	1925	Aqua America	WTR	A-	1939
Bank of Montreal	BMO	A+	1829	Abbott Laboratories	ABT	A	1926	Compass Bancshares	CBSS	A+	1939
Bank of Nova Scotia	BNS	A	1834	Becton, Dickinson	BDX	A	1926	ONEOK Inc.	OKE	A	1939
Toronto-Dominion Bk.	TD	A-	1857	Owens & Minor	OMI	A-	1926	Wells Fargo	WFC	A	1939
Amer Express	AXP	A-	1870	Protective Life Corp.	PL	A	1926	Burlington N. Santa Fe	BNI	A-	1940
Royal Bank Canada	RY	A	1870	Rohm & Haas	ROH	A	1927	Seacoast Banking FL	SBCF	A-	1940
Exxon Mobil	XOM	A-	1882	Univl Corp.	UVV	A	1927	Knight Ridder Inc.	KRI	A	1941
UGI Corp.	UGI	A-	1885	Altria Group	MO	A+	1928	VF Corp.	VFC	A-	1941
Johnson Controls	JCI	A+	1887	Hormel Foods	HRL	A	1928	AMETEK, Inc.	AME	A-	1942
Imperial Oil Ltd..	IMO	A	1891	Gannett Co.	GCI	A	1929	Florida Public Utilities	FPU	A-	1942
Procter & Gamble	PG	A	1891	McCormick & Co. Vtg.	MKC.V	A-	1929	New Plan Excel Realty Tr	NXL	A	1942
First Merchants Corp.	FRME	A	1894	Hershey Foods	HSY	A	1930	Old Republic Int'l	ORI	A	1942
Colgate-Palmolive	CL	A+	1895	McClatchy Co Cl. A	MNI	A-	1930	AmSouth Bancorp	ASO	A	1943
First Horizon Na'tl	FHN	A+	1895	Meredith Corp.	MDP	A-	1930	Energen Corp.	EGN	A	1943
Mellon Financial	MEL	A-	1895	Synovus Financial	SNV	A-	1930	Tootsie Roll Industries	TR	A	1943
Northern Trust	NTRS	A-	1896	Weston (George) Ltd.	WN	A-	1930	FPL Group	FPL	A	1944
General Mills	GIS	A-	1898	Anheuser-Busch Cos..	BUD	A+	1932	Johnson & Johnson	JNJ	A+	1944
General Electric	GE	A-	1899	Illinois Tool Works	ITW	A+	1933	Masco Corp.	MAS	A	1944
Bristol-Myers Squibb	BMY	A-	1900	Torchmark Corp..	TMK	A	1933	ALLETE Inc.	ALE	A-	1945
Church & Dwight	CHD	A	1901	Walgreen Co.	WAG	A+	1933	BancorpSouth	BXS	A-	1945
Pfizer, Inc.	PFE	A	1901	BB&T Corp.	BBT	A	1934	Brown-Forman Cl. A	BF.A	A	1945
Bank of America	BAC	A-	1903	Badger Meter	BMI	A-	1934	Bombardier Inc Cl. A	BBD.MV	A	1946
CH Energy Group	CHG	A-	1903	Noland Co.	NOLD	A-	1934	MacDermid, Inc.	MRD	A-	1946
Sunoco Inc.	SUN	A-	1904	Pitney Bowes	PBI	A-	1934	Sara Lee Corp.	SLE	A-	1946
Wiley(John)SonsCl. B	JW.B	A-	1904	Sensient Technologies	SXT	A-	1934	Sterling Bancorp	STL	A+	1946
Ameren Corp.	AEE	A-	1906	Vulcan Materials	VMC	A-	1934	Dover Corp.	DOV	A-	1947
Gillette Co.	G	A-	1906	Haverty Furniture	HVT	A-	1935	Emerson Electric	EMR	A	1947
OGE Energy	OGE	A-	1908	Kimberly-Clark	KMB	A	1935	Genuine Parts.	GPC	A	1948
Mercantile Bankshares	MRBK	A	1909	Merck & Co.	MRK	A+	1935	Southern Co.	SO	A-	1948
Ingersoll-Rand Cl. A	IR	A	1910	Power Corp of Canada	POW.SV	A+	1935	Parker-Hannifin	PH	A-	1949
State Street Corp.	STT	A	1910	Questar Corp.	STR	A-	1935	Smucker (J.M.)	SJM	A-	1949
UST Inc	UST	A-	1912	Tompkins Trustco	TMP	A	1935	Trustmark Corp.	TRMK	A	1949
Jefferson-Pilot	JP	A+	1913	Westamerica Bancorp	WABC	A	1935	Carlisle Cos.	CSL	A+	1950
Wrigley,(Wm) Jr	WWY	A	1913	Comerica Inc.	CMA	A	1936	Equitable Resources	EQT	A	1950
Wachovia Corp	WB	A-	1914	Commerce Bancshares	CBSH	A+	1936	Churchill Downs	CHDN	A-	1951
Wilmington Trust Corp.	WL	A+	1914	Ecolab Inc.	ECL	A	1936	New Jersey Res.	NJR	A	1951
Int'l Bus. Machines	IBM	A-	1916	Nat'l City Corp..	NCC	A	1936	Enbridge Inc.	ENB	A	1952
3M Co.	MMM	A-	1916	Supervalu Inc.	SVU	A-	1936	Fifth Third Bancorp	FITB	A+	1952
Mine Safety Appl.	MSA	A-	1918	United Technologies	UTX	A+	1936	PepsiCo Inc.	PEP	A+	1952
Avon Products	AVP	A	1919	Valley Nat'l Bancorp	VLY	A	1936	Schering-Plough	SGP	A-	1952
Courier Corp.	CRRC	A	1919	Hancock Holding	HBHC	A-	1937	Reynolds & Reynolds Cl. A	REY	A-	1953
GATX Corp.	GMT	A-	1919	MDU Resources Group	MDU	A	1937	Cincinnati Financial	CINF	A-	1954
CLARCOR Inc.	CLC	A	1921	Baldor Electric	BEZ	A	1938	Diebold, Inc.	DBD	A	1954
Bemis Co.	BMS	A	1922	Marshall & Ilsley	MI	A	1938	HNI Corp.	HNI	A-	1955
Scripps(E.W.) Cl. A	SSP	A-	1922	Otter Tail	OTTR	A	1938	Thomas Industries	TII	A-	1955
Marsh & McLennan	MMC	A-	1923	AGL Resources	ATG	A-	1939				
Popular Inc.	BPOP	A+	1923	Ameron Int'l	AMN	A-	1939				

on a regular basis. In fact, banks became even more generous in their dividend policies with the 2003 tax law that reduced the dividend tax rate.

In 2003, Citigroup boosted its quarterly payment 75 percent and said it would reduce stock repurchases. Wachovia increased its quarterly dividend 21 percent and raised its target payout ratio to a range of 50 percent, from 30 to 35 percent, while Bank of America hiked its quarterly payment by 25 percent. Standard & Poor's believes that most banks over the longer term will have dividend payout ratios in the 40 to 50 percent range.

Continuation of the industry consolidation trend also appears in the cards as banks move to compete more efficiently in a less regulated environment. Compared with the banking systems of most developed countries, the U.S. industry is still highly fragmented, despite the many mergers over the years. According to the Federal Deposit Insurance Corp. (FDIC), the number of banks it has insured steadily declined to 7,700 in 2004 from 14,628 in 1975. Thousands of smaller players continue to try to compete with industry leaders in terms of pricing and services, no easy task. The trend of larger banks acquiring smaller regional banks at premium prices should remain in force in the years ahead.

Key Measures

When evaluating a bank stock, these are some of the profitability measures you should investigate:

Return on assets (ROA). This is a bank's net income divided by its total average assets during a given period. A rising ROA trend is generally positive. Historically, most banks' ROA range from 0.6 to 1.5 percent. Regional and community banks with a lower cost of funds and a higher-yielding loan mix have higher net interest margins.

Yield on earning assets (YEA). Divide interest income on earning assets (loans, short-term money market investments, lease financings, and taxable and nontaxable investment securities) by the average value of these assets during the same period. Because it reflects general interest-rate levels, the YEA can fluctuate considerably over time. If a bank's YEA is high relative to that of other banks, it may indicate a high-risk portfolio of earning assets, particularly high-risk loans. If the YEA is substantially lower than that of other banks, it may indicate that the bank's portfolio has several problem loans that are yielding less than they should or that the bank has overly conservative lending policies.

Rate paid on funds (RPF). The cost of obtaining a bank's funds, also known as yield on earning assets, discussed above, is calculated by dividing the interest expense on the funds a bank uses to support earning assets by the total average level of funds employed in that way. RPF varies with the general level of interest rates and is affected by the makeup of the bank's liabilities. The greater the proportion of a bank's noninterest-bearing demand accounts, low-interest-rate savings accounts, and equity, the lower its RPF will be.

Net interest margin (NIM). This equals the difference between the yield on earning assets and the rate paid on funds. A NIM of less than 3 percent is generally considered low; more than 6 percent is regarded as high because of the difficulty to sustain it. NIM tends to be higher at small retail banks than at large wholesale banks.

Real Estate Investment Trusts

Real Estate Investment Trusts (REITs), which are companies that buy, develop, manage, and sell real estate assets, allow participants to invest in a professionally managed portfolio of real estate properties. These properties include shopping centers, hotels, office buildings, restaurants, and health care facilities.

REITs are exempt from federal corporate income taxes and from most state income taxes. In return for the tax exemption, REITs must pay at least 90 percent of their taxable income to shareholders every year in the form of dividends. They must also invest at least 75 percent of their total assets in real estate and generate 75 percent or more of their gross income from rents or mortgage interest.

Basically, there are three types of REITs. *Equity REITs*, which are by far the most common, invest in or own real estate and make money from the rents they collect. *Mortgage REITs* lend out money to owners and developers or invest in financial instruments secured by mortgages. *Hybrid REITs* invest in both properties and mortgages.

Net income is not generally used to measure the performance of a REIT, mainly because, for accounting purposes, the value of real estate depreciates regularly over time. Since more often than not market property values rise, the depreciation deduction from net income artificially lowers the reported earnings of REITs.

Key Measures

The chief REIT profitability measure is funds from operations (FFO), which is similar to cash flow. Funds from operations are net income, excluding gains or losses from debt restructuring and sales of property, plus depreciation and amortization. Most REITs report both net income and funds from operations.

The average REIT payout ratio, based on funds from operations, is close to 90 percent. A ratio above 90 percent could mean that the REIT does not have enough capital left to maintain its properties or to use as a buffer during a real estate downswing. You're better off buying a REIT that has a lower yield, not only because of the safety factor, but also because the company usually is in a good position to increase the dividend.

Before you invest in a particular REIT, determine if its operators are experienced in buying and selling properties, as well as in managing them. Management should have an appreciable percentage of their net worth invested in the company. Also, avoid REITs that are highly leveraged. Funds from operations should cover interest costs by a margin of at least two to one.

You want to invest in a REIT that carries a high S&P quality ranking. A B+ rank should be the minimum. In the REIT sector, especially, an investor wants to buy a stock that has had steady earnings and dividend growth.

It's especially important that you buy a package of REITs (at least three or four) for diversification. Or you could buy a mutual fund that specializes in REITs. Three of the better-situated funds are shown in Figure 4-3.

FIGURE 4-3 **Funds**

FUND	SYMBOL	EXPENSE RATIO	PHONE NUMBER
Fidelity Real Estate Inv.	FRESX	0.57%	800-544-8888
T. Rowe Price Real Estate	TRREX	1.00	800-638-5660
Vanguard REIT Index	VGSIX	0.21	800-635-1511

Water Utilities

Increased demand for improved water quality, along with aging systems, is expected by Standard & Poor's to translate into positive long-term prospects for water utilities, the stocks of which generally provide above-average yields. Water utilities in the United States are seeking rate hikes from their respective state commissions to offset rising infrastructure costs as municipalities turn toward privatization to repair their decaying water systems.

Major growth is seen in desalination (a process by which salt is removed from seawater as a source for drinking water), especially in Nevada, Arizona, California, and Texas, where the population continues to expand. In addition, Standard & Poor's believes there will be further consolidation in the industry by the major U.S.-based, investor-owned water utilities. S&P also anticipates that companies in the group will continue to raise their dividends.

Two well-situated water utilities are:

Aqua America (WTR)
S&P earnings and dividend rank: A–
Through subsidiaries, Aqua America (formerly Philadelphia Suburban Corp.) is the largest U.S.-based publicly traded water utility. It provides water and waste services in Pennsylvania, Ohio, Illinois, Texas, New Jersey, Indiana, North Carolina, Virginia, Florida, Maine, Missouri, New York, and South Carolina. The company aims to expand its customer base through regional acquisitions.

American States Water (AWR)
S&P earnings and dividend rank: B+
This utility's primary operating unit is Southern California Water Co., which serves about 252,000 water customers and 23,000 electric customers. Its customer base covers 75 communities in 10 counties throughout California. In January 2005 the California Public Utilities Commission enacted a rate increase for Southern California Water that will provide additional revenues of $2.8 million annually.

Energy Stocks

The fortunes of oil and gas companies are tied to overall supply and demand, which are reflected in oil and gas prices. Price changes affect industry sectors differently. High prices for oil and natural gas, for instance, benefit upstream (that's industry jargon for exploration and production) companies, but hurt the downstream (refining) companies in the form of higher raw materials costs. For integrated oil companies, such as ExxonMobil, the business diversification between the upstream and downstream tends to mitigate the effects of oil and gas price fluctuations. Because the integrated companies are usually more leveraged to the exploration and production part of the business, however, these companies generally benefit from higher prices for oil and gas.

Key Measures

An oil company's operating margin is a measure of how efficiently it functions. It is determined by dividing operating income (revenues minus operating expenses) by revenues. The operating margin indicates the profitability of basic operating activities before accounting for interest expense and income taxes.

Another good measure is the ratio of long-term debt to total capitalization. Because the oil industry is relatively capital intensive, debt ratios for certain industry participants may be higher than for companies in service-related industries. But because of their more stable cash flow, the integrated oil companies tend to be less leveraged than smaller independent exploration and development companies or refining and marketing companies.

As for the key valuation measure of the stocks—the price-earnings ratio (P/E)—the faster growing companies carry higher multiples, while the stagnant firms' P/Es are lower, as is the case with any industry. Also, the stocks of large, international integrated companies have higher multiples because their geographic and business diversification tends to stabilize their earnings, which somewhat offsets commodity price and geopolitical risk.

Telecommunications Stocks

Before AT&T's breakup into the seven Bell operating companies in 1984, buying the shares of Ma Bell or of the large independent companies was a sure thing for investors whose goal was a steady dividend stream. Investing in telecom stocks now has become a minefield. AT&T's monopoly shattering has resulted in intense telecom competition, increasing deregulation, reduced profits, and dividend cuts and omissions.

At the same time, pressure from wireless and cable companies muddied the waters of the wireline companies. Wireless service has become an increasingly attractive option for telecom customers since service quality and affordability have improved considerably. Wireline carriers have had to invest in wireless technology in order to stay competitive.

The acquisition in 2005 of AT&T by SBC Communications, the nation's second largest regional phone company and the 1984 offspring of AT&T, reflected the radically changed course of the telecom industry. In effect, the child wound up taking care of the parent. San Antonio–based SBC has some 50 million local telephone customers, mostly in the Midwest and South. It also owns 60 percent of Cingular Wireless, which serves more than 46 million wireless customers.

Key Measures

In gauging the appeal of an established telephone company's stock, the price-earnings ratio is a key valuation tool, along with its cash flow. For comparison purposes, the benchmarks are the P/E ratios on the S&P Integrated Telecommunications Services index and the S&P 500 index. Here are profiles of four of the more promising telecom companies:

CenturyTel (CTL)
S&P earnings and dividend rank: A
Dividends paid since 1974
Following the sale in 2002 of its wireless operations to Alltel for $1.6 billion in cash, CenturyTel focuses solely on wireline local telecommunications. The company plans to pursue acquisitions of underserved incumbent local exchange carrier markets to promote efficiencies via synergies with its existing network and to drive long-term earnings growth through enhanced service offerings. CTL operates more than 2 million telephone access lines, primarily in rural and suburban areas in 22 states, with operations concentrated in Wisconsin, Louisiana, Michigan, and Ohio. In 2005 it appeared that CenturyTel's prospects were more favorable than those of the Baby Bells, based on CTL's limited competitive pressures from wireless and cable carriers, and its higher earnings quality. Analysts' consensus five-year per-share earnings growth rate is 4 percent.

Sprint Corp. (FON)
S&P earnings and dividend rank: B
Dividends paid since 1939
This company's Sprint PCS wireless business in 2005 contributed more than 45 percent of revenues, while the wireline segment was split between the local telephone and global markets. The local telephone division is the largest independent U.S. incumbent local exchange carrier. In late 2004, Sprint and Nextel Communications announced a proposed merger of the two companies that closed in the second quarter of 2005. The new company has a balanced mix of consumer, business, and government customers. The merger is expected to accelerate the company's business mix away from weak long distance operations and toward higher wireless growth. Analysts'

consensus per-share earnings growth over five years is estimated at 13 percent.

Verizon Communications (VZ)
S&P earnings and dividend rank: B
Dividends paid since 1984

Verizon was formed through the $60 billion merger of Bell Atlantic Corp. and GTE Corp in 2000. At the end of 2004, Verizon was the largest U.S. provider of wireline communications, with 53 million access lines, and it was the second largest wireless carrier, with 43.8 wireless customers. The domestic telecom segment, which serves a territory consisting of 32 states and the Distict of Columbia, generated more than 50 percent of operating revenues. In February 2005, Verizon agreed to acquire MCI Inc. for $6.7 billion in stock and cash. The deal was expected to close in early 2006. Verizon anticipates benefits from an increased presence in the commercial market and in the deployment of wireless and wireline broadband networks and services.

Citizens Communications (CZN)
S&P earnings and dividend rank: B–
Dividends paid since 2004

CZN stock yielded more than 7 percent from its $1 annual dividend in July 2005. The company provides wireline services to rural areas and small- and medium-size towns and cities, including the Rochester, New York, metropolitan area (its largest market) as an incumbent local exchange carrier. It also provides companies local exchange carrier services to business customers and to other communications carriers in the West via Electric Lightwave. Because of its focus on rural areas and small cities, Citizens Communications is somewhat insulated from the cutthroat competition for customers in urban areas. Cash flow in recent years has been excellent. CZN paid a $2 special dividend in 2004 and initiated quarterly dividends of 25 cents. In the first quarter of 2005, 56 percent of free cash flow was paid out in dividends.

Pharmaceutical Stocks

The pharmaceutical industry has proved itself to be a dynamic one, having reinvented itself many times over the years in the face of changing market models and government regulation. Continued increased consumption of prescription drugs seems assured, thanks to the aging of the baby boom generation and rising average life expectancy. The elderly (those 65 and older) account for more than one-third of the nation's total consumption of prescription medications. The world's elderly population is estimated to surge 89 percent over the next 20 years, while the total world population is expected to climb only 26 percent.

Key Measures

In analyzing a drug stock, start by examining the company's recent and historical sales performance. Has sales growth been consistent or volatile? How has growth been achieved—through volume, pricing, acquisitions, or via a combination of these?

The operating margin is also important. Pharmaceutical companies normally have high operating profit margins (operating earnings as a percentage of sales). In the early 1990s, operating ratios as high as 40 percent were fairly common among leading drug makers. In recent years, margins have contracted because of reduced pricing flexibility, but the industry average still exceeds 30 percent. That's more than twice that of the average corporation in the S&P 500. The high margin reflects drug companies' very low raw material costs and lower-than-average selling, general, and administrative expenses per dollar of sales. Though substantial costs are incurred during a drug's R&D phase, once those costs have been covered, the lion's share of revenues flows directly to profits. Companies that can consistently develop valued-added, widely used drugs with long lives can command margins well above the industry average.

Changes in a company's operating margin over a period of years can reveal management's effectiveness in improving company profitability. Restructuring and cost streamlining can play a major role in a company's profit margin.

Pretax, Net Returns, and ROE

Other critical drug company measures are the pretax and net returns. Drug industry pretax and net income returns are typically well above the averages in other industries. Drug makers' net earnings as a percentage of sales averaged about 17 percent over the five years ending in 2003, compared with 4.5 percent for other industries.

The pharmaceutical business is less capital intensive than most other industries, and tends to have lower interest expense and depreciation as a percentage of sales. Profit margins have also been enhanced by lower tax rates, R&D credits, and tax credits from manufacturing operations in Ireland and other areas. Lower-than-average drug industry tax rates also reflect the large portion of sales derived from countries with tax rates below those of the United States.

Finally, return on equity (ROE, or net earnings as a percentage of average stockholders' equity) is considered a key measure of management's effectiveness in the pharmaceutical industry. The average ROE of more than 25 percent ranks among the highest of all industries. The elevated ratio is essentially a function of the industry's relatively high profit margins.

Preferred Stocks

Some investors looking for income turn to preferred stocks, which are a cross between stocks and bonds, though they behave more like bonds. Preferred stocks usually have a fixed dividend, a prior claim (ahead of common stock) on the income and assets of the issuing company, and have no voting rights. Their investment quality is rated like bonds. Some preferred issues are convertible into common stock at fixed exchange rates.

Most preferred stocks are cumulative; that is, the dividends will accrue even if they are not actually paid. The majority of preferreds are redeemable, or "callable," which means that the issuer has the right to call the shares after a stated date.

Participating preferred stocks may receive additional dividends based on a predetermined formula using the issuer's profits. The participation dividend will be less than the amount paid to common shareholders, but this feature can add to the value of preferred shares. Most preferreds are nonparticipating.

Corporations normally have only one issue of common stock, but there may be several issues of preferred stock. Stocks that have first preference in the distribution of dividends are referred to as first preferred or preferred A; the next in the series is called second preferred or preferred B; and so on.

Key Measures

As with any investment, preferred stock has its advantages and disadvantages. The pluses:

> The dividend is predictable and usually carries a high yield.

> Preferred stocks generally are safe investments, with a good track record of paying dividends.

> They can be bought and sold like common stock.

The minuses:

> Preferred stock dividends do not qualify for the low 15 percent tax rate.

> Like bonds, if inflation and interest rates rise, the value of the preferred stock declines (of course, if inflation and interest rates fall, the value of the preferred climbs).

> Investors don't participate in the growth of the company and any resultant capital gains that common shareholders receive.

> Preferred stocks don't have the safety of a bond, because dividends can be passed.

Preferred stock is largely owned by corporations since the tax law allows them to exclude 70 percent of preferred dividends from income taxes.

You can invest in preferred stock via closed-end funds (see Chapter 7), which is a good way to go for long-term investors. Some examples: Nuveen Quality Preferred Income Fund (ticker symbol: JTP), John Hancock Preferred Income Fund (HPI), Preferred Income Opportunity Fund (PFO), and BlackRock Preferred Opportunity Trust Fund (BPP). These funds typically use leverage to increase yield and employ interest-rate hedges and swaps to protect against interest-rate fluctuations. You can get preferred stock information online at www.preferredsonline.com.

Master Limited Partnerships

Master Limited Partnerships (MLPs) have not been widely regarded as traditional income vehicles for the average investor because of their tricky nature and former bad reputation. But they are worth investigating because of their high yields (typically 6 percent to more than 8 percent) and relative safety.

MLPs are similar to REITs because they don't pay income taxes. In order to escape taxes, 90 percent of an MLP's income must come from the exploration, development, mining or production, processing, refining, transportation, or marketing of any mineral or natural resource subject to depletion allowances. The income can also be derived from rent from real property, certain gains from the sale of real property or capital assets, interest, and dividends.

MLPs trade like stocks. Close to 50 at this writing are actively traded, mostly on the New York Stock Exchange. Owners of the issues are considered limited partners, or unitholders, not shareholders. The limited partners have a claim on profits and have no legal liability. The general partner runs the business and collects a fee. MLPs pass depreciation deductions to the limited partners, so the income is tax sheltered.

Cash distributions often exceed partnership income, and when they do, the difference is regarded as a return of capital to the unitholder and taxed at the capital gains rate when the unitholder sells. Cash distributions normally are relatively steady, which results in MLP units trading like bonds, falling when interest rates rise and climbing when interest rates decline.

MLPs got their start in the 1980s, when Congress, in order to encourage oil and gas exploration, gave energy companies the right to spin off production and transportation assets into separately traded Master Limited Partnerships. Unfortunately, in the early years investors were badly burned by some scam artists who peddled more than $100 billion worth of tax shelters with questionable assets structured as limited partnerships. Unlike the situation now, these partnerships were not publicly traded.

MLP unitholders receive Form K-1, which is similar to the form 1099-DIV that stockholders receive from companies that pay dividends. In most cases the unitholder must fill out a Schedule E form: Supplemental Income and Loss (from rental real estate, royalties, partnerships, S corporations, estates, trusts, etc.). Using Turbo Tax or other tax software eases tax filing.

Specific MLPs

MLPs' high yields and steady cash flows make them attractive, but before investing in one, it may be prudent to consult a tax adviser to help determine the tax implications. Some of the better-known MLPs include:

Pipelines. Amerigas Partners (APU) sells propane at retail to consumers in 46 states. Kinder Morgan Energy Partners (KMP) owns and operates natural gas, gasoline, and other petroleum product pipelines. Teppco Partners (TPP) owns and operates pipelines transporting refined petroleum products. Valero (VLI) owns and operates crude oil and refined product pipelines and associated facilities mostly in Texas, New Mexico, Colorado, Oklahoma, California, and New Jersey.

Natural Resources. Alliance Resource Partners (ARLP) operates coal mines in four states. Crown Pacific (CRPP.OB) owns and operates timberlands and wood product manufacturing facilities in Oregon and Washington. Natural Resource Partners (NRP) owns, but does not operate, coal properties in the Appalachia, IL Basin, and Powder River Basin areas of the United States.

Real Estate. America First Real Estate Investment Portfolio (AFREZ) owns residential apartment complexes in Florida, North Carolina, Michigan, Tennessee, Ohio, Illinois, and Virginia. Real Estate Partners (ACP) owns and manages undeveloped land and residential, hotel, casino, and resort properties in 31 states. New England Realty Associates (NEN) owns and manages residential apartment buildings, condominium units, and commercial properties in Massachusetts and New Hampshire. The partnership terminates at the end of 2017.

Miscellaneous. Airlease, Ltd. (AIRL.OB) leases commercial jet aircraft to passenger airlines and freight carriers. Alliance Capital Management (AC) operates mutual funds and provides investment management services to private clients, individual and institutional investors. Cedar Fair (FUN) owns and operates amusement parks in six states.

Points to Remember

➤ Traditional income stocks include electric, water and gas utilities, real estate investment trusts (REITs), banks, energy companies, and pharmaceutical firms. Utilities and REITs typically carry the highest yields, but banks, energy companies, and drug firms have a history of above-average dividend hikes over the long term. Some telecom stocks, though not the safe dividend haven they used to be, are also worth considering.

➤ In assessing the traditional dividend payers, various valuation measures should be applied. Price-earnings ratios and payout ratios head the list.

➤ Some income investors buy preferred stock, which is a cross between stocks and bonds, though they behave more like bonds. Preferred stocks are mainly owned by corporations since the tax law allows them to exclude 70 percent of preferred dividends from taxes.

➤ Preferred stock pros: The dividend is highly predictable and usually carries a high yield; most have a good track record of paying dividends; and they can be bought and sold like common stock.

➤ Preferred stock cons: The dividends do not quality for the low 15 percent tax rate; investors don't participate in the growth of the company and any resultant capital gains that common shareholders receive; and preferreds don't have the safety of a bond because dividends can be passed.

➤ Master Limited Partnerships (MLPs), with their high yields and tax advantages, are attractive for some investors. MLPs are similar to REITs because they don't pay income taxes. MLP investors are considered limited partners, or unitholders.

➤ There are close to 50 MLPs that are actively traded, mostly on the New York Stock Exchange. They fall into different categories: pipelines, natural resources, real estate, and miscellaneous.

(The preceding industry information has been provided courtesy of Standard & Poor's *Industry Surveys*.)

CHAPTER 5

Dividends as a Hedge against Inflation

Inflation is sometimes called a silent risk because of its quietly eroding nature. The continuing rise in the level of prices paid for goods and services is a serious threat to your financial future. What appears to be a satisfactory nest egg today will look pretty lean 10 years from now and downright anorexic in 20 years.

As measured by the consumer price index, inflation has been relatively tame in recent years, averaging less than 3 percent annually. But even that mild rate, which is a far cry from the double-digit numbers of the late 1970s and early 1980s, can play havoc with your purchasing power. After 10 years of 3 percent inflation, $1,000 today would be worth only $744, a decline of 26 percent. In 30 years, a 3 percent annual inflation rate would mean that what you buy today for $80,000 would cost you nearly $200,000.

A 3 percent increase per year in the inflation rate doubles prices in 24 years. A 4 percent annual inflation rate cuts your purchasing power in half in 18 years, while a 6 percent rate results in prices doubling in only 12 years.

Investing in stocks of companies that regularly increase their dividends is one of the best ways to stay ahead of inflation over the longer term. Some investors regard bonds as safer than stocks, but since bond payments are fixed, you have inflation, or interest rate, risk. If you buy a bond for $1,000 that yields 6 percent, you receive

$60 a year in interest for however long you own it. That $60 will shrink in terms of purchasing power after a few years of even mild inflation. And if interest rates are increasing, the price of the bond will usually fall; if you sell the bond prior to its maturity, you would incur a capital loss.

Figure 5-1 shows the advantage of buying stocks with growing dividends. The table demonstrates what happens to a hypothetical $10 stock that pays a 25-cent annual dividend when the dividend rises 10 percent a year and the share price increases by the same percentage. At the end of 10 years, your dividend yield remains 2.5 percent of the most recent share price. But for long-term investors, the best way to value your dividend is to view it as a yield on your original investment. Though the value of your investment has risen over the years, your cost has not changed. The stock you bought for $10 is now worth $23.57, but you still paid $10 for it. And now you're receiving a 59-cent annual dividend, which means that the yield on your cost is 5.9 percent.

A 5.9 percent yield is not only generous, but keep in mind that as long as the dividend isn't cut, your annual yield on your original investment will never fall below 5.9 percent. And if the company has

FIGURE 5-1 Effects of an Increasing Dividend

Year	Stock Price ($)	Dividend ($)	Current Yield (%)	Yield on Cost (%)
1	10.00	0.25	2.5	2.5
2	11.00	0.28	2.5	2.8
3	12.10	0.30	2.5	3.0
4	13.31	0.33	2.5	3.3
5	14.64	0.37	2.5	3.7
6	16.11	0.40	2.5	4.0
7	17.72	0.44	2.5	4.4
8	19.49	0.49	2.5	4.9
9	21.43	0.54	2.5	5.4
10	23.57	0.59	2.5	5.9

a history of strong dividend boosts, the yield is likely to go higher. Your capital gain is also not factored into the equation.

An Example of Profiting from Dividends

Cintas Corp. (stock symbol: CTAS) is not exactly a household name. The Cintas Corp. manufactures corporate uniforms that it rents to customers in such industries as airlines, hotels, and grocery stores. Services provided to the rental markets include the cleaning of uniforms, as well as ongoing replacements. Cintas also offers ancillary products, such as the rental or sale of entrance mats, fender covers, towels, and mops.

These are pretty mundane businesses. But they've paid off big time. When the company went public in 1983, the stock sold for $0.93 (adjusted for splits). The dividend amounted to $0.006 a share, for a yield of 0.6 percent. By 2005 the dividend had climbed to $0.32, but the yield in early 2005, at 0.7 percent, remained about the same as in 1983. On the original cost in 1983, however, the yield amounted to 34 percent. So in 22 years the yield went from 0.6 percent to 34 percent. As of 2005, Cintas had increased its dividend at a compound rate of 27 percent annually since going public in 1983. At the same time, the share price of Cintas soared from $0.93 in 1983 to $44 in early 2005, a 4,631 percent gain.

Of course, not many investors had the foresight to invest in Cintas back in 1983. But if 10 years ago you had been attracted to the company because of its 12-year history of strong gains in earnings, cash flows, and steady dividend hikes, you still would have done well. The average price of the stock in 1995 was $11 and the dividend amounted to $0.07 a share, for a yield of 0.6 percent. By early 2005 the yield on your original investment was 2.9 percent (higher than the yield on the S&P 500), with a price appreciation of 400 percent.

Unlikely to Break the String

Although there are no guarantees, companies that regularly increase dividends are a good bet to continue doing so and are ideal for long-term investors. As Peter Lynch, who racked up an outstanding 10-year record as manager of Fidelity's highly successful Magellan Fund, said, "The dividend is such an important factor in the success of many stocks that you could hardly go wrong by making an entire portfolio of companies that have raised their dividends for 10 or 20 years in a row." Lynch also observed: "Companies that don't pay dividends have a sorry history of blowing the money on a string of stupid diversifications."

Figure 5-2 lists more than 100 companies that have boosted their dividends to shareholders every year for the 10 years through the 2005 indicated dividend. To weed out companies that make only nominal yearly dividend increases, we eliminated stocks with 10-year cumulative dividend growth under 250 percent. That is a considerable edge on inflation, which in the 1994–2004 10-year period has seen prices rise 31 percent.

Many of these stocks now provide above-average yields on their 1995 prices. Assuming there are no dividend cuts, with just the dividends from these issues, the returns on the stocks over 10 years will outpace the average annual total return of 11.9 percent that Standard & Poor's has posted since 1926. If price appreciation were factored in, the returns are juicy indeed.

Companies that consistently raise their dividends at a healthy rate are sending a signal to the investment community that they can well afford to share their profits, that their cash flow is not likely to stagnate, and that they are optimistic about their businesses' future. In fact, studies have suggested that increasing the dividend has been a reliable indicator of higher earnings ahead.

Companies also pay increasing dividends to create investor loyalty. As we noted earlier, a stock is less likely to be dumped by an individual who is looking forward to the next quarterly payment. And when that payment represents a double-digit return on the original investment, the incentive to hold is even greater. That helps to support the price of the stock.

We have to emphasize again that there are no guarantees in investing. So we can't promise that every stock in Figure 5-2 will continue to hike its dividend annually for the next 10 years. An example of a

FIGURE 5-2A Stocks with Strong 10-Year Yields

COMPANY	TICKER SYMBOL	QUALITY RANKING	1995 AVG PRICE	2005 INDICATED RATE	% YIELD ON 1995 AVG PRICE	1995-2005 DIVD INCREASE (%)
ACE Limited	ACE	B	44.98	0.84	1.9	404
AFLAC Inc.	AFL	A	38.72	0.44	1.1	423
Alabama Nat'l Bancorp	ALAB	A	63.65	1.35	2.1	800
Alberto-Culver	ACV	A+	52.44	0.46	0.9	332
Allied Irish Banks ADS	AIB	NR	42.49	1.52	3.6	311
American Int'l Group	AIG	A+	68.35	0.50	0.7	553
Anchor Bancorp Wisc.	ABCW	A	27.60	0.50	1.8	567
AptarGroup Inc.	ATR	A	51.91	0.60	1.2	362
Arrow Financial	AROW	A-	27.99	0.92	3.3	268
Arrow International	ARRO	B+	33.30	0.60	1.8	757
Astoria Financial	AF	A-	37.40	1.20	3.2	1,100
Automatic Data Proc.	ADP	A+	43.00	0.62	1.4	282
BancFirst Corp.	BANF	A	70.41	1.12	1.6	300
Bank of Nova Scotia	BNS	A	32.40	1.28	4.0	313
Barclays plc ADS	BCS	NR	44.34	1.77	4.0	372
Becton, Dickinson	BDX	A	59.96	0.72	1.2	251
Brown & Brown	BRO	A+	46.96	0.32	0.7	300
Century Bancorp(MA)	CNBKA	A	28.74	0.48	1.7	300
Cintas Corp.	CTAS	A+	43.83	0.32	0.7	380
Citigroup Inc.	C	A+	48.28	1.76	3.6	1,660
City National	CYN	A	68.28	1.44	2.1	454
Coastal Financial Corp.	CFCP	A+	15.04	0.18	1.2	351
Commerce Group Inc.	CGI	B+	67.72	1.32	1.9	474
Commercial Federal	CFB	B+	27.55	0.54	2.0	1,116
Community Investors Bancorp	CIBI	B+	13.50	0.36	2.7	914
CORUS Bankshares	CORS	A-	49.73	1.40	2.8	730
Cullen/Frost Bankers	CFR	A	46.30	1.06	2.3	272
Doral Financial	DRL	A+	40.35	0.72	1.8	1,018
Eaton Vance	EV	A-	27.08	0.32	1.2	688
Empire Ltd. Cl. A	EMP.NV	B+	33.25	0.48	1.4	368
Expeditors Int'l,Wash	EXPD	A+	55.95	0.22	0.4	1,367
Federal Home Loan	FRE	A+	61.64	1.20	1.9	300
Fifth Third Bancorp	FITB	A+	45.30	1.40	3.1	421
First Bancorp	FBP	A	47.40	0.56	1.2	951
First Bancorp (NC)	FBNC	A-	25.51	0.68	2.7	344
First Nat'l Lincoln Corp.	FNLC	NR	17.50	0.48	2.7	930
First Oak Brook Bancshrs	FOBB	A-	30.45	0.72	2.4	586
First of Long Island	FLIC	A	46.24	0.84	1.8	254
First State Bancorporation	FSNM	A	36.49	0.56	1.5	446
FNB Corp (FL)	FNB	B+	19.45	0.92	4.7	267
Forest City Ent. Cv. Cl. B	FCE.B	NR	64.39	0.40	0.6	621
Forest City Enterp. Cl. A	FCE.A	NR	63.25	0.40	0.6	621
Gallagher(Arthur J.)	AJG	A+	29.95	1.12	3.7	362
Golden West Financial	GDW	A+	61.95	0.24	0.4	312
Great West Lifeco	GWO	A+	28.65	0.78	2.7	550
Harley-Davidson	HDI	A+	62.10	0.50	0.8	1,011
Harte-Hanks Inc.	HHS	B+	26.59	0.20	0.8	801
Home Depot	HD	A+	40.58	0.40	1.0	848
IBERIABANK Corp.	IBKC	A+	59.39	1.12	1.9	647
Illinois Tool Works	ITW	A+	90.45	1.12	1.2	261
Independent Bank	IBCP	A	30.45	0.76	2.5	513
Int'l Bancshares	IBOC	A	36.60	0.80	2.2	1,368
Irwin Financial	IFC	A	22.94	0.40	1.7	264
Johnson & Johnson	JNJ	A+	66.22	1.14	1.7	256
Lakeland Financial	LKFN	A+	38.57	0.84	2.2	354

(cont'd on next page)

FIGURE 5-2B Stocks with Strong 10-Year Yields (Continued)

COMPANY	TICKER SYMBOL	QUALITY RANKING	1995 AVG PRICE	2005 INDICATED RATE	% YIELD ON 1995 AVG PRICE	1995–2005 DIVD INCREASE (%)
Laurel Cap Group	LARL	B+	23.30	0.80	3.4	422
Linear Technology	LLTC	A	39.20	0.40	1.0	967
Luxottica Group ADS	LUX	NR	21.20	0.19	0.9	469
M&T Bank	MTB	A+	100.20	1.60	1.6	540
MAF Bancorp	MAFB	A	43.38	0.92	2.1	595
MBNA Corp.	KRB	A+	25.54	0.56	2.2	425
McDonald's Corp.	MCD	A	32.98	0.55	1.7	319
McGrath RentCorp	MGRC	A-	43.22	0.88	2.0	274
Medtronic, Inc.	MDT	A-	52.90	0.34	0.6	477
Mercury General	MCY	B+	55.45	1.72	3.1	330
Metro Inc. Cl. A	MRU.SV	A+	27.55	0.40	1.5	900
Movado Group	MOV	B+	19.35	0.16	0.8	532
Natl Bk of Canada	NA	A-	52.26	1.68	3.2	320
NewMil Bancorp	NMIL	A	29.36	0.80	2.7	627
Northeast Indiana Bancorp	NEIB	B+	20.38	0.60	2.9	869
Northrim Bancorp	NRIM	A	23.97	0.38	1.6	262
Nucor Corp.	NUE	B	63.39	0.60	0.9	371
Old Second Bancorp	OSBC	A	32.99	0.48	1.5	256
Pacific Capital Bancorp	PCBC	A	28.66	0.72	2.5	383
Paychex Inc.	PAYX	A+	31.53	0.52	1.6	1,365
People's Bank	PBCT	B+	37.65	1.16	3.1	308
Pfizer, Inc.	PFE	A	26.86	0.76	2.8	339
Pier 1 Imports	PIR	A-	18.04	0.40	2.2	1,438
Popular Inc.	BPOP	A+	26.48	0.64	2.4	365
Power Financial	PWF	A+	32.75	0.81	2.5	436
Praxair Inc.	PX	A	45.42	0.72	1.6	350
Provident Bankshares	PBKS	A	33.61	1.06	3.2	401
RenaissanceRe Holdings	RNR	A-	47.88	0.76	1.6	1,326
Roper Industries	ROP	A	63.70	0.43	0.7	278
Ross Stores	ROST	A+	27.97	0.20	0.7	597
Royal Bancshares(PA)	RBPAA	A	24.64	1.00	4.1	1,145
Royal Bank Canada	RY	A	58.99	2.20	3.7	273
Sandy Spring Bancorp	SASR	A	33.43	0.80	2.4	390
Savannah Bancorp	SAVB	A	27.75	0.54	1.9	1,127
Seacoast Banking FL	SBCF	A-	20.03	0.56	2.8	256
SEI Investments	SEIC	A	36.92	0.20	0.5	567
Sigma-Aldrich	SIAL	A+	62.63	0.76	1.2	322
SLM Corp.	SLM	A-	48.14	0.76	1.6	429
Southwest Bancorp(OK)	OKSB	A	19.35	0.30	1.6	292
Sovran Self Storage	SSS	B+	41.10	2.42	5.9	357
State Street Corp.	STT	A	43.40	0.68	1.6	312
Sterling Bancorp	STL	A+	24.96	0.76	3.0	595
Sterling Bancshares	SBIB	A	14.74	0.24	1.6	280
Stryker Corp.	SYK	B+	50.03	0.09	0.2	800
Suffolk Bancorp	SUBK	A+	33.74	0.76	2.3	285
Summit Bancshares	SBIT	A	19.00	0.28	1.5	409
Synovus Financial	SNV	A+	27.36	0.73	2.7	376
Sysco Corp.	SYY	A+	34.60	0.60	1.7	445
T.Rowe Price Group	TROW	A	61.29	0.92	1.5	475
TCF Financial	TCB	A	27.47	0.85	3.1	473
Toronto-Dominion Bk.	TD	A-	40.60	1.60	3.9	264
Trustmark Corp.	TRMK	A	27.83	0.80	2.9	262
U.S.B. Holding	UBH	A	23.09	0.52	2.3	1,227
Wal-Mart Stores	WMT	A+	51.49	0.52	1.0	441
Washington Mutual	WM	A	41.89	1.84	4.4	438
Wells Fargo	WFC	A	59.90	1.92	3.2	327
West Coast Bancorp (OR)	WCBO	A-	24.37	0.37	1.5	285
Westamerica Bancorporation	WABC	A	52.40	1.20	2.3	387
Wiley(John)Sons	JW.B	A	34.70	0.30	0.9	310

good dividend-paying stock that fell out of bed is the Florida-based Winn-Dixie Stores, one of the biggest U.S. food retailers in terms of supermarket sales. The company had paid a dividend since 1934 and frequently raised it over the years. However, undercut by Wal-Mart and other stores in the highly competitive Sunbelt, Winn-Dixie has fallen on hard times. It slashed its annual dividend from $1.02 a share to $0.36 in 2002; to $0.20 in 2003; and to $0.15 in 2004. The company omitted the dividend in 2005 and filed for Chapter 11 bankruptcy in February of that year.

We like to regard Winn-Dixie as the exception that proves the rule and strongly advocate buying select companies with long histories of rising dividends. You'll see some outstanding candidates in Figure 5-2. Again, for diversification purposes and to lower your risk, choose a package of these stocks. And keep your eye on them.

If you examine the list, you may be surprised that there is not one electric utility among the stocks. Though many utilities increase their dividends annually, those hikes in recent years have rarely outpaced the inflation rate. Utilities generally have higher yields and are appealing if you need current income. But if you're planning to retire 10 or more years from now, your retirement income stream will be higher if you invest in stocks that raise their dividends at a brisk pace.

Financial services companies dominate the list of steadily increasing dividend payers, with regional banks standing out. As the banking industry continues to consolidate (see Chapter 4), many of the regionals will likely be bought out, which adds a potential kicker.

Not surprising, the list has some familiar "big brand" names. These highly profitable and well-run companies include Home Depot, Wal-Mart, McDonald's, and Harley-Davidson.

There are three prominent health care companies in our list: Pfizer, Johnson & Johnson, and medical device maker Medtronic. Despite talk of lowering medical and pharmaceutical costs and some problem drugs, these companies enjoy high profit margins, and they should continue to reward investors with increasing dividends.

Not all companies on the list will do in the next 10 years what they did in the last 10. You need to do your homework. Investigate the

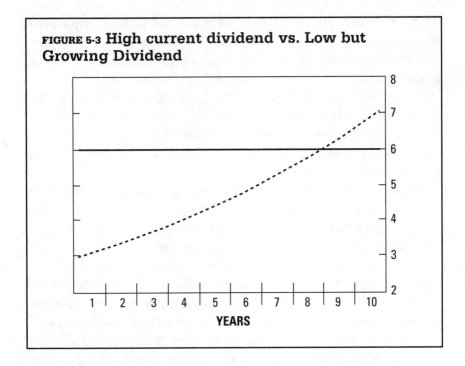

FIGURE 5-3 **High current dividend vs. Low but Growing Dividend**

companies carefully before you invest in their stocks and keep in mind that, for the best returns, you must diversify across industries.

Given a choice between a high current dividend and a low but growing one, we believe that you should always choose the latter (unless you desperately need the income now). The simple chart in Figure 5-3 shows you why. Let's say Joe's $100 investment returns a steady $6 annually. Mary invests an equal amount in a stock that pays only $3 a year, but the company raises its dividend 10 percent annually. In the early years, Joe is clearly ahead. But by year nine, Mary's annual return has outpaced Joe's, and it will continue to grow as compounding works its magic.

Points to Remember

➤ Inflation is sometimes called a silent risk because of its quietly eroding nature. The continuing rise in the level of prices paid for goods and services is a serious threat to your financial future.

➤ A 3 percent increase per year in the inflation rate doubles prices in 24 years. A 4 percent annual inflation rate cuts your purchasing power in half in 18 years, while a 6 percent rate results in prices doubling in only 12 years.

➤ Investing in stocks of companies that regularly increase their dividends is one of the best ways to stay ahead of inflation over the longer term.

➤ You should view a stock's current dividend as a yield on what you paid for the stock (your cost basis). Although the dividend rose, your cost didn't.

➤ Stocks with dividends that grow into a well-above-average yield on your cost outperform the historical total return of the S&P 500 with the stocks' dividends alone.

➤ Although most companies that have boosted their dividends regularly for a decade will continue to do so, some obviously won't. It's important, therefore, to invest in a basket of these stocks.

➤ Make sure your portfolio is diversified across several industries to avoid putting all your eggs in one basket.

➤ Stocks that offer low current yields but increasing dividends are a better choice for long-term investors than high-yield stocks with modest or marginal earnings growth.

CHAPTER 6

Magnify Your Returns via Dividend Reinvestment

I f you don't need the income from dividend-paying stocks and mutual funds, an excellent way to build your portfolio and increase your potential return at the same time is through dividend reinvestment plans. Most of these plans allow partial reinvestment of dividends, so you can have your cake and eat it too if your income requirements are modest.

Dividend reinvestment provides a powerful boost to a portfolio's long-term return because of compounding. Take the S&P 500 as an example. From 1994 to 2004, the index was up a hefty 138.4 percent in terms of capital appreciation, despite the 2000–2002 severe bear market. But factor in reinvested dividends and the figure balloons to 186 percent—a sizable difference. Over the longer term, the variance has been more impressive. From the end of 1974 to the end of 2004, the S&P 500 with dividends reinvested racked up a 13.7 percent annual return versus a 10 percent annual return without payments.

That's what you call the magic of compounding, which is the way your investment grows on the initial money you invested and on the interest or dividends earned. When someone asked Albert Einstein what was the most important thing he learned from mathematics, he replied: "Compound interest. It's the most powerful force on earth." (We saw the compounding effect of dividend reinvesting illustrated in Figure 1-2, in Chapter 1.)

In his classic book *The Intelligent Investor*, Benjamin Graham, who is regarded as the father of investment analysis, gives the following example that dramatizes the force of dividend reinvestment. If an investor put $15 a month in the 30 stocks of the Dow Jones Industrial Average from August 1929 (two months before the market crashed) to the start of 1949 and reinvested the dividends, the $3,600 investment would have increased to more than $8,500, for an 8 percent average annual total return. Not bad, considering the Dow Jones index skidded 69 percent in that period.

DRIPs

Dividend reinvestment plans (DRIPs) have a long history. Though mutual funds and closed-end funds gave investors the option of buying more stock with reinvested dividends virtually since their inception, individual companies were not allowed to offer these plans until 1968. In that year, Citibank offered DRIPs on companies for which it acted as transfer agent. In 1977, Allegheny Power was the first to come out with its own plan. There are now more than 1,000 DRIPs, and the number is climbing.

In order to participate in a DRIP, you must own at least one share of stock. The share or shares also must be in your name, not a "street name." Under "street name" ownership, the shares are held by the broker and maintained in the investor's account.

Once you're a shareholder of record, you can enroll in the company's DRIP. Contact the shareholder relations department or the company's transfer agent for a DRIP application and prospectus. You can also get information online at such Web sites as www.dripcentral.com, www.wall-street.com, and www.investorguide.com.

You should buy your first share or shares from a discount broker, or you could purchase it from several different organizations, such as those below.

> The National Association of Investment Clubs (NAIC) has more than 100 participating DRIP companies. You can buy only one share or a fraction of a share. There is a membership fee, and it costs $7 to buy a share in a company.

> NetStockDirect. This Web site (www.netstockdirect.com) not only lists companies that offer DRIPs, but also offers a discount-type brokerage service, ShareBuilder, where you can invest for $4 per trade in 4,000 different companies. ShareBuilder is not an official DRIP site, but it is a way to invest in a DRIP manner, such as reinvesting dividends, even in those companies that don't have a DRIP.

> BUYandHOLD (www.buyandhold.com) is similar to ShareBuilder. You can invest in a DRIP fashion in companies that don't have DRIPs. BUYandHOLD charges $6.99 per month, which includes two purchases per month. Additional buys are $2.99 each. It allows unlimited monthly transactions for $14.99 a month, or if you open an IRA, only $2.99 per trade.

> First Share, Inc. (1-800-683-0743). This is a membership organization ($18 a year) that assists investors in acquiring their first qualifying share of a DRIP stock. It links members with investors willing to sell a single share in a company. Members pay sellers the share's market value plus $7.50. You also pay First Share $10 per transaction.

> Moneypaper. This organization (Web site: www.moneypaper.com, telephone number 1-800-388-9993) allows you to buy initial shares of more than 1,000 DRIP companies through its brokerage arm. The stock purchase fee is $20 for subscribers to Moneypaper's monthly newsletter ($90 annually) and $30 for nonsubscribers.

Folios

Most of the companies described above offer what are known as "folio services," which are a cross between a mutual fund and an online brokerage account with DRIP characteristics. These firms keep their brokerage fees low by "window trading," which involves collecting customer orders and then placing them in bulk form at predetermined times or "windows."

Another of these companies is Foliofn. At their Web site (www.foliofn.com), you can buy up to 50 stocks by simply entering the ticker symbol and the dollar amounts. Or you can choose up to 75 prepackaged folios, such as the folio utility, which are the 15 stocks in the Dow Jones Utility Average, a folio of bank stocks, REIT stocks, or a folio of the 10 highest-yielding stocks in the Dow Jones Industrial Average, known as the "Dogs of the Dow," which we will discuss in Chapter 8.

There is no minimum account size, and you can purchase fractional shares of the stocks in the folios. An annual membership fee of $199 ($19.95 a month) allows you to build one folio and includes up to 200 free trades monthly. Or if you don't want the membership, you pay $4 for each buy and sell order you place. The Foliofn Web site also offers such research data as P/E ratios, yields, earnings estimates, income statements, and balance sheets, as well as daily, weekly, and monthly prices and volumes.

The folio approach may work out fine if you have sufficient money to start. But if you have less than $5,000 to $10,000, buying dozens of stocks can eat into your return.

DSPs

Direct stock plans (DSPs) get our vote as the preferred way to reinvest dividends. With DSPs there's no need to use a broker at all. DSPs have a shorter history than DRIPs. At the end of 1994 the Securities and Exchange Commission (SEC) made changes in so-called open availability dividend reinvestment plans, with the result that these plans became much easier and far less costly for a company to offer. Direct stock plans allow investors to make initial purchases directly from the companies versus the nonavailability plans (DRIPs), where, as discussed above, you must own at least one share to get into the plan.

DSPs have become very popular both with companies and investors. There are more than 400 in existence, and a number of new ones pop up each year. Although there are some fees to open an account and some plans charge $1 or so for optional cash purchases (see below), DSPs are far cheaper than buying stock through a broker, even a discount house. (You'll find a list of our favorite DSPs with their features in Chapter 10.)

A number of DSPs and DRIPs permit you to open an Individual Retirement Account. If you open a traditional IRA, you don't have to worry about taxes until you start to draw down the money at a later date (you can start to withdraw without a penalty when you reach age $59^{1/2}$). If you qualify for a Roth IRA (your income can't exceed a certain amount), you don't pay any taxes when you withdraw the money if you're over $59^{1/2}$ and have been in the Roth IRA for at least five years. Companies that offer IRAs include ExxonMobil, Federal National Mortgage, McDonald's, Allstate Corp., and Wal-Mart Stores.

Advantages of DRIPs and DSPs

For the long-term investor, dividend reinvestment plans offer a convenient and low-cost way to build a stock portfolio. By participating in a DRIP or a DSP, your stake in a company increases dramatically over time. (We saw how the S&P 500 index has grown considerably with the magic of compounding via dividend reinvesting.)

For example, if in 1994 you had invested $1,000 in the beverage and snack company Pepsico and reinvested the dividends, your money would have grown to $3,291 in 2004, for an average annual rate of return of 12.6 percent.)

Of course it can also work the other way. As an extreme example, $1,000 invested in Eastman Kodak in 1994 would have dwindled to $793 in 2004. The moral: You can't buy and just hold; you've got to monitor. Do your homework.

Incidentally, companies also benefit from DRIPs and DSPs. They would not offer dividend reinvestment plans if they did not get something from them. DRIPs and DSPs attract small investors who are more loyal to a company than the big institutions, such as mutual funds, pension plans, and banks. Smaller investors tend to hold stocks longer, which reduces volatility, and are more apt to buy the company's products or services. Also, if a company issues new shares for its dividend reinvestment plans, it is an inexpensive way to raise capital. That's a key reason the capital-intensive utilities and banks have the heaviest DRIP and DSP representation.

Optional Cash Purchases

One of the most attractive features of both DRIPs and DSPs is the optional cash purchase. At one time only a handful of companies that had DRIP plans allowed you to buy shares with optional cash payments (OCPs) in addition to plowing back the dividends. And the maximum amount you could invest via OCPs was relatively low, with the money invested only monthly or quarterly.

The vast majority of DRIPs and DSPs now allow much larger maximum optional cash payments, while keeping the minimums low. With the direct stock plans, the money is usually invested weekly. All of the DSPs and many of the DRIPs permit investing via automatic debits from checking or savings accounts each month, which encourages disciplined investing—the key to a successful financial future.

Each plan has a minimum investment to get started, ranging from $50 to $1,000, but if you sign up for the automatic debit feature, plans with high initial cash requirements usually waive the payment.

Dollar Cost Averaging

You get the benefit of dollar cost averaging when you buy shares via the optional cash payment feature of DRIPs and DSPs. This systematic buying program entails the investment of similar dollar amounts at fixed intervals. You buy fewer shares when prices are high, more shares when they are low. Over the years, your average cost per share using this formula method of investing will likely be lower than the average of your purchase prices, providing the stock or mutual fund is in a basic long-term uptrend.

The best way to take full advantage of dollar cost averaging is to have a set amount of money taken out of your checking or savings account monthly. Here's an example of how dollar cost averaging plays out if you automatically buy $200 worth of a blue-chip stock directly from the company every month:

1. The first month, the stock trades for $60 a share. Your $200 buys 3.3 shares. One of the big positives in buying from most mutual funds or via dividend reinvestment plans is that you can purchase fractional shares.

2. The next month, the stock sells for $50 a share. Your $200 investment now buys four shares.

3. The third month, the stock rises to $65, and your $200 investment buys 3.1 shares.

4. The fourth month, the stock slips back to the $60 level, and your $200 buys 3.3 shares again.

At the end of four months you've invested $800 to purchase 13.7 shares at an average price of $58.39, which is lower than the $60 price it traded at four months earlier. You have a profit of $1.61 a share because when the stock dropped, you bought more shares.

Value Averaging

Value averaging is another form of dollar cost averaging. The difference is that you don't make the same investment each month in a stock or mutual fund as you would in dollar cost averaging. Instead, you vary the amount invested so that the value of the portfolio increases by a fixed sum or percentage at each interval.

Say that instead of investing $300 every month, you want the value of your investment to rise by $300 each month. In the first month, the value of your investment rose $100. Under value investing, you would add $200 to your investment in order to achieve your goal of having the investment gain $300 each month. Since you want the investment to increase only $300, if the investment rose $400 in any one month, you would sell $100 worth of the investment. On the other hand, if the value of the investment fell $100, you would have to cough up $400: $100 to make up for the loss plus $300 to increase the value of the portfolio.

With value averaging you know how much your portfolio will be worth at the end of your investment time frame, but you don't know how much it will cost out of pocket. Under dollar cost averaging, you know how much you'll invest, but you don't know what the value will be at the end of your investment time frame.

Value averaging obviously is a more aggressive approach than dollar cost averaging. Besides having to invest more money at times, value averaging entails trading and tax costs, since you have to sell stock to stay within your targeted investment value. Also, you have to spend more time monitoring your portfolio than with dollar cost averaging.

Enrolling and Exiting a DSP

To get started in a direct stock plan, you simply send for the prospectus, complete the authorization form that's included, and mail it to the bank or firm administering the plan. You can also enroll online in some companies. Most companies have their dividend reinvestment prospectuses online, as well as information on how to obtain the authorization form. The number one transfer agent handling DSPs is Computershare (formerly EquiServe, which was the result of a merger between First Chicago Trust Company of New York and Boston EquiServe). Computershare can be accessed at www. computershare.com, and you can view your account on the Computershare Web site. NetStockDirect also allows you to enroll in some plans online.

At one time, if you wanted to sell a DSP, you had to notify the company in writing. Now, more and more DSP plans permit you to sell over the telephone or online.

Plan participants receive periodic statements showing the amount of full and fractional shares purchased, and the prices paid. You will receive a 1099 form at the end of the year, because even though you don't receive the dividends, they are taxable. But when you sell the shares, the dividends on which you were taxed are added to your cost basis, which reduces your capital gains tax. It's important, therefore, to keep year-end statements.

Diversify Your Choices

To build an effective, diversified dividend reinvestment portfolio, stick with a mix of good quality stocks (those ranked at least B+ by Standard & Poor's) that have a history of boosting their dividends The mix should include an energy company, a health care firm, and a utility, as well as a company in each of these sectors: financial, consumer products, and technology.

You should not own more than 15 stocks in your portfolio. You can get adequate diversification with that number, providing the stocks are not closely correlated. If there are more than 15 stocks in a portfolio, you lower your chances for above-average gains, and your risk is not reduced very much.

Technology Stocks Get in on the Act

Not that long ago you didn't have much of a choice if you wanted to invest in technology stocks via dividend reinvestment plans. IBM was about the only pure player. Now, partly thanks to the lower tax rate on dividends, the number of tech companies that have initiated dividends and offer DRIPs and DSPs are growing. Counted among the technology plans, in addition to Microsoft, are Analog Devices (ticker symbol: ADI), Hewlett-Packard (HPQ), Intel (INTC), Maxim Integrated Products (MXIM), Qualcomm (QCOM), Texas Instruments (TXN), XM Satellite (XMSR), Xilinx (XLNX), and Yahoo! (YHOO). The last two companies don't pay dividends, but still offer direct purchase plans. As we mentioned, DSPs and DRIPs can be an inexpensive way for a company to raise capital.

As more tech companies move out of their high growth stage, we should see an increasing number starting to pay dividends. At the same time, many of these companies are flush with cash. In the fourth quarter of 2005, the 78 tech companies in the S&P 500 held $140 billion in cash. Some good candidates to initiate dividends as well as to start offering DSPs and DRIPs include Cisco Systems (CSCO), Dell Computer (DELL), Electronic Arts (ERTS), and Intuit (INTU).

Disadvantages of DRIPs and DSPs

No investment is perfect, and dividend reinvestment plans have their drawbacks. For one, you don't have close control in timing purchases or sales. To better time a sale, you can request a stock certificate from your plan company after you've acquired 100 shares and sell them through a discount broker. Also, more companies now allow you to sell over the telephone or on the Internet.

Another minus for dividend reinvestment plans is that you may stick with a plan of a company whose long-term fundamentals are lackluster. The key to buying a DRIP or DSP is not the enticing features of the plan, but the quality of the underlying stock. You have to do your homework. The dividend reinvestment stocks we recommend in Chapter 10 have historically had strong earnings and dividend records, as well as leading positions in their market places, but you must stay on top of them. Anything can happen down the road, as we've seen with Ma Bell and some other former blue chips.

A final drawback we've already mentioned is that if you're not in an IRA, you must report your dividends as taxable income even though you don't actually receive them. This is a minor disadvantage, though, especially in view of the more favorable tax treatment.

The many positives of DRIPs and DSPs clearly offset the negatives, particularly for the investor who takes advantage of the plans' automatic debit feature. The old adage applies here: "What you don't have, you don't miss." You will be pleasantly surprised to see how much, in how little time, your stake in a company grows when you invest on a regular basis and reinvest the dividends.

Points to Remember

➤ Dividend reinvestment provides a powerful boost to a portfolio's long-term return because of compounding, which is the way your investment grows on the initial money you invested and on the interest or dividends earned.

➤ Dividend reinvestment plans (DRIPs) provide a good way to build your portfolio on a systematic basis. Most of these plans allow you to not only reinvest the dividends but also to purchase additional shares.

➤ With DRIPs, you have to own at least one share to join the plan. You can buy the first share through a discount broker or via several different companies, such as First Share and Moneypaper. Various online firms also offer folio services, which are a cross between a mutual fund and a brokerage account.

➤ Direct stock plans (DSPs) are more attractive than DRIPs in that you don't need to use a broker. You buy the shares directly from the companies. Although there are some fees involved, DSPs are far cheaper than buying stock through a broker.

➤ A number of DRIPs and DSPs permit you to open either traditional or Roth Individual Retirement Accounts (IRAs).

➤ When you take advantage of the optional cash purchase feature offered by most of the plans and set up an automatic debit from your savings or checking account, you get the benefit of dollar cost averaging, whereby over the years your average cost per share will likely be lower than the average of your purchase prices.

➤ Companies also benefit from dividend reinvestment plans since they attract smaller investors who tend to hold stocks longer, which reduces volatility, and these investors are more apt to buy the company's products or services. And if a company issues new shares for its plan, it's a cheap way to raise capital.

➤ In building a DRIP or DSP portfolio, diversification is important. Stick with a mix of good quality stocks that have a history of boosting their dividends. The mix should include an energy company, a health care firm, and a utility, as well as a company in the consumer products, technology, and telecommunications sectors. You don't need more than 15 stocks in your DRIP or DSP portfolio, providing they are not closely correlated.

➤ There are a few disadvantages in dividend reinvestment plans, such as limited control over timing of purchases and sales. The pluses, though, far outweigh the minuses.

CHAPTER 7

Dividend-Oriented Mutual Funds and ETFs That Let You Sleep at Night

O ne of the basic tenets of a successful investment program is diversification. The importance of this concept was forcefully brought home in the blazing bull market of 1990–2000, which saw the S&P 500 index jump at least 20 percent in each of those years and the Nasdaq index rocket 1,400 percent in the 10-year period.

Investors got caught up in the so-called "dot-com" stocks and funneled their money into these Internet start-up companies, many of which eventually crashed and burned. Dot-com morphed into dot-bomb.

Though not a dot-com company, Enron has become a classic example of investor madness. The darling of Wall Street, Enron was considered a creative, innovative company. Among other things, Enron bought electricity from utilities and sold it to consumers. When it came out that the company had overstated its profits by more than $580 million from 1997 to 2001, it went belly up and had the dubious honor of being the biggest bankruptcy in U.S. history. Stockholders, especially employees who had all their retirement money in the shares, were left empty-handed.

It's doubtful that all investors have learned their lesson. The gambling instinct inevitably comes to the fore when the market is juiced up and everybody seems to be making money in the latest hot stock or sector. Odds are, though, that the type of investor who is attracted to solid dividend-paying stocks will not be sucked in. These people are on the right track. They believe that the investment race does not belong to the swift trader hopping on board every speculative vehicle but to the rational long-term investor who knows that buying a diversified portfolio of stocks that pay dividends and regularly increase them are the engines that power a secure financial future.

Good Diversification Vehicles

Mutual funds and exchange traded funds (ETFs) provide an easy and convenient way to diversify. Income investors can choose various mutual funds that invest in money market instruments, bonds, and/or preferred stocks; these are called *income* funds, or *balanced* funds. They focus on both stocks and bonds. Their main objective is income, with capital gains a secondary consideration.

For dividend investors seeking a combination of income and capital appreciation, *equity income* funds (also called *large value*) and *growth and income* funds (also known as *large blend*) can fit the bill.

Growth and Income

This type of fund aims for steady, though not high, income payouts, while placing equal weight on capital appreciation. Many of the stocks in the S&P 500 index are found in growth and income funds. The majority of the funds are large-capitalization portfolios (capitalization is arrived at by multiplying the number of outstanding shares of a company by the stock price), with various percentages in different industries, known as "sector weightings."

Growth and income funds are less susceptible to economic recessions and to sectors going in and out of investment favor. They generally seek growth of capital and current income and invest primarily in stocks with above-average yields and the potential to appreciate in price. Typically, the price-earnings ratios of the stocks in growth and income funds are below that of the S&P 500. Both Morningstar and Standard & Poor's, which rank mutual funds, call these funds "large blend."

Equity Income

This type of fund seeks relatively high current income and growth of income by investing 60 percent or more of their portfolios in stocks. Risk is generally low. Managers of equity income funds normally attempt to provide yields that are at least 50 percent higher than the yield of the S&P 500. Big dividend payers, such as utilities, financials, health care, energy, and consumer staples, can be found in the typical equity income portfolio.

Despite the conservative nature of growth and income funds and equity income funds, studies have shown that, over the longer term, they come close to matching the performance of more aggressive funds, such as those in the growth and small cap categories. Moreover, the dividend-oriented funds as a whole have chalked up strong records with fewer down years and less steep declines than the more aggressive funds. Over the 15-year period ending in 2004, the average annual total return of the Lipper equity income funds category was 10.3 percent. Since January 2003, when the lower tax rate on dividends was passed, the number of equity income funds jumped to over 240, or more than 35 percent, as of the first quarter of 2005, compared with an increase of only 6 percent for all stock funds.

Sales Charges

The dividend-oriented funds we recommend later in this chapter are all no-load, which means there is no sales charge to buy them. By purchasing a no-load fund directly from the fund company, you don't pay a commission and all of your money is invested.

For example, $5,000 invested in a 5 percent front-load fund results in a $250 sales charge and only $4,750 investment in the fund. If a load fund is held for many years, the effect of the load, if paid up front (back loads are paid when investors redeem their shares), is not diminished as quickly as many believe. If the money paid for the load had been working for you, as in a no-load fund, it would have been compounding over the entire period. A fee difference of only 1 percent for a $100,000 investment earning an 8 percent annual return can reduce the value of your investment by $70,000, or about 13 percent over a 20-year period.

Some observers maintain that load versus no-load is not an important issue, and that the key to picking a fund is the manager's performance. But for every strong-performing load fund, there is a similar no-load or low-load fund. In fact, studies have shown that no-load funds have a superior record to load funds over the longer term.

You should be aware that funds have various ways of tacking on sales charges. At one time an 8.5 percent front-end sales commission— the maximum allowed by the National Association of Securities Dealers—was common. Now, few, if any, funds charge that much. The loads usually range between 3 and 6 percent. Most charge about 5 percent. The lower fees reflect mutual funds' goal to build assets, since management fees are based on a percentage of a fund's total assets.

Watch the Classes

Be aware, however, of hidden fees with the various classes of mutual funds:

➤ Class A shares charge a front-end load.

➤ Class B shares typically have a 12b-1 fee (for sales and marketing expenses) and a back-end load that decreases the longer the fund is held. These shares usually carry contingent deferred sales charges for up to six years. Class B shares appear to be on the way out, with regulators going after brokers for recommending these second-class investments when the more attractive A shares are available.

➤ Class C shares are those that have a level load, which typically levies an annual charge of 1 percent of your account balance. Since the fund takes away from you 1 percent every single year, the level load winds up being the most expensive type of load for long-term investors.

In 2005 the brokerage units of American Express, J.P. Morgan Chase, and Citigroup were censured and fined for improperly pushing mutual funds. They recommended Class B shares and Class C shares without disclosing that A shares might have been a more advantageous way to invest.

Examine Expense Ratios

Just because a fund does not impose a sales charge doesn't mean it's a good buy. You have to look at the expense ratio, as well as at the long-term performance. The expense ratio, expressed as "total operating expenses" in the fund's prospectus, represents a percentage of the fund's average assets. A fund's expenses include a management fee, administrative costs, 12b-1 distribution fees, and other operating expenses. The management, or advisory, fee generally represents the largest percentage of a fund's total operating expenses. It is an ongoing annual charge paid to the fund's portfolio managers.

New rules mandating increased disclosure of how fees are set went into effect at the end of the first quarter in 2005. In the past, funds usually discussed in very general terms how fees were set, and that disclosure was buried in something called "Statement of Additional Information," which was rarely seen by mutual fund holders. Now, funds are required to discuss specific circumstances of the fund and how the board evaluated each factor. Also, the fund has to reveal the extent to which economies of scale would be realized as the fund grows, and whether fee levels reflect these economies of scale for the fund investors.

So in addition to making sure the fund you're thinking of buying is no-load, you must take a close look at its expense ratio. Index funds, such as those that track the S&P 500 index or the Russell 5000 index, typically charge about 0.2 percent of assets. The expense ratio of actively managed funds averages 1.4 percent annually. If you buy a fund through a broker, you will pay on average another 0.4 percent, which adds up to 1.8 percent. We would in general not recommend any fund that has an expense ratio over 1 percent, and we advise buying those funds that you can purchase directly from the companies.

You can compare mutual fund costs and fund classes using an online calculator at the Securities & Exchange Commission Web site (www.sec.gov). Click on "investor information" and "calculators."

Exchange Traded Funds (ETFs)

Exchange traded funds, or ETFs, are similar to mutual funds, but they trade on stock exchanges like regular stocks, and as such, their prices are determined by supply and demand. To keep commission costs as low as possible, you should buy ETFs only through discount or online brokers.

An ETF is actually a basket of stocks that is based on an index. The official definition of an ETF, according to the AMEX (where the vast majority of ETFs are traded), is "a registered investment company under the Investment Company Act of 1940, which has received certain exemptive relief from the SEC to allow secondary market trading in the ETF shares. ETFs are index-based products, in that each ETF holds a portfolio of securities that is intended to provide investment results that, before fees and expenses, generally correspond to the price and yield performance of the underlying bench market index."

Unlike closed-end funds (mutual funds are called open-end), which trade at a premium or discount to their net asset value (NAV), ETFs are priced in line with their intrinsic value. As a result, investors can get in or out of the shares anytime at a price close to NAV. This is helpful especially when the market is in a free fall. Mutual fund holders can only sell their investment at the closing price on any day. Also, ETFs can be sold short and bought on margin.

ETFs generally are more tax efficient than mutual funds because the trading turnover tends to be much lower. As a result, capital gains distributions are kept to a minimum. That translates to lower taxes and keeps commission costs down.

Another advantage of ETFs is that their expense ratios are typically about half those of similar mutual funds. For example, the expense ratio of iShares S&P 500 index is only 0.09 percent, versus 0.18 percent for the Vanguard 500 Index Fund. One more plus is that, unlike a mutual fund, ETFs don't have to keep high cash reserves to meet redemptions; ETFs are never forced to sell securities in a falling market if a large number of investors want to bail out.

The first ETF, Standard & Poor's Depositary Receipts (SPDR), less formally known as "Spiders," began trading on the American Stock Exchange in January 1993. Spiders is by far the largest ETF. There are now more than 160 ETFs with assets exceeding $200 billion, and the number is climbing. From 2000 to 2005, ETFs grew 37 percent annually, compared with less than a 2 percent increase for mutual funds.

Barclays Global Investors (iShares) is the Goliath in the ETF field, with a 70 percent share. Other companies offering ETFs include Vanguard (Vipers, or Vanguard Index Participation Equity Receipts) and Merrill Lynch (HOLDRs, or Holding Company Depositary Receipts). HOLDRs must be bought or sold in 100-share lots, while ETFs can be purchased in odd lots. Also with HOLDRs, which are sector funds that concentrate in one industry, the portfolios don't add or delete stocks unless the company is acquired or goes out of business.

Among the most heavily traded ETFs are:

SPDR Trust Series securities (symbol: SPY), which track the S&P 500 index

Nasdaq-100 Trust Series I (QQQ), which track the Nasdaq 100 index

Diamonds Trust Series I (DIA), which track the Dow Jones Industrial Average

SPDR Trust Series (MDY), which track the S&P 400 Mid Cap index

One disadvantage of ETFs is that you have to pay a commission to buy and sell them. Another is that ETFs don't necessarily trade at the net asset value of their underlying holdings; that is, an ETF could potentially trade above or below the value of the underlying portfolios. However, historically, the difference has been extraordinarily small.

One more negative for smaller investors is that you can't dollar cost average in an ETF via an automatic plan, as you can in a mutual fund, where the fund can take out money from your checking account each month to buy more shares. Of course, you can dollar cost average in an ETF, but investing small sums is not cost effective because of brokerage commissions. It's generally recommended that those who want to make periodic investments in ETFs should invest at least $1,000 per ETF since the transaction cost would then represent a smaller percentage of the account.

ETFs, though, may become more attractive for smaller investors. At this writing, the Nasdaq stock exchange is working on a new exchange traded fund service that would allow investors without a brokerage account to accumulate money and occasionally purchase shares of the Nasdaq 100 Trust, or Cubes (QQQQ)—a proxy for the technology sector. In this way the small investor can dollar cost average. Nasdaq hopes to price trades at $1 or $2 each; the exact costs would be determined by how often investors send in money and when the cash would be invested. If the pilot program is successful, it could be expanded to include other Nasdaq funds that invest in American Depositary Receipts of international company shares.

Web sites that offer detailed information on ETFs include www.amex.com, www.ishares.com, www.holdrs.com, and www.streettracks.com.

Recommended Dividend-Oriented Mutual Funds

The following listed funds have good long-term performance records, are no-load, have relatively low expense ratios, and boast high S&P performance rankings. The S&P fund performance rankings range from 1 STAR (lowest) to 5 STARS (highest).

Fidelity Dividend Growth (FDGFX)

S&P 10-year performance ranking: 4 STARS

Average annualized 10-year total return (ended March 2005): 13.7 percent

Expense ratio: 0.65 versus 1.37 for peers

Minimum initial investment: $2,500. IRA: $500. Subsequent: $250

Telephone number: (800) 544-8544

Fidelity Equity Income (FEQIX)

S&P 10-year performance ranking: 3 STARS

Average annualized 10-year total return (ended March 2005): 10.97

Expense ratio: 0.69 versus 1.40 for peers

Minimum initial investment: $2,500. IRA: $500. Subsequent: $250

Telephone number: (800) 544-8544

Parnassus Income Trust Equity Income Fund (PRBLX)

S&P 10-year performance ranking: 5 STARS

Average annualized 10-year total return (ended March 2005): 11.8 percent

Expense ratio: 0.95 versus 1.15 for peers

Minimum initial investment: $2,000. IRA: $500. Subsequent: $50

Telephone number: (800) 999-3505

T. Rowe Price Equity Income Fund (PRFDX)

S&P 10-year performance ranking: 4 STARS

Average annualized 10-year total return (ended March 2005): 12.4 percent

Expense ratio: 0.78 versus 1.37 for peers

Minimum initial investment: $2,500. IRA: $1,000. Subsequent: $100

Telephone number: (800) 638-5660

USAA Income Stock (USISX)

S&P 10-year performance ranking: 3 STARS

Average annualized 10-year total return (ended March 2005): 9.09 percent

Expense ratio: 0.79 versus 1.40 for peers

Minimum initial investment: $3,000. IRA: $260. Subsequent: $50

Telephone number: (800) 531-8181

Vanguard Equity Income Fund/Investor (VEIPX)

S&P 10-year performance ranking: 4 STARS

Average annualized 10-year total return (ended March 2005): 12.0 percent

Expense ratio: 0.32 versus 1.37 for peers

Minimum initial investment: $3,000. IRA: $1,000. Subsequent: $100

Telephone number: (800) 662-2739

Vanguard Growth & Income Fund/Investor (VQNPX)

S&P 10-year performance ranking: 4 STARS

Average annualized 10-year total return (ended March 2005): 11.9 percent

Expense ratio: 0.42 versus 1.15 for peers

Minimum initial investment: $3,000. IRA: $1,000. Subsequent: $100

Telephone number: (800) 662-2739

Recommended Dividend Oriented ETFs

The following exchange traded funds all have low expense ratios and are attractive for income-oriented investors who do not want to funnel money gradually or through automatic investment plans into mutual funds via dollar cost averaging.

iShares Dow Jones Select Dividend Index (DVY)

Since its inception in 2003, the iShares Dow Jones Select Dividend Index has become one of the fastest growing exchange traded funds. Investing exclusively in dividend-paying stocks, the fund tracks the performance of the Dow Jones Dividend Index, which includes 100 of the highest-yielding stocks in the broader Dow Jones U.S. Total Market Index. The benchmark and DVY invest in stocks of companies that have increased their dividends over the previous five years and that pay out less than 60 percent in earnings.

For the one-year period ended February 2005, DVY had a total return of 11.6 percent versus a total return of 7.0 percent for the S&P 500. DVY does not pay out dividends to fundholders; instead, the payments go toward buying additional shares of stock.

iShares S&P Global Financial Sector (IXG)

This exchange traded fund's objective is for long-term maximum capital appreciation by investing primarily in stocks of companies within the financial sector, including banks, diversified financial, and insurance. Top holdings in early 2005 included Citigroup, Bank of America, HSBC Holdings, Wells Fargo & Co., Royal Bank of Scotland, Wachovia, and UBS AG.

For the three-year period that ended February 2005, iShares S&P Global Financial Sector had an average annualized total return of 11.7 percent versus a total return of 4.6 percent for the S&P 500 index.

Select Sector SPDR: Utilities (XLU)

Part of the Select Sector SPDR Funds family, Select Sector SPDR: Utilities seeks long-term maximum capital appreciation by investing primarily in stocks of electric, gas, water, and multi-utility companies. Utilities included in the ETF in mid-2005 included TXU Corp., FPL Group, Teco Energy, and PG&E Corp.

For the five-year period ended February 2005, XLU recorded an average annualized total return of 7.3 percent, compared with a total return of 1.4 percent for all equity utilities sector funds. The fund has outperformed its peer group index (S&P 500 Utilities Sector index) in two of the last five years.

PowerShares High Yield Dividend Achievers (PEY)

PEY invests in the 50 highest-yielding stocks of companies that have raised their annual dividends in every year for at least the past 10. Unlike the iShares Dow Jones Select Dividend Index, stocks in PowerShares High Yield Dividend Achievers are weighted according to their dividend yield, not by market capitalization size.

When launched in early 2005, the fund attracted more than $135 million in assets and yielded 3.5 percent.

iShares Dow Jones U.S. Utilities Sector (IDX)

This ETF, as with Select SPDR: Utilities, looks for long-term capital appreciation by investing mainly in different types of utilities. In early 2005, top holdings of the fund included Exelon Corp., Duke Energy, and Southern Co.

For the three-year period ended February 2005, iShares Dow Jones U.S. Utilities Sector had an average annualized total return of 9.3 percent versus a total return of 9.0 percent for all equity utilities sector funds.

S&P Quality Rankings Global Equity Managed Trust (BQY)

This closed-end exchange traded fund seeks to provide current income and capital appreciation by investing primarily in high quality stocks with above-average dividends. Launched in late 2004, the trust's investment process begins with the universe of equity securities of issuers contained in the S&P Quality Rankings, which are intended to capture in a single ranking the growth and stability of a U.S. company's earnings and dividends over the most recent 10 years. The S&P International Quality Rankings are intended to capture in a single ranking the growth and stability of a non-U.S. issuer's earnings and dividends over the most recent seven years.

Closed-End Funds

Unlike open-end mutual funds that issue and redeem shares at net asset value (NAV), closed-end funds have a fixed number of shares outstanding. They increase the number of shares only when raising new capital through secondary offerings, and they can buy back shares on the open market. Since supply and demand determine their share prices, closed-end funds may sell at discounts or premiums to NAV. The funds are traded like individual stocks on the stock exchanges.

With closed-end funds, managements are not forced to sell low as investors exit a falling market or to buy high with new money. These funds can take a longer-term view than mutual funds that are subject to net redemptions, and can also hold illiquid stocks that might put other funds in a bind.

Dividend-oriented closed-end funds include Adams Express (symbol: ADX), Tri-Continental Corp. (TY), Eaton Vance Tax-Advantaged Global Dividend Fund (ETG), Nuveen Tax-Advantaged Total Return Strategy Fund (JTA), Dreman/Claymore Dividend & Income Fund (DCS), and Cohen & Steers, REIT & Utility Income Fund (JNC).

A listing of closed-end funds can be found in *Standard & Poor's Stock Guide*, which is published monthly.

Withdrawal Plans

When you wish to start drawing on your nest egg to provide a steady income stream, you might consider setting up a systematic withdrawal plan. Virtually all mutual funds offer these plans, which permit you to set a monthly, quarterly, semi-annual, or annual schedule to receive regular payments from your fund (either directly to you or to your bank account). You can adjust your withdrawals should your expenses change, or you can cancel the plan if you no longer need the periodic income.

There are three withdrawal plan options:

1. You can set up a fixed dollar amount.

2. You can set up a specific type of fixed dollar amount designed to pay you the entire value of your account over a certain period of time.

3. You can receive a percentage of your account value.

How do you determine how much you can safely take out of your mutual funds without running out of money? A rule of thumb is that if you plan to be in retirement for 20 to 25 years, you should withdraw 4 to 5 percent. If you expect to be retired for 30 years or more, you should trim your withdrawal to 3 to 4 percent.

The withdrawal amount can be increased by the annual inflation rate. For example, a $13,000 per-year withdrawal from a fund with a value of $400,000 can be raised to $13,390 the next year, assuming a 3 percent inflation rate. There are various retirement income calculators on the Internet that you can use to put in different withdrawal rates.

T. Rowe Price and Vanguard, among others, also offer personalized services, for a fee of around $500, which include free annual reviews (if you have a certain amount invested). They give you computerized planning and modeling geared to your specific needs and time schedule.

T. Rowe Price was the first to offer a computerized modeling program to help assure retirees that they are invested appropriately and are withdrawing money at a rate that will meet their retirement goals. The program uses "Monte Carlo" modeling, which is a statistical method to project outcomes. The modeling takes into account all possible scenarios for gains and losses, using financial market history since 1921. The program then comes up with the probabilities of success for a variety of alternative investment and withdrawal strategies.

Instead of "Monte Carlo" modeling, Vanguard uses "Time Path Analysis." This involves taking data that go back to 1960 and testing the "sensitivity" of each investment and withdrawal scenario, based on historical experiences.

According to T. Rowe Price, those who take out only 3 percent a year can be fairly conservative with their investments. They can leave most of their money in cash (such as money market funds, CDs, and short-term Treasuries) and bonds. However, you will need a considerable amount of stocks if you want to use a greater withdrawal rate.

T. Rowe Price found that with a withdrawal rate of 4 percent, a $500,000 initial nest egg would probably still be worth a median $395,000 after 30 years if the portfolio was invested 60 percent in stocks, 30 percent in bonds, and 10 percent in cash. On the other hand, if the stock investments were reduced to 20 percent of the portfolio, the median value was only $180,000. (The median value marks the halfway point, with half the "Monte Carlo" simulations ending in a higher balance and half ending lower.)

Most investment professionals believe that the majority of retirees need at least 25 to 45 percent of their portfolios in stocks to generate returns that will keep them ahead of inflation over the long term.

Points to Remember

➤ A good way for dividend-oriented investors to diversify is through no-load mutual funds and exchange traded funds (ETFs) that concentrate on companies that pay dividends and consistently raise them.

➤ The importance of diversification was brought home in the 2000–2002 deep bear market, when investors lost their shirts when they focused on the so-called new economy Internet stocks and the shares of such companies as Enron and WorldCom.

➤ Two types of mutual funds whose holdings are concentrated in dividend payers are growth and income and equity income. A few dividend-oriented fund recommendations: Fidelity Dividend Growth (FDGFX), Parnassus Income Trust Income (PRBLX), T. Rowe Price Equity Income (PRFDX), Vanguard Equity Income (VEIPX), and Vanguard Growth & Income (VQNPX).

➤ Exchange traded funds (ETFs) are similar to mutual funds, but they trade on stock exchanges like regular stocks, and as such, their prices are determined by supply and demand. ETFs actually are baskets of stocks, usually based on a market index.

➤ Advantages of ETFs: tax efficiency, low expense ratios, ease of trading, and they can be sold short and bought on margin.

➤ Disadvantages of ETFs: You must pay a commission to buy and sell them, and they don't necessarily trade at the net asset value of their underlying holdings. Historically, however, the difference has been quite small.

➤ We recommend these dividend-oriented ETFs: iShares Dow Jones Select Dividend Index (DVY), iShares S&P Global Financial Sector (IXG), Select SPDR: Utilities (XLU), PowerShares High Yield Dividend Achievers (PEY), iShares Dow Jones U.S. Utilities Sector (IDX), and S&P Quality Rankings Global Equity Managed Trust (BQY).

➤ Closed-end funds are unlike open-end mutual funds in that they don't issue and redeem shares at net asset value (NAV). Closed-end funds increase shares outstanding only when raising new capital through secondary offerings, and they can buy back shares on the open market.

➤ Since supply and demand determines closed-end share prices, they may sell at discounts or premiums to NAV.

➤ There are a variety of dividend-oriented closed-end funds. *Standard & Poor's Stock Guide*, which is published monthly, lists them.

➤ Withdrawal plans are available from mutual funds for those looking for an income stream in retirement. These plans permit you to set a monthly, quarterly, semi-annual, or annual schedule to receive regular payments.

➤ There are various retirement income calculators on the Internet that you can use to put in different withdrawal rates, or you can get personalized service for a fee from some mutual fund companies.

➤ Those who withdraw only 3 percent a year have greater flexibility with their investments.

➤ Investment professionals recommend that most retirees need at least 25 to 45 percent of their portfolios in stocks to generate returns that will keep them ahead of inflation.

CHAPTER 8

Dividend Strategies

I n this chapter we'll take a look at some of the dividend investment strategies that have been around awhile. These strategies are, in effect, formula-type, similar to dollar cost averaging, which we discussed in Chapter 6.

To review, dollar cost averaging, which simply entails buying a fixed dollar amount of a stock at specific time intervals, offers the potential for profits with reduced market risk. It frees you of the problems of attempting to time market fluctuations, which studies show is a futile effort, and instead to put those swings to work for you. When the price of your stock or mutual fund is low, your money buys more shares; when the price is higher, you receive fewer shares for your money. As a result, the average amount you pay for each share—the average cost per share—likely will be lower than the average price per share.

Stocks that pay dividends and have a history of regularly increasing payments are especially good for dollar cost averaging. This type of stock can help provide a regular money flow for periodic investments, particularly when you have an unexpectedly large bill due that makes it difficult to come up with the money you need to invest. Of course, as we mentioned in Chapter 6, the best way to realize the maximum gains from these stocks is to reinvest the dividends, if you can afford to do so.

Dogs of the Dow

The Dow dividend strategy, or the "Dogs of the Dow" as it is popularly known, has many adherents. The strategy is simplicity itself. At the end of every year, you buy the 10 highest-yielding stocks of the 30 in the Dow Jones Industrial Average, putting equal amounts of money into the 10 issues. Hold the stocks until the end of the following year, and repeat the process.

The fact that the 10 stocks have the highest yield means, of course, that their stock prices are depressed (remember that the yield is figured by dividing the dividend by the price). More often than not, the issues offer good value. They are all well-known, large-capitalization stocks of companies that for the most part are not likely to go out of business. Usually, company-specific problems that have caused investors to shun the stocks can be fixed. Or it may be just a question of time before unfavorable industry conditions can be reversed, such as high interest rates that would adversely affect financial stocks or a recession that would depress the stocks of companies whose fortunes are closely tied to the economy (called cyclical stocks).

In the meantime, you are receiving above-average dividend yields. Even if one or two of the companies cut or omit their dividends, you still garner a solid average yield from the other "Dogs." As with the S&P 500 index, dividends have historically accounted for more than 40 percent of the average total return on all of the Dow Industrial stocks.

The Dogs' strategy of buying stocks of Dow companies that are out of investor favor actually goes way back. In *The Intelligent Investor*, Benjamin Graham refers to a study published in the June 1951 issue of the *Journal of Finance* that documents a strategy of investing in depressed Dow stocks from 1917 to 1950, as well as another study from 1933 to 1969. The studies examined strategies of buying either the six or 10 issues in the Dow Industrial Average trading at the lowest price-to-earnings multiples and rebalancing them every one to five years. The study showed that the strategy was unprofitable from 1917 to 1933, but was a big winner in 1937–1969, outperforming both the Dow Jones Industrial Average and the 10 issues of the Dow that carried the highest P/E multiples.

In recent years the performance of the Dogs of the Dow has been inconsistent. In 2003 the Dogs beat the Dow Jones Industrial

Average by more than 3 percentage points. It fell behind the Dow in 2004, with the Dogs gaining 4.5 percent and the Dow index rising 5.3 percent. Contributing to the lag were such 2004 losers as Merck, falling 30 percent because of the company's problems with its Vioxx arthritis pain drug, which had to be pulled from the market; General Motors, whose shares slid 25 percent because of high pension costs, weak sales, and market share losses; and big commercial banker Citigroup, which slipped 1 percent, partly due to regulatory violations in Japan.

The Dogs of the Dow also did not beat the Dow Jones index in 1998 and 1999, when dividend stocks were shunned in favor of high-tech issues. In those years, the Dogs were up 10.7 and 4 percent, respectively, compared with the Dow Jones Industrial Average gain of 16.1 percent in 1998 and 25.2 percent in 1999.

The Dogs, though, did better in the 2000–2002 bear market. They climbed 6.4 percent in 2000, versus a 6.6 percent decline in the Dow Jones Industrial Average; slid 4.9 percent in 2001, compared with a 7.2 percent drop in the Dow; and fell 8.9 percent in 2002, versus a sharp loss of 16.8 percent for the Dow. (See Figure 8-1 for a list of the 2005 Dogs.)

FIGURE 8-1 **Dogs of the Dow for 2005**

Stock/Symbol	Price/Yield on 12/31/04
SBC Communications/SBC	25.77/5.01%
General Motors/GM	40.06/4.99%
Altria/MO	61.10/4.78%
Merck/MRK	32.14/4.73%
Verizon/VZ	40.51/3.80%
JP Morgan Chase/JPM	39.01/3.49%
Citigroup/C	48.18/3.32%
DuPont/DD	49.05/2.85%
Pfizer/PFE	26.89/2.83%
General Electric/GE	36.50/2.41%

The Puppies and Pigs

Variations on the Dogs of the Dow abound. There is the "Flying Five," where you buy the five lowest-priced stocks among the 10 highest yielders on the Dow, keep them for a year, and then, like the Dogs, sell those that no longer qualify and buy the new Flying Five. This strategy carries more risk than the Dogs since you don't have as much diversification. There is also the strategy that calls for buying only the five top-yielding stocks in the Dow. But here again you are less diversified.

Then there are the Pigs of the Dow. This strategy differs from the Dogs in that you buy the five worst-performing stocks of the Dow at the end of each year, rather than the highest yielders. The Pigs originated in 2002 when Philip Durell, editor of the *Inside Value* online newsletter, decided to track the five worst Dow performers in that year. Durell admits that the strategy, though showing good results in 2003, 2004, and when backtested from 1931, has its limitations. (Backtesting, which many believe is suspect because of survivorship bias, involves testing an investment strategy using historical data and then seeing whether it has predictive validity on current data.) Durell prefers broader research, since the Pigs strategy often misses the best-performing Dow stocks and ignores other potentially profitable undervalued stocks outside the Dow Industrials. At the same time, Durell rightly observes that stocks do not become undervalued only at year-end.

Although buying undervalued stocks can be a winning strategy, the Dogs of the Dow and its variations have some inherent problems. Trading costs and taxes erode returns when buying and selling the required number of stocks each year. Also, as the popularity of the strategy has grown, more investors are hopping on board and bidding up the 10 Dow Dogs at the end of each year, which limits the profit potential.

UITs and Mutual Funds Based on the Dogs

A reflection of the Dogs' popularity is the number of brokerage houses that offer unit investment trusts based on the strategy. (Unit investment trusts, in contrast to continually managed mutual funds, are unmanaged fixed portfolios of stocks or bonds that are held for a specified term.) Offered by such brokers as Merrill Lynch, Salomon Smith Barney, Morgan Stanley, Dean Witter, and Van Kempen, the UITs are called the "Select 10 Portfolio." The UITs are invested in the 10 highest-yielding Dow stocks and then turned over 12 months later. Fees are above average, though they might be somewhat lower than what it would cost you to buy small amounts of stocks in 10 companies from a broker.

Mutual funds based on the Dogs strategy are not pure plays, since the SEC does not allow mutual funds to limit investments to 10 stocks. These funds include Hennessy Balanced Fund and Hennessy Total Return (800-966-4354).

About twice a month the Hennessey Balanced Fund buys the 10 stocks that meet the criteria of those in the Dow Jones Industrial Average with the highest dividend yield (the Dogs). The fund uses 50 percent of its investable cash and 50 percent in U.S. short-term Treasury securities. The Hennessy Total Return Fund invests 75 percent of its investable cash in the 10 Dogs of the Dow and the remaining 25 percent in short-term Treasury securities.

These Hennessey funds have high expense ratios (well over 1 percent), and you may be better off investing in the T. Rowe Price Equity Income fund, Vanguard Equity Income Investor Shares, or Payden Growth & Income Fund. These no-load, low expense funds, which boast good long-term records, invest in a diversified portfolio of large-cap stocks with high dividends. You might also consider the Exchange Traded Fund iShares Dow Jones Select Dividend Index Fund, which we discussed earlier.

Other Investment Strategies

S&P 10 Highest Dividend Yielders

Jeremy Siegel, in his book *The Future for Investors*, says that it pays to apply the Dogs of the Dow strategy to the 100 largest companies in the S&P 500 index (see Appendix 3 for a list of these firms). He questions why choosing the 10 highest-yielding stocks should be limited to the Dow Jones Industrials, which make up only 25 percent of the total market value of stocks.

Siegel found that picking the 10 highest-yielding stocks among the 100 largest-cap stocks in the S&P 500 paid off somewhat better than the 10 Dogs of the Dow. From 1957 to 2003, the S&P 10 beat the Dow 10 by more than 1 percent a year.

Geraldine Weiss's Theory

Geraldine Weiss, author of *The Dividend Connection* and *Dividends Don't Lie*, has been championing the theory that a stock's underlying value is in its dividends, not in its earnings. She emphasizes that the blue-chip companies are more predictable than newer companies with an erratic record of earnings and dividends. She defines a blue chip as stock of a company that (1) has raised its dividend at least five times in the past 12 years, (2) has at least 5 million shares outstanding, (3) has at least eight institutions holding its stock, (4) has seen earnings improve in at least seven of the last 12 years, (5) has a record of at least 25 years of uninterrupted dividends, and (6) has a Standard & Poor's Quality ranking of A+ or A.

According to Ms. Weiss's theory, a stock's price is driven by its yield. When a stock offers a high dividend yield, investors will buy, resulting in a higher price and a lower dividend yield. When the yield declines, the stock will languish until it falls far enough to make the yield attractive again.

Her research has shown that stocks typically fluctuate between extremes of high dividend yield and low dividend yield. These recurring extremes can be used to establish a channel of undervalued and overvalued prices. The tops and bottoms of cycles are determined by charting the dividend yield of a stock over a long enough period of time for the dividend-yield pattern to emerge. By calculating the historic points at which a stock turns down, or reverses a slide and turns up, the future behavior of that stock can be anticipated.

Relative Dividend Yield

The relative dividend yield strategy, as put forward by Anthony Spare, a money manager based in San Francisco, is similar to

Geraldine Weiss's technique. The two most common measures of whether a stock is over- or undervalued are the price-to-earnings ratio and the price-to-book value (assets minus liabilities). But Spare's strategy calls for comparing the stock's dividend yield with the yield of the S&P 500 index. If a stock's yield is considerably higher than that of the index, the stock is a buy.

To calculate the relative dividend yield, divide the yield of the S&P 500 into the stock's yield. When the result is well above 1.0 (the yield is more than 100 percent of that of the S&P 500), it is a signal to buy the stock.

Anthony Spare, in his book *Relative Dividend Yield*, says that a company's dividend represents a payout percentage of "normal" or sustainable earnings power. Reported earnings for most companies, he believes, present an unreliable method of valuation. Stocks with cyclical earnings or that have earnings problems typically sell at their highest P/E multiples when their prices are depressed. When reported profits are strong and the company is doing well, the multiples are lower.

Spare further states that the dividend policy at most large corporations is taken very seriously; changes are not made lightly. "Just as the oil companies did not raise dividends as much as earnings increased in the late 1970s (also in 2004–2005) when oil prices were escalating and profit margins reached very high levels, so they did not cut dividends in the mid-1980s when product prices dropped sharply and earnings plunged." He maintains that his use of dividends provides the same information the "normal earnings" P/Es would provide, but in a more direct manner. Spare concludes that the use of dividends doesn't require the arbitrary choice of time periods to be averaged to arrive at normal earnings, nor does it require assumptions about future profit margins and sales levels.

As in the Dogs of the Dow strategy and Ms. Weiss's approach, most of Spare's stocks with buy signals are depressed and the companies are encountering difficulties, usually temporary. But investors are compensated for being patient by a good dividend stream, as is the case with the other dividend strategies.

Dividend Yields vs. Dividend Increases

Goldman Sachs in 2003 did an interesting study of dividend-based investment strategies. Using 10 years of data for companies in the S&P 500 at the end of 2002, the well-regarded investment broker tested the following four strategies:

1. Invest in the 50 stocks with the highest dividend yields.

2. Invest in the 50 stocks with the lowest yields.

3. Invest in the 50 stocks with the largest dividend increases.

4. Invest in the stocks with dividend cuts (in a normal year, fewer than 50 companies reduce their payments).

Returns were calculated for each portfolio for the 12 months before and 12 months after each portfolio's formation.

Goldman found that portfolios employing a low-yield strategy outperformed the benchmark portfolio by 3.6 percent annually. In sharp contrast, the high-yield strategy resulted in portfolios that were underdiversified and underperformed the benchmark portfolio by 6.6 percent annually.

Stocks with large dividend increases were the second best performers. They outpaced the benchmark portfolio by 2.4 percent annually in the year before the dividend increase, but underperformed the benchmark portfolio by 0.8 percent annually in the year after the increase.

Goldman Sachs concluded that the stocks of companies with low yields and high dividend increases had higher profitability (as measured by return on equity) and higher expected earnings growth (as measured by earnings yields) than stocks with high yields and dividend cuts. And ultimately these low-yield stocks produced better returns for investors.

We agree with the Goldman Sachs results. The strategy of buying stocks with relatively low yields and a record of sizable dividend increases, as well as at least a 10-year history of steady dividend boosts, gets our vote as the best blueprint for a winning long-term investment portfolio.

Points to Remember

There are a number of dividend investment strategies. The most popular are:

➤ The Dow dividend strategy, or the Dogs of the Dow, entails buying the 10 highest-yielding stocks of the 30 in the Dow Jones Industrial Average at the end of each year. You invest equal amounts of money in the 10 stocks. These blue-chip issues usually offer good value and are often only temporarily depressed because of company-specific problems that can be fixed or because their industries are experiencing problems because of a poor economy that may soon turn around.

➤ The Flying Five strategy, where you buy the five lowest-priced stocks among the 10 Dow highest yielders, keep them for a year, and then, like the Dogs, sell those that no longer qualify and buy the new "Flying Five." There is also a strategy that calls for buying only the five top-yielding stocks in the Dow. These strategies carry more risk since you are less diversified.

➤ The Pigs of the Dow strategy involves buying the five worst-performing stocks of the Dow Jones Industrial Average rather than the highest yielders.

➤ The performance of the Dogs and their variations has been spotty.

➤ There are several mutual funds and UITs based on the Dogs of the Dow. They include the Hennessey Balanced Fund and the Hennessy Total Return Fund. These vehicles, however, carry high fees.

➤ The S&P 10 is another variation on the Dogs of the Dow. This strategy calls for picking the 10 highest-yielding stocks among the 100 largest-cap stocks in the S&P 500 index. According to Jeremy Siegel, the S&P 10 has outperformed the Dogs of the Dow by 1 percentage point annually from 1957 to 2003.

➤ It may be a better strategy to invest in no-load, low expense funds that boast good long-term records and have a diversified portfolio of large-cap stocks with high dividends, such as T. Rowe Price Equity Income Fund, Vanguard Equity Income Investor Shares, and Payden Growth & Income Fund.

➤ Aids in determining when to buy or sell stocks are Geraldine Weiss's technique of dividend yield patterns or Anthony Spare's relative dividend yield, which compares a stock's yield with that of the S&P 500 index.

➤ A study by Goldman Sachs comparing investing in (1) high-yield stocks, (2) low-yield stocks, (3) stocks of companies with the largest dividend increases, and (4) stocks of companies that cut their dividends found that low-yield stocks performed best. Investing in stocks with large dividend increases produced the second best performances. Buying high-yield stocks proved the worst strategy.

➤ We advise sticking with lower-yielding stocks that have a record of good-sized dividend increases in every year of at least the past 10.

CHAPTER 9

What Can Go Wrong

W e have assumed in this book that President George W. Bush will be successful in making the lower dividend tax rate permanent or at least extending it beyond 2008. But what if he fails? At this writing, the President's Social Security privatization proposal appears to be moribund, which may hamper his pushing through the permanent tax cuts. The huge federal budget deficit has due to the 2003 tax reductions and the Iraq War, which could well lead to ramped-up inflation, made Congress leery, in spite of the current Republican majority.

If the favorable dividend tax rates are not made permanent or extended, we still believe that dividend-paying stocks should be an important part of investors' portfolios. As we have discussed, not only do stocks that pay dividends reduce volatility, but they have historically performed better than issues that don't have a payout. Dividends indicate that a company's finances are healthy. A corporation that has paid a dividend over a long period usually has a record of increasing revenues, profits, and cash flow. Steady increases in payments also reflect management's confidence that the company will continue to enjoy its good fortune. Most important, unlike earnings, dividends are real and can't be manipulated.

Throughout the book, we've mentioned companies that have paid dividends for many years are a good starting point for investment, and you'll find more in the next chapter and in the appendices. Odds are that they will continue to provide above-average returns; though, as we pointed out, due diligence on your part is essential before plunking down your money to buy them.

Even if dividends revert to being taxed at ordinary income rates, they should still play a key role in building portfolios and providing a steady income stream. But in that scenario, it would be prudent for income-oriented investors to supplement dividend-paying stocks with other investments such as Treasury Inflation Securities (TIPS) and I Bonds.

TIPS

Treasury Inflation Protected Securities are indexed to the consumer price index (CPI). When you're paid interest, twice a year, the principal is adjusted to reflect inflation, as measured by the CPI. For example, say you buy a $1,000 TIPS with a 3.5 percent interest rate. Your first semiannual payment will be adjusted to compensate for any changes in the CPI. If the index climbs 1 percent, your interest payment will be calculated as though your bond were worth 1 percent more, or $1,010. Every six months the value of the bond will be recomputed using the same method. When the bond matures, you'll receive its current recalculated value, so your money won't be worth less because of inflation either in your payments or your principal.

The main drawback of TIPS is that you have to pay federal taxes each year on the compensatory additions to principal, even though you don't actually see the money until you redeem the security. However, TIPS are exempt from state and local income taxes.

Mutual funds that invest in these securities are required to pay you the adjustment for inflation each year, but taxes are still owed. The Vanguard Inflation-Protected Securities Fund (VIPSX) has the lowest expense ratio of this type of fund, at 0.18 percent. In the year ending 2004, the fund's average annualized return was 3.26 percent, and since inception in June 2000, it has been 9.75 percent.

If you want to invest in TIPS via an exchanged traded fund (ETF), there's iShares Lehman TIPS Bond Fund (TIP).

I Bonds

The inflation-protected U.S. Savings bond known as the I Bond is not only exempt from state and local taxes, but is not federally taxable until it's redeemed, which can be as many as 30 years away. The return on the I Bond is based on two rates: a fixed rate that lasts for up to 30 years, and a rate based on inflation, which is adjusted every six months (on November 1 and May 1).

You can buy the bonds through banks in denominations ranging from $50 to $10,000. They can also be purchased for $1,000 via the Web site www.savingsbonds.gov. An individual can't purchase more than $30,000 worth of the bonds per calendar year. One drawback to the bonds is that they are pieces of paper, certificates, whose safe keeping is the responsibility of the investor. They cannot be held in a brokerage account. The Bureau of the Public Debt will replace lost, stolen, or destroyed bonds if the holder can provide the serial number, issue date, and taxpayer identification.

I Bonds are purchased at face value, with no sales charge, and can be redeemed beginning after six months. The issue date is the month and year when payment is received by the issuing agent. Designed as a long-term savings vehicle, the bonds have a penalty for early redemption. An I Bond redeemed within the first five years loses three months of earnings. Thus, an I Bond redeemed at 17 months will pay 14 months of earnings. Under certain circumstances, returns on the bonds are federally tax exempt if the proceeds are used to pay college tuition and fees.

The Treasury Department has created a program called the Savings Bond Wizard, available at www.savingsbondwizard.com, that helps investors keep track of their holdings. The Wizard shows your bond inventory in a spreadsheet format, and the program displays the current value and interest rate for each bond; checks for valid combinations of serial number, series, denominations, and issues date; shows the yield to date, the next accrual date, and the final maturity date for each bond; recalculates bond values and interest for different redemption dates; and allows for an update of the bond database every six months.

TIPS and I Bonds are safe investments. But because of that, their returns are usually nothing to write home about.

Corporate Bonds

Bonds of corporations, which should be part of a well-diversified portfolio, offer higher yields than other types of bonds. These bonds are especially attractive to retirees since, like dividend-paying stocks, they provide a steady income stream.

Like other bonds—such as those issued by the U.S. government— corporate bonds can be held until maturity (when the final principal payment is due) or they can be sold in the secondary market, where the price can rise or fall depending on interest rates (bond prices move inversely to interest rates), the economy, or company-specific news. Whatever the price move, the coupon (the fixed interest rate for the life of the bond) remains the same.

Because of the uncertainty associated with running a business, corporate bonds are among the riskiest of the different types of bonds. But they provide yields that are usually higher than the inflation rate. If you want less risk, you would purchase corporate bonds with high credit ratings. The two biggest rating agencies are Standard & Poor's and Moody's. S&P's top rating is AAA, while Moody's is Aaa. The ratings run the gamut from triple A to D (in payment default).

If you own an individual bond and plan to hold it until maturity, you needn't be overly concerned about market risk (price fluctuations) and interest rate risk. If you invest via a bond mutual fund, though, you have to factor in these two risks because fund managers can buy and sell bonds as often as they feel it necessary to meet the fund's objective. As a result, you risk loss because of fluctuations in the fund's value.

Municipal Bonds

"Muni bonds," which are issued by state, county, or city governments, are exempt from federal tax and are generally state tax-free for residents of the state in which they're issued. A muni that's free of federal, state, and city taxes is known as "triple tax-free."

Because they're attractive to higher-income investors, triple tax-free munis generally offer a lower interest rate than equivalent taxable bonds. Depending on the investor's tax rate, however, the return may be higher than on a regular bond. To calculate the tax-equivalent yield for someone in the highest federal tax bracket of 35 percent, divide the coupon yield, say 3.5 percent, by 1.0 minus 0.35, or 0.65 (the formula is tax-exempt yield divided by 1.0 minus the tax bracket). This gives a hypothetical tax-equivalent yield of 5.4 percent, and it would be increased by any state and local tax deduction.

Attractive no-load, low-expense-ratio, single-state muni bond funds include:

California: Fidelity Spartan CA Muni (FCTFX 800-544-8544)

Florida: T. Rowe Price FL Muni (FLTFX 800-638-5660)

Maryland: T. Rowe Price Tax Free MD Bond (MDXBX 800-638-5660)

New York: Vanguard NY Long Term Tax Exempt (VNYTX 800-662-2739

Ohio: Vanguard OH Long Term Tax Exempt (VOHIX 800-662-2739)

Pennsylvania: Vanguard PA Long Term Tax Exempt (VPAIX 800-662-2739)

Dividend-Paying Stocks Offer the Most Potential

While bonds offer portfolio diversification and an income stream, we hope that you have been convinced by reading this book that investing in stocks of companies that have strong dividend records is the better way to meet your long-term investment objectives.

Putting money regularly in well-situated dividend-payers, whether via individual issues, DRIPs, DSPs, mutual funds, closed-end funds, or ETFs, will go a long way toward giving you financial peace of mind.

Points to Remember

➤ Even if the Bush administration is not successful in making the lower dividend tax rate permanent, dividend-paying stocks should be an important part of an investor's portfolio.

➤ Not only do stocks that pay dividends reduce volatility, but they have historically performed better than issues that don't pay dividends.

➤ Dividends indicate that a company's finances are strong. A corporation that has paid a dividend over a long period usually has a record of increasing revenues, profits, and cash flow. Steady increases in payments also reflect management's confidence that the company will continue to enjoy its good fortune.

➤ The many tables in this book (and the write-ups in the next chapter) are a good starting point for investment. Odds are that these companies will continue to provide above-average returns, though due diligence on your part is essential before investing in them.

➤ It may be prudent for income-oriented investors to supplement dividend-paying stocks with other investments such as Treasury Inflation Securities (TIPS), I Bonds, and corporate bonds.

CHAPTER 10

Selected Stocks Worth Buying

To sum up the theme of this book, buying quality stocks that have strong dividend records and favorable prospects is a solid, relatively safe way to invest for the long term. And invest you must if you are to meet your financial goal for retirement, college tuition, home purchase, travel, or—most important—peace of mind in this age that is hardly characterized by job security. The market's ups and downs notwithstanding, stocks over the long haul have outperformed other assets—including bonds, gold, and real estate—by a wide margin. From 1928 to 2004, stocks, as measured by the S&P 500 index, delivered an impressive average annual total return of 11.9 percent.

So far, we've listed scores of stocks that fit various dividend criteria. The thumbnail sketches of stocks in this chapter may help you narrow the field. We divided the stocks into three separate groups. Some equities clearly fit into more than one category. We made the final selection in each group with an eye toward industry diversification.

We believe all these stocks have long-term appeal. But as we've stated more than once in this book, you can never just buy and hold. You must stay on top of your investments. In other words, buy, hold, and monitor. With so much useful market information on the Internet, the task of following stocks has become easier.

Group 1: Stocks You Can Buy Directly

The following stocks are for those investors who don't depend on dividend income to meet living expenses. Many of the plans, however, offer partial dividend reinvestment; that is, they give participants the option to receive dividends on part of the shares held in the plan while reinvesting dividends on the remainder. Each of the companies we profiled permits you to bypass a broker and buy shares directly if you join their dividend reinvestment plan (there are a few companies that don't pay dividends that offer direct purchase). Each also permits optional cash payments. As we saw in Chapter 6, direct stock purchase plans (DSPs) and dividend reinvestment plans (DRIPs) are a convenient and inexpensive way to build a portfolio.

Keep in mind that companies often make changes to their dividend reinvestment plans. So it is important that you consult with the company and obtain a current prospectus before investing.

The eight stocks described below make up a diverse group, with representation in these sectors: energy, consumer staples, consumer discretionary, financials, health care, and information technology. We believe they have above-average long-term earnings and dividend growth prospects.

Bank of America (BAC) (Figure 10-1)

100 North Tryon Street

Charlotte, NC 28255

(888) 279-3457

$1,000 initial investment or automatic monthly investments of $50

Optional cash purchases: $50 to $120,000 annually

Dividends paid since 1903

S&P earnings and dividend rank: A–

Bank of America provides a wide range of banking and financial services and products to 28 million households and 2 million businesses. Its primary market areas are the Mid-Atlantic, Midwest, Southeast, Southwest, Northwest, and West, as well as selected international markets. Bank of America has offices in 30 states. Operations are divided into consumer and commercial banking asset management, global

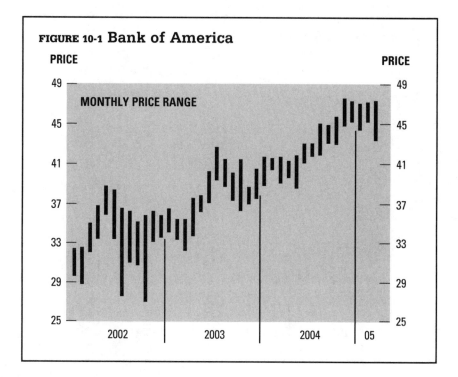

FIGURE 10-1 **Bank of America**

PRICE

MONTHLY PRICE RANGE

49, 45, 41, 37, 33, 29, 25

2002   2003   2004   05

corporate and investment management, and equity investments. In 2004 the company acquired FleetBoston Financial for $47.2 billion.

Standard & Poor's estimates long-term per-share annual earnings growth for the company of 10 to 12 percent. The consensus estimate of Wall Street analysts, as carried in Standard & Poor's *Earnings Guide*, is for five-year average annual earnings growth of 9 percent.

ExxonMobil (XOM) (Figure 10-2)

5959 Las Colinas Blvd.

Irving, TX 75039-2298

(800) 252-1800

$250 initial investment or automatic monthly investments of at least $50 for five consecutive months

Optional cash purchases: $50 to $250,000 annually

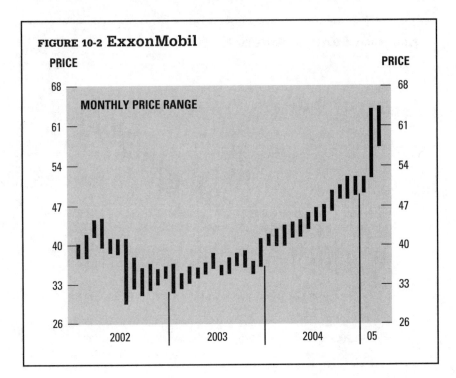

FIGURE 10-2 ExxonMobil

Dividends paid since 1882

S&P earnings and dividend rank: A–

In a corporate family reunion 88 years in the making, the Federal Trade Commission in 1999 allowed Exxon and Mobil to reunite in one of the largest mergers in history. In 1911, the Supreme Court ordered the breakup of John D. Rockefeller's Standard Oil Trust, resulting in a spinoff of 34 companies, two of which were Standard Oil Co. of New Jersey (later Esso and then Exxon) and Standard Oil Co. of New York (later Mobil). In 2004, Exxon estimated that it had achieved about $10 billion in synergies and efficiencies from the merger.

ExxonMobil, which is the world's largest publicly owned integrated oil company, is the number one refiner in the world and the second biggest refiner in the United States. It maintains the largest portfolio of proved oil reserves and production in North American and is the number one net producer of oil and gas in Europe. The company is also a major manufacturer and marketer of basic petrochemicals. Expected continuation of relatively high crude oil prices and rising worldwide demand bode well for XOM.

The consensus of analysts is a five-year average annual earnings growth estimated at 7 percent.

Fifth Third Bancorp (FITB) (Figure 10-3)

38 Fountain Square Plaza

Cincinnati, OH 45623

(888) 294-8285

$500 initial investment

Optional cash purchases: $50 to $5,000 per transaction

Dividends paid since1952

S&P earnings and dividend rank: A+

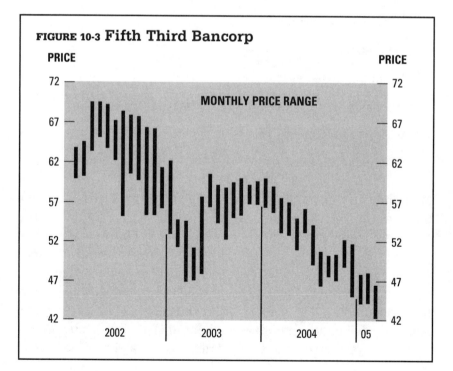

FIGURE 10-3 Fifth Third Bancorp

Cincinnati-based Fifth Third Bancorp has a track record of 31 consecutive years of higher earnings through 2004, a feat that few companies have accomplished. FITB, which operates throughout Ohio, Kentucky, Indiana, Michigan, Illinois, Florida, West Virginia, and Tennessee, has consistently been ranked as one of the most efficient large U.S. banks, as measured by the efficiency ratio (non-interest expense to operating revenue). Its loan portfolio has been about evenly divided between commercial and consumer.

Standard & Poor's believes the company's ability to generate peer-leading loan, deposit, and revenue growth while keeping expenses under control should remain intact. As a result, above-average profit growth is expected to continue.

The analysts' consensus estimate is for a five-year average annual earnings growth rate of 12 percent.

General Electric (GE) (Figure 10-4)

3135 Easton Turnpike

Fairfield, CT 06431-0001

(800) 786-2543

$250 initial investment

Optional cash purchases: $10 to $10,000 per transaction

Dividends paid since 1899

S&P Quality ranking: A+

Multi-industry, media, and financing giant General Electric conducts business through two segments—GE Industrial and GE Capital. The company's Industrial segment is comprised of nine operating divisions: Power Systems (power-utility generators), Aircraft Engines (jet engines), Medical Systems (medical diagnostic equipment), Consumer Products (appliances and lighting), Industrial Systems (electric motors), NBC (broadcasting and cable), Plastics, Specialty Materials (silicones, additives, industrial diamonds), and Transportation Systems (locomotive and railroad equipment). The Capital

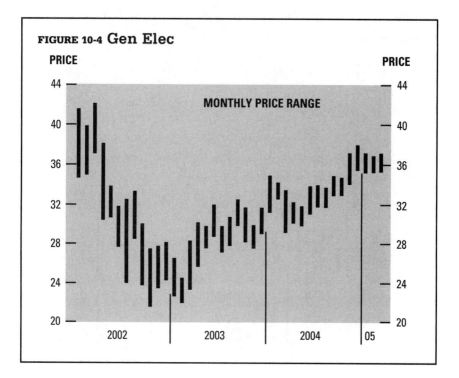

FIGURE 10-4 Gen Elec

segment is comprised of Insurance, Commercial Finance, Consumer Finance, and Equipment Leasing.

Longer term, Standard & Poor's estimates a per-share annual compound profit growth rate of about 10 percent. The consensus of analysts is a five-year average annual earnings growth rate of 11 percent.

International Business Machines (IBM) (Figure 10-5)

One New Orchard Road

Armonk, NY 10504

(888) 426-6700

$500 initial investment or automatic monthly investments of at least $50 for 10 consecutive months

Optional cash purchases: $50 to $250,000 annually

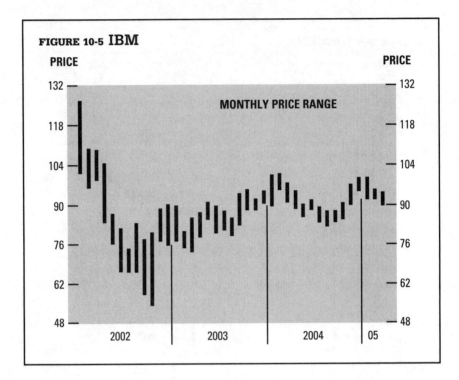

FIGURE 10-5 IBM

Dividends paid since1916

S&P earnings and dividend rank: A–

IBM, still the world's largest computer company, is no longer just a computer vendor. Computer hardware accounts for about 32 percent of sales. IBM has focused on key areas such as services and software. Given the Internet's use as a business tool in streamlining everything from supply chain management to customer service, IBM's goal was to leverage its capabilities in offering e-business (electronic business) products and services. Thus, certain key growth engines, services, and software have gained momentum in the company. Also, IBM Global Services has been growing at an average double-digit rate over the past several years.

Standard & Poor's believes that the sale of IBM's PC unit to Leovo Group in 2005 will enable the company to maintain an even better focus on profitable growth areas in services and software, where it has more of a competitive advantage.

Analysts estimate a five-year average annual earnings growth rate of 11 percent.

Pfizer Inc. (PFE) (Figure 10-6)

235 East 42nd Street

New York, NY 10017-5755

(800) 733-9393

$500 initial investment

Optional cash purchases: $50 to $120,000 annually

Dividends paid since1901

S&P Quality ranking: A

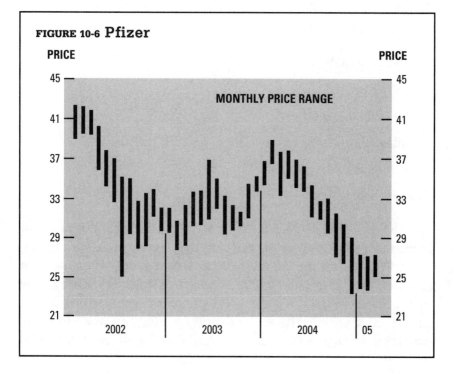

FIGURE 10-6 Pfizer

Pfizer traces its roots back to 1849, when it was founded by Charles Pfizer and Charles Erhart as a chemical products company. Following its acquisitions of Warner-Lambert in 2000 and Pharmacia Corp. in 2003, Pfizer now ranks as the world's largest prescription pharmaceuticals company, accounting for about 11 percent of the global market.

The breadth and depth of the company's drug portfolio throughout the global pharmaceutical market is unmatched. About 15 of Pfizer's drugs are the leaders in their respective therapeutic markets; five are among the world's top selling products; and 10 generate sales exceeding $1 billion annually.

Despite some recent problems with the Celebrex COX-2 inhibitor, Standard & Poor's believes that per-share profit growth in coming years will be healthy, thanks to its strong drug pipeline.

The consensus estimate of analysts is a five-year average annual earnings growth rate of 9 percent.

Procter & Gamble (PG) (Figure 10-7)

One Procter & Gamble Plaza

Cincinnati, OH 45202-3315

(800) 764-7483

$250 initial investment

Optional cash purchases: $100 to $120,000 annually

Dividends paid since1891

S&P earnings and dividend rank: A

Procter & Gamble's goal is to create the most successful global brands in every category everywhere that it competes. With brands like Crest toothpaste, Pampers disposable diapers, Gillette razors, and Tide detergent in its family of products, the company believes that it has assembled a portfolio of premier consumer brands in a variety of categories. It sells about 300 products in more than 160 countries. P&G shored up its dominant position in the wet shaving category with the 2005 acquisition of Gillette.

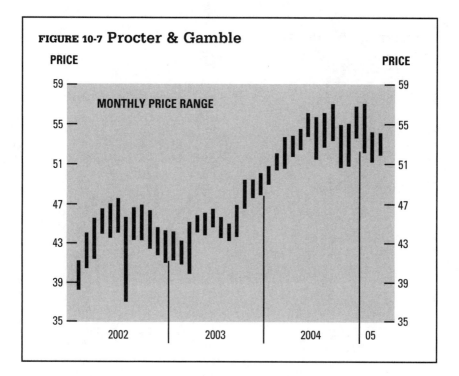

FIGURE 10-7 **Procter & Gamble**

The company plans to maintain its historically strong revenue and earnings growth rate by focusing on faster growing categories such as beauty and health care and faster growing markets in developing countries. Long-term objectives are to deliver 4 to 6 percent sales growth, double-digit net operating earnings growth, and free cash flow equal to 90 percent or more of net earnings.

Analysts estimate that the average annual per-share earnings five-year growth rate will be 11 percent.

Wal-Mart Stores (WMT) (Figure 10-8)

702 SW 8th Street

Bentonville, AR 72716

(800) 438-6278

$250 initial investment or automatic monthly investments of at least $25

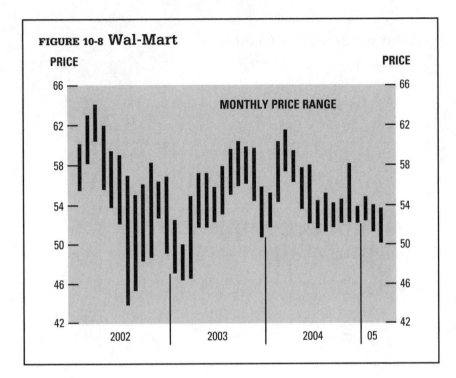

FIGURE 10-8 Wal-Mart

Optional cash purchases: $50 to $150,000 annually

Dividends paid since 1973

S&P earnings and dividend rank: A

Wal-Mart, the largest retailer in North America, has set its sights on other parts of the world. In addition to the thousands of stores in North America, the company has hundreds of stores in Argentina, Brazil, Canada, China, Germany, Korea, Mexico, Puerto Rico, and the United Kingdom.

Wal-Mart's operations are divided into three divisions: Wal-Mart, Sam's Club, and International. The average U.S. Wal-Mart discount store has about 98,000 square feet and carries a wide variety of general merchandise. The average Supercenter is much larger, with about 187,000 square feet. Most Supercenters, which carry a broader assortment of groceries, developed from the relocation or expansion of Wal-Mart discount stores. The company's Neighborhood Markets, which offer groceries, pharmaceuticals, and general merchandise, have an average size of about 43,000 square feet. The company has successfully increased productivity and passed on cost reductions to customers via an everyday low pricing strategy. In 2004 it achieved about $12 billion in price rollbacks.

The analysts' consensus estimate is for a five-year average annual earnings growth rate of 14 percent.

Group 2: Stocks with Outstanding Dividend Growth

The seven stocks that follow, all taken from the table in Figure 5-2, pages 65–66 at the end of this chapter, have superior records of dividend growth. Each has increased its payments to shareholders by at least 250 percent from 1995 to the indicated 2005 rate. You should consider these issues as excellent long-term holdings. Even if you are close to or in retirement, your portfolios generally should contain companies that rapidly boost their dividends. Over time you will be better off than if you buy stocks that have a high current yield but provide little in the way of dividend growth. As we saw in Chapter 5, stocks with strong dividend growth can offset the eroding effect of inflation.

AFLAC Inc. (AFL) (Figure 10-9)

1932 Wynnton Road

Columbus, GA 31999

706-323-3431

Dividends paid since 1973

S&P earnings and dividend rank: A

AFLAC provides supplemental health and life insurance through its subsidiary, American Family Life Assurance Company of Columbus, which operates in the United States and Japan. Most of AFLAC's policies are individually underwritten and marketed at worksites through

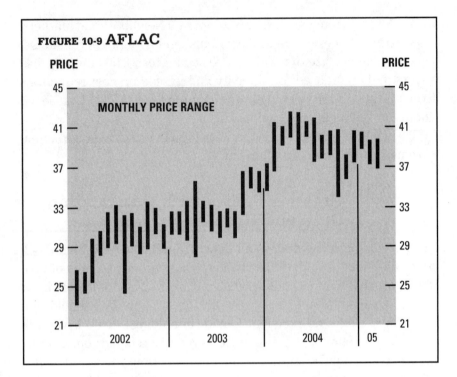

FIGURE 10-9 AFLAC

independent agents, with premiums paid by the employee. The company is believed to be the world's leading underwriter of individually issued policies marketed at worksites. Japan accounts for the majority of the company's revenues.

AFLAC Japan's insurance products are designed to help pay for unreimbursed costs under Japan's national health insurance system and include cancer plans, care plans, general medical expense plans, medical/sickness riders to cancer plans, living benefit life plans, and accident plans. AFLAC U.S. sells cancer plans and various types of health insurance, including accident and disability, fixed-benefit dental, personal sickness and hospital indemnity, hospital intensive care, long-term care, and short-term disability plans. The company also offers several life insurance plans in the United States and Japan.

The analysts' consensus five-year earnings estimate is for an average annual rate of 14 percent.

City National Corp. (CYN) (Figure 10-10)

400 North Roxbury Drive

Beverly Hills, CA 90210

(310) 888-6000

Dividends paid since 1994

S&P earnings and dividend rank: A

City National, which operates in the dynamic southern California market, has built an enviable private banking franchise. It is the second largest independent commercial bank headquartered in California.

Internal growth has been augmented by an aggressive acquisition campaign. CYN has established positions in key regional submarkets in southern and northern California that it views as having attractive demographic characteristics. Since 2000, it has acquired Oakland-based Civic Bancorp, with more than $502 million in assets; the

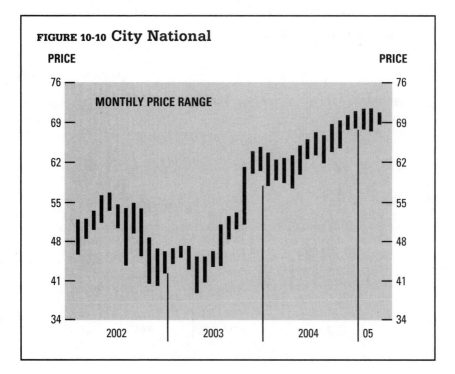

FIGURE 10-10 City National

Pacific Bank, a $775 million asset bank headquartered in San Francisco; Reed, Conner & Birdwell, a Los Angeles-based investment manager with $1.2 billion in assets under administration; and Convergent Capital Management, a privately held Chicago-based company, and substantially all of its assets under management holdings, including its majority ownership interests in eight asset management firms and minority interests in two more, which, combined, managed some $8.5 billion. All told, as of 2005, City National had more than $16 billion in assets under investment management.

Analysts estimate that average annual earnings will grow at a rate of 9 percent over five years.

Home Depot (HD) (Figure 10-11)

2455 Paces Ferry Road

Atlanta, GA 30339-1834

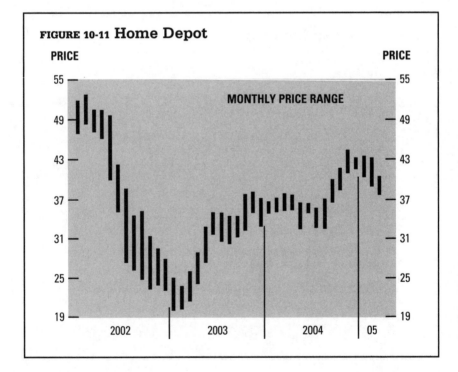

FIGURE 10-11 Home Depot

(770) 433-8211

Dividends paid since 1987

S&P earnings and dividend rank: A+

Founded in 1978, Home Depot is the world's largest home improvement retailer and the second largest U.S. retailer, with more than $72
billion in revenues. Home Depot stores average 107,000 square feet
plus 22,000 square feet of garden center and storage space. They
stock 40,000 to 50,000 items. The company also offers installation
services; in 2004, it acquired Installed Products U.S.A., a roofing and
fencing installed services business, and RMA Home Services, a
replacement windows and siding installed services business.

Home Depot Landscape Supply stores are designed to extend the
reach of Home Depot's garden departments by focusing on professional landscapers and avid do-it-yourself garden enthusiasts. EXPO
design centers, which average about 100,000 square feet, sell more
upscale products and services, primarily for home decorating and
remodeling projects. Unlike Home Depot, they do not sell building
materials and lumber. The recent and likely additional acquisitions
are expected to help maintain positive earnings momentum.

Over the longer term, rising U.S. home ownership should continue
to drive market growth. Also, as baby boomers spend more time at
home with their families, they are likely to allocate a larger portion
of their disposable income to their homes than in previous years.

The analysts' consensus five-year average annual earnings estimate
is 9 percent.

McDonald's Corp. (MCD) (Figure 10-12)

McDonald's Plaza

Oak Brook, IL 60523

(630) 623-3000

Dividends paid since1976

S&P earnings and dividend rank: A

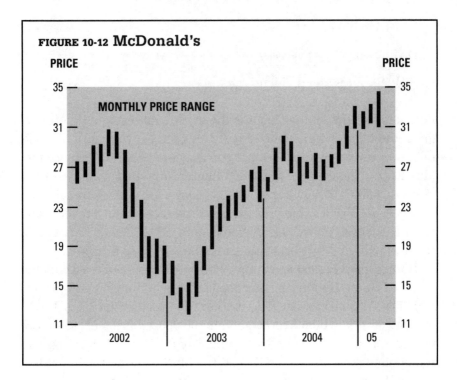

FIGURE 10-12 McDonald's

With one of the world's most widely known brand names, McDonald's serves about 49 million customers daily. The company operates and licenses more than 31,000 restaurants in some 120 countries. McDonald's also operates and franchises more than 1,000 restaurants under its Partner Brands concepts: Boston Market and Chipotle Mexican Grill. It has a minority interest in a U.K.-based quick service restaurant, Pret A Manger.

After several disappointing years in the United States, sales trends have rebounded since 2003. The company has attributed this to a new corporate strategy that focuses on product development and investment in existing properties, rather than on expansion and price discounting. McDonald's operating priorities include fixing operating inadequacies in existing restaurants; and taking a more integrated and focused approach to growth, with emphasis on increasing sales, margins, and returns in existing restaurants. The company is expected to rack up strong sales growth as it shifts its menu to more upscale fare, which would enable it to significantly increase the amount of the average check.

Analysts estimate that McDonald's will rack up an 8 percent average annual earnings growth rate over five years.

Medtronic, Inc. (MDT) (Figure 10-13)

710 Medtronic Parkway

Minneapolis, MN 55432-5604

(763) 514-4000

Dividends paid since 1977

S&P earnings and dividend rank: A–

Medtronic, formed in 1949, boasts leading positions in many medical device categories, including cardiac rhythm management, neurological/spinal, vascular, and cardiac surgery markets. Cardiac rhythm

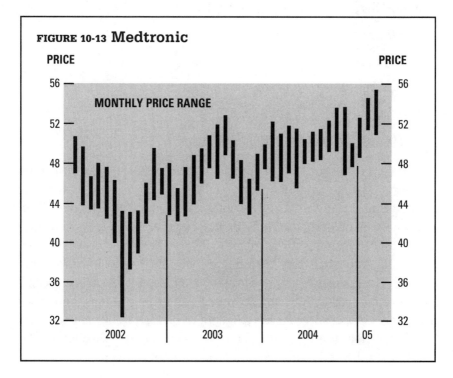

FIGURE 10-13 Medtronic

management products, which account for close to 50 percent of revenues, include implantable pacemakers to treat slow or irregular heartbeats. Implantable cardioverter defibrillators treat abnormally fast heartbeats by sending electrical impulses or an electrical shock to restore normal rhythm.

The company's neurological and diabetes products include implantable neurostimulation systems, external and implantable drug administration devices, continuous gluocose monitoring systems, hydrocephalic shunts and drainage devices, surgical instruments, and diagnostic equipment.

Positive long-term fundamentals include growing global demand for quality health care, an aging population, and rising research and development expenditures, which is expected to lead to a steady flow of new diagnostic and therapeutic products.

The earnings estimate by analysts is a 15 percent average annual five-year growth rate.

Sysco Corp. (SYY) (Figure 10-14)

1390 Enclave Parkway

Houston, TX 77077-2099

(281) 584-1390

Dividends paid since 1970

S&P earnings and dividend rank: A+

Sysco (not to be confused with tech company Cisco Systems) is the largest marketer and distributor of food-service products in the United States and Canada. The company was formed in 1970 when shareholders of nine companies exchanged their stock for Sysco common stock. Sysco has grown significantly, with sales increasing from $115 million to more than $29 billion via internal expansion and acquisitions. The company provides products and services to about 400,000 restaurants, hotels, schools, hospitals, retirement homes, and other food-service operations. It has a fleet of more than 8,500 vehicles from nearly 200 distribution facilities and self-serve centers throughout the continental United States, Alaska, and parts of Canada.

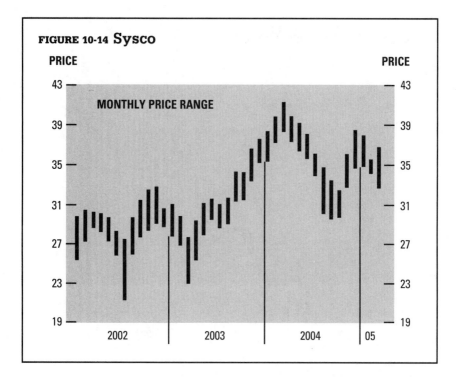

FIGURE 10-14 Sysco

PRICE

MONTHLY PRICE RANGE

The company is emphasizing the sale of Sysco-branded products, which typically carry wider margins than other branded products. The company should benefit from favorable industry trends, including increased dining out and efficiency gains from industry consolidation. There are considerable cross-selling opportunities, since current customers receive only about 35 percent of their products through the company.

Analysts expect Sysco's earnings to grow at an average annual five-year rate of 14 percent.

T. Rowe Price Group (TROW) (Figure 10-15)

100 East Pratt Street

Baltimore, MD 21202

(410) 345-2000

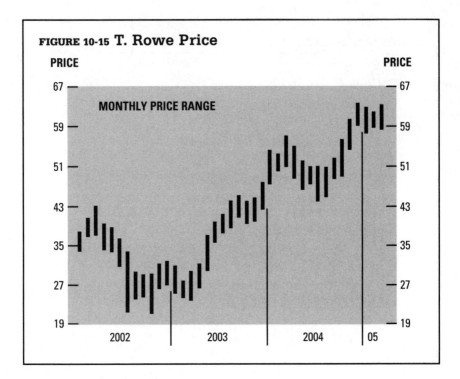

FIGURE 10-15 T. Rowe Price

Dividends paid since 1986

S&P earnings and dividend rank: A

T. Rowe Price Group is the successor to an investment counseling business formed by the late T. Rowe Price in 1937. It is now the investment advisor to the T. Rowe price family of no-load mutual funds and is one of the largest publicly held U.S. mutual fund complexes. Assets under management amounted to $235 billion at the end of 2004.

TROW also manages private accounts for individuals and institutions. Its assets under management are accumulated from a diversified client base that is accessed across several distribution methods. The company's broad line of no-load mutual funds makes it easy for investors to reallocate assets among funds, which is not the case at some smaller fund companies. This contributes to increased client retention.

Longer-term prospects are enhanced by industry consolidation, which could increase TROW's market share, and by favorable demographics, higher retirement savings, and international expansion.

Analysts estimate a five-year average annual earnings growth rate of 13 percent.

Group 3: Good Quality Stocks with Higher Yields

In this section we suggest a portfolio for investors looking for current income. Often these investors are retirees who count on stock dividends to pay some of their living costs. As individuals live longer, the number of years the average person spends in retirement increases. The issues highlighted here all have yields that are at least twice that of the S&P 500 (as of mid-2005). All of the stocks, moreover, carry an S&P Quality rank of at least A–, indicating a decade or more of above-average earnings and dividend growth and stability.

Even if you are retired and need investment income for regular expenses, we recommend you add some low-yielding, growing dividend stocks to your portfolio mix such as those in Group 2 and in the table in Figure 10-24. Since it is likely that you will spend many years in retirement, it's essential that growth be an important part of your total return.

Altria Group (MO) (Figure 10-16)

120 Park Avenue

New York, NY 10017-5592

(917) 663-4000

Dividends paid since 1928

S&P earnings and dividend rank: A+

Formerly Philip Morris Cos., Altria is a holding company with worldwide subsidiaries that manufacture various consumer products, including cigarettes and packaged foods. Majority-owned Kraft Foods is the largest packaged food company in North America; it

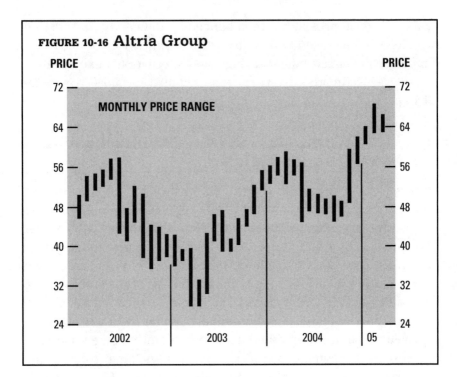

FIGURE 10-16 Altria Group

produces a wide variety of coffee, confectionery, cheese and grocery, and processed meat products in Europe and around the globe. In 2002 the company sold its Miller Brewing Co. subsidiary to South African Brewers, plc., receiving over $3 billion worth of shares in the newly formed company, SABMiller, which represented a 36 percent economic interest and a 24.9 percent voting interest.

The many lawsuits against the tobacco industry have been hanging over Altria. But as of mid-2005, Standard & Poor's believed that litigation pressures were easing, primarily due to a ruling in the Department of Justice case rejecting a $280 billion claim against the industry.

Analysts estimate a five-year average annual earnings growth rate of 9 percent.

Ameren Corp. (AEE) (Figure 10-17)

1901 Chouteau Avenue

St. Louis, MO 63103

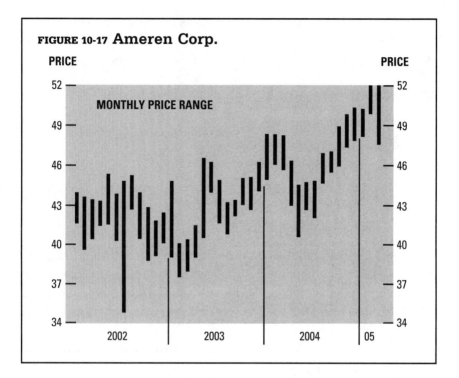

FIGURE 10-17 Ameren Corp.

(314) 621-3222

Dividends paid since 1906

S&P earnings and dividend rank: A–

Ameren, Missouri's largest electric utility, acquired Illinois Power in 2004, which increased its customer base by 46 percent to 3.2 million. The holding company was formed in 1997 through the merger of AmerenUE, the holding company for Union Electric Co., and CIPSCO, the holding company for Central Illinois Public Service. In 2003, Ameren acquired CILCORP, the holding company for Central Illinois Light, in a transaction valued at $1.4 billion. AmerenEnergy Generating Company was formed in 2000 when, as a result of Illinois deregulation, AmerenCIPS (which serves electric and natural gas customers in central and southern Illinois) transferred its Illinois power plants to the new, unregulated electric generating subsidiary.

Standard & Poor's expected the Illinois Power acquisition to start to contribute to earnings in 2005. The consensus estimate for Ameren is average annual profits of 4 percent over five years.

Citigroup (C) (Figure 10-18)

399 Park Avenue

New York, NY 10041

(212) 559-1000

Dividends paid since 1986

Earnings and dividend rank: A+

Operating in more than 100 countries, Citigroup is a diversified global financial services company. Subsidiaries include such familiar names as Citicorp, Smith Barney, and Student Loan Corp. The company spun off all but 9.9 percent of its Travelers Property Casualty unit in 2002.

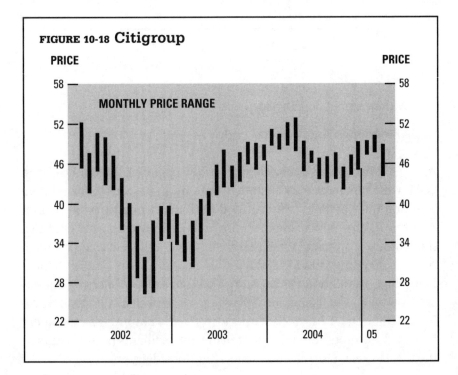

FIGURE 10-18 Citigroup

Operations are in four segments: Global Consumer, Global Corporate and Investment Bank, Global Investment Management, and Private Client Services. The Global Consumer segment, which provides banking, lending, insurance, and investment services, has accounted for the majority of net income. Global Consumer includes Cards, which provides MasterCard, VISA, and private label products.

The company's longer-term revenue and earnings prospects were regarded by Standard & Poor's as above average. The analysts' consensus estimate is for average annual five-year earnings growth of 11 percent.

Kimco Realty (KIM) (Figure 10-19)

333 New Hyde Park Road

New Hyde Park, NY 11042-0020

(800) 285-4626

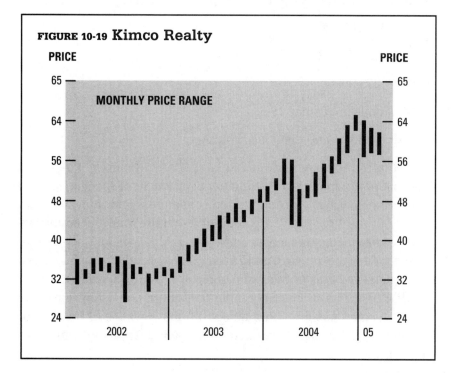

FIGURE 10-19 Kimco Realty

Dividends paid since 1992

Earnings and dividend rank: A+

Since 1966, Kimco has specialized in the acquisition, development, and management of well-located shopping centers with strong growth potential. The real estate investment trust's portfolio consists of some 700 property interests, including neighborhood and community shopping center properties, retail store leases, ground-up development projects, and undeveloped land located in 41 states, Canada, and Mexico. Kimco believes its neighborhood and community shopping center properties is the largest held by a publicly traded REIT.

Kimco's investment objective, which it has met over the years, is to increase cash flow, current income, and, consequently, the value of its existing portfolio of properties.

Analysts look for Kimco to record a five-year average annual earnings growth rate of 8 percent.

RPM International (RPM) (Figure 10-20)

2628 Pearl Road

Medina, OH 44258

(330) 273-5090

Dividends paid since 1969

S&P earnings and dividend rank: A–

RPM International was founded in 1947 as Republic Powdered Metals. The company is an international producer of specialty paints, protective coatings, roofing systems, sealants, and adhesives. Its family of products, which are marketed in more than 140 countries, includes brand names such as Carboline, DAP, Day-Glo, Rust-Oleum, Tremco, Flecto, Stonhard, and Zinsser. These products mainly serve the structural waterproofing and corrosion control markets.

RPM historically has been able to deliver consistent earnings growth, regardless of economic conditions, because of its diverse product portfolio, which caters to both the industrial and consumer end markets.

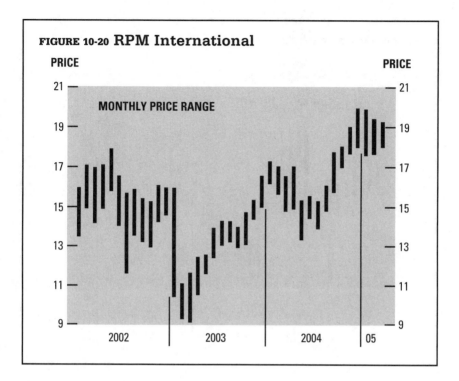

FIGURE 10-20 **RPM International**

Analysts estimate a five-year average annual earnings growth rate of 9 percent.

Sara Lee (SLE) (Figure 10-21)

3 First National Plaza

Chicago IL 60602

(312) 726-2600

Dividends paid since 1946

S&P earnings and dividend rank: A–

Sara Lee, best known for its baked goods, also boasts many other branded food and nonfood products, ranging from Ball Park franks to the Wonderbra. The company aims to build leadership brands in three highly focused global businesses: food and beverages, intimates and underwear, and household products. In recent years Sara

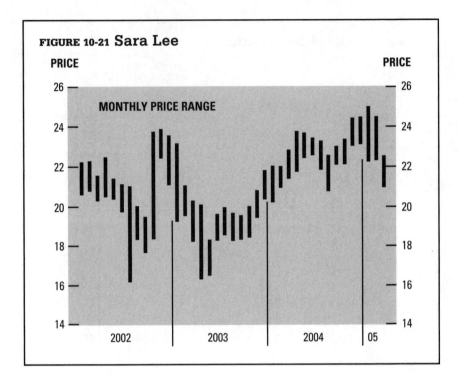

FIGURE 10-21 Sara Lee

Lee has worked to reshape and refocus itself around its three core businesses. It divested several businesses, including its PYA/Monarch food-service operation and its Coach leather goods unit. Sara Lee regarded these businesses as valuable companies that did not fit its narrower business focus. It has been using proceeds from divestitures to repurchase stock, retire debt, and fund acquisitions.

Standard & Poor's believes Sara Lee's restructuring plan has significant potential to create a higher margin company with a more predictable earnings stream and better long-term growth prospects.

Analysts expect SLE's five-year annual earnings growth rate to average 7 percent.

Weingarten Realty SBI (WRI) (Figure 10-22)

2600 Citadel Plaza Drive

Houston, TX 77008

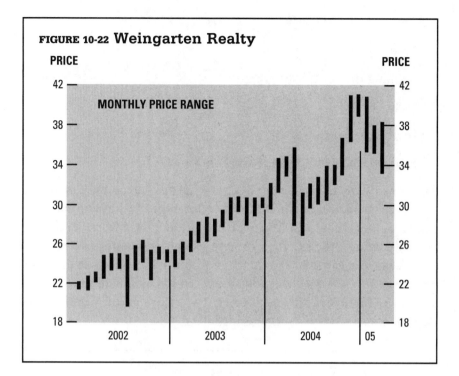

FIGURE 10-22 **Weingarten Realty**

Dividends paid since 1958

S&P earnings and dividend rank: A–

This real estate investment trust focuses primarily on the development, acquisition, and ownership of neighborhood and community
shopping centers, and, to a lesser extent, on industrial properties.
Weingarten seeks to increase cash flow and portfolio value via intensive management of its existing portfolio, renovation of properties,
and acquisition and development of income-producing real estate
where returns on investment exceed the cost of capital. More than
45 percent of the building square footage of its properties is located
in Texas, but the trust continues to expand its holdings outside the
state. The two largest tenants are Kroger and Safeway supermarkets.

Standard & Poor's expects Weingarten, which has a history of
making prudent acquisitions, to continue active acquisition efforts
and disposition activities.

Wilmington Trust (WI) (Figure 10-23)

1100 North Market Street

Wilmington DE 19890

(302) 651-1000

Dividends paid since 1914

S&P earnings and dividend rank: A+

Formed in 1903 to manage the wealth of the duPont family, Wilmington Trust has grown to become the fifteenth largest U.S. personal trust manager and the largest financial institution in Delaware, with more than 40 branch offices. The company groups its operations into three core businesses: regional banking, corporate financial services, and advisory fee-based services. In recent years, acquisitions of asset management firms have enhanced the offerings of Wilmington's private client advisory services business.

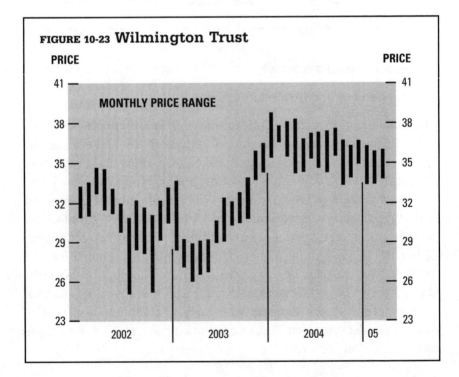

FIGURE 10-23 Wilmington Trust

The company is expanding its trust businesses faster than its traditional banking business, with the result that income from trust and other fee-based activities accounts for about 50 percent of Wilmington Trust's total revenues, versus about 30 percent for its peers.

Analysts estimate that WI will record a five-year average annual earnings growth rate of 8 percent.

Dividend Aristocrats

The companies in the table in Figure 10-24 are a unique group. They are all members of the S&P 500 index and each of them has increased its dividend in every year of the past 25. Six of them—Altria Group, Bank of America, General Electric, McDonald's, Procter & Gamble, and Wal-Mart—have been highlighted above.

FIGURE 10-24 S&P 500 Dividend Aristocrats

Cash payments based on ex-dividend dates from Jan. 1 to Dec. 31 of each year

COMPANY	TICKER SYMBOL	CASH DIVIDENDS PAID EACH YEAR SINCE	SECTOR	COMPANY	TICKER SYMBOL	CASH DIVIDENDS PAID EACH YEAR SINCE	SECTOR
Abbott Laboratories	ABT	1926	Health Care	Johnson & Johnson	JNJ	1944	Health Care
ALLTEL Corp.	AT	1961	Telecommunication Services	Johnson Controls	JCI	1887	Consumer Discretionary
Altria Group	MO	1928	Consumer Staples	KeyCorp	KEY	1963	Financials
AmSouth Bancorp	ASO	1943	Financials	Kimberly-Clark	KMB	1935	Consumer Staples
Anheuser-Busch Cos.	BUD	1932	Consumer Staples	Leggett & Platt	LEG	1939	Consumer Discretionary
Archer-Daniels-Midland	ADM	1927	Consumer Staples	Lilly (Eli)	LLY	1885	Health Care
Automatic Data Proc.	ADP	1974	Industrials	Lowe's Cos.	LOW	1961	Consumer Discretionary
Avery Dennison Corp.	AVY	1964	Industrials	Masco Corp.	MAS	1944	Industrials
Bank of America	BAC	1903	Financials	May Dept. Stores	MAY	1911	Consumer Discretionary
Bard (C.R.)	BCR	1960	Health Care	McDonald's Corp.	MCD	1976	Consumer Discretionary
Becton, Dickinson	BDX	1926	Health Care	McGraw-Hill Companies	MHP	1937	Consumer Discretionary
CenturyTel Inc.	CTL	1974	Telecommunication Services	Merck & Co.	MRK	1935	Health Care
Chubb Corp.	CB	1902	Financials	Nucor Corp.	NUE	1973	Materials
Clorox Co.	CLX	1968	Consumer Staples	PepsiCo Inc.	PEP	1952	Consumer Staples
Coca-Cola Co.	KO	1893	Consumer Staples	Pfizer, Inc.	PFE	1901	Health Care
Comerica Inc.	CMA	1936	Financials	PPG Industries	PPG	1899	Materials
ConAgra Foods	CAG	1976	Consumer Staples	Procter & Gamble	PG	1891	Consumer Staples
Consolidated Edison	ED	1885	Utilities	Regions Financial	RF	1968	Financials
Donnelley(R.R.)& Sons	RRD	1911	Industrials	Rohm & Haas	ROH	1927	Materials
Dover Corp.	DOV	1947	Industrials	Sigma-Aldrich	SIAL	1970	Materials
Emerson Electric	EMR	1947	Industrials	Stanley Works	SWK	1877	Consumer Discretionary
Family Dollar Stores	FDR	1976	Consumer Discretionary	Supervalu Inc.	SVU	1936	Consumer Staples
First Horizon National	FHN	1895	Financials	Target Corp.	TGT	1965	Consumer Discretionary
Gannett Co.	GCI	1929	Consumer Discretionary	TECO Energy	TE	1900	Utilities
General Electric	GE	1899	Industrials	3M Co.	MMM	1916	Industrials
Grainger (W.W.)	GWW	1965	Industrials	U.S. Bancorp	USB	1930	Financials
Heinz (H.J.)	HNZ	1911	Consumer Staples	VF Corp.	VFC	1941	Consumer Discretionary
Household Int'l	HI	1926	Financials	Wal-Mart Stores	WMT	1973	Consumer Discretionary
Jefferson-Pilot	JP	1913	Financials	Walgreen Co.	WAG	1933	Consumer Staples

Dividend Reinvestment Plans of Companies in the S&P 1500

The companies listed in this section are in the S&P 1500, which consists of the S&P 500 composite index, Mid Cap 400 index, and Small Cap 600 index. All of the companies have dividend reinvestment plans that are worth looking into. For a list of companies that boast a five-year (2000–2005) annual dividend growth rate of at least six percent, see Appendix 2.

As we mentioned earlier, these plans are an attractive, low-cost, convenient way to build stock positions. Not only can you reinvest the dividends, but most of the plans also allow you to buy additional shares via an automatic investment plan or by sending in various amounts when you have the extra money. You'll be pleasantly surprised how quickly you can accumulate a good-sized nest egg using these programs.

When you decide on which plans to join, you should monitor the companies closely. There's no such thing as buying and ignoring. As former president Ronald Reagan said, "Trust, but verify."

3M Company (MMM)
Leading maker of Scotch tapes and coated abrasives.
(800) 401-1952
www.mmm.com

Optional cash purchases: $10 to $10,000 quarterly

Dividends paid since 1916

S&P earnings and dividend rank: A–

A

Abbott Laboratories (ABT)

Major maker of health care and nutritional products.

(888) 332-2268

www.abbott.com

Optional cash purchases: $10 to $20,000 annually

Dividends paid since 1926

S&P earnings and dividend rank: A

Acuity Brands (AYI)

Manufacturer of residential and commercial lighting fixtures.

(800) 432-0140

www.acuitybrands.com

Initial shares can be purchased directly from the company: $500 minimum or automatic monthly investments of at least $50 for 12 consecutive months.

Optional cash purchases: $25 to $100,000 annually

Dividends paid since 2002

S&P earnings and dividend rank: not ranked.

Aetna (AET)

Provider of insurance and financial services.

(800) 446-2617

www.aetna.com

Initial shares can be purchased directly from the company: $500 minimum or automatic monthly investments of at least $50 for 10 consecutive months.

Optional cash purchases: $50 to $250,000 annually

Dividends paid since 2001

S&P earnings and dividend rank: not ranked

AFLAC (AFL)

Insurance company (see page 160).

(800) 235-2667

www.aflac. com

Initial shares can be bought directly from the company: $1,000 minimum.

Optional cash purchases: $50 to $250,000 annually

Dividends paid since 1973

S&P earnings and dividend rank: A

Agilysys (APD)

Electronic components distributor.

(800) 622-6757

www.agilysys.com

Optional cash purchases: $25 to $5,000 monthly

Dividends paid since 1965

S&P earnings and dividend rank: B+

AGL Resources (ATG)

Large natural gas utility based in Georgia.

(800) 633-4236

www.aglresources.com

Initial shares can be purchased directly from the company: $250 minimum.

Optional cash purchases: $25 to $5000 monthly

Dividends paid since 1939

S&P earnings and dividend rank: A–

Air Products & Chemicals (APD)

Manufactures industrial chemicals, equipment, and gases.

(877) 322-4941

www.airproducts.com

Initial shares can be purchased directly from the company: $500 minimum or automatic monthly investments of at least $100 for five consecutive months.

Optional cash purchases: $100 to $200,000 annually

Dividends paid since 1954

S&P earnings and dividend rank: B+

Albany International (AIN)

Largest maker of engineered fabrics for papermaking machines.

(312) 360-5395

www.albint.com

Optional cash purchases: $10 to $5,000 monthly

Dividends paid since 2002

S&P earnings and dividend rank: B

Albemarle Corp. (ALB)

Manufacturer of industrial chemicals.

(800) 622-6757

www.albermarle.com

Dividends paid since 1994

S&P earnings and dividend rank: B+

Albertson's Inc. (ABS)

Major food and drugstore retailer.

www.albertsons.com

Dividends paid since 1960

S&P earnings and dividend rank: A–

Alcoa (AA)

Leading aluminum producer in the United States.

(800) 317-4445

www.alcoa.com

Optional cash purchases: $25 to $5,000 monthly

Dividends paid since 1939

S&P earnings and dividend rank: B+

Alexander & Baldwin (ALEX)

Provider of ocean shipping, with interests in real estate and agribusiness.

(800) 356-2017

www.alexanderbaldwin.com

No optional cash purchases; need at least 25 shares to participate in the plan

Dividends paid since 1902

S&P earnings and dividend rank: B+

Allegheny Technologies (ATI)

Important maker of stainless steel and specialty metals.

(800) 842-7629

www.alleghenytechnologies.com

Initial shares can be purchased directly from the company: $1,000 minimum.

Optional cash purchases: $100 to $10,000 monthly

Dividends paid since 1996

S&P earnings and dividend rank: B–

Allergan (AGN)

Maker of ophthalmic and dermatological products.

(781) 575-2726

www.allergan.com

Optional cash purchases: $10 to $50,000 annually

Dividends paid since 1989

S&P earnings and dividend rank: B

ALLETE Inc. (ALE)

Electric utility operating in Minnesota and Wisconsin.

(800) 535-3056

www.allete.com

Initial shares can be purchased directly from the company: $250 minimum.

Optional cash purchases: $10 to $100,000 annually

Dividends paid since 1945

S&P earnings and dividend rank: A–

Alliant Energy (LNT)

Utility holding company for Wisconsin Power & Light.

(800) 356-5343

www.alliant-energy.com

Initial shares can be purchased directly from the company: $250 minimum or automatic monthly investments of at least $25.

Dividends paid since 1946

S&P earnings and dividend rank: B

Allstate Corp. (ALL)

Large property/liability/life insurer.

(800) 355-5191

www.allstate.com

Initial shares can be purchased directly from the company: $500 minimum or automatic monthly investments of at least $50 for 10 consecutive months.

Optional cash purchases: $100 to $150,000 annually

Dividends paid since 1993

S&P earnings and dividend rank: B+

ALLTELL Corp. (AT)

Diversified telecommunications and information services company.

(877) 446-3628

www.alltel.com

Optional cash purchases: $50 to $25,000 quarterly

Dividends paid since 1945

S&P earnings and dividend rank: B+

Altria Group (MO)

Formerly Philip Morris, the company is a major supplier of cigarettes and has a sizable investment in Kraft Foods and SABMiller.

(800) 442-0077

www.altria.com

Initial shares can be purchased directly from the company: $500 minimum or automatic monthly

investments of at least $50 for 10 consecutive months.

Optional cash purchases: $50 to $250,000 annually

Dividends paid since 1928

S&P earnings and dividend rank: A+

AMB Property (AMB)

Real estate investment trust.

(800) 331-9474

www.amb.com

Initial shares can be purchased directly from the company: $500 minimum.

Optional cash purchases: $500 to $5000 monthly

Dividends paid since 1997

S&P earnings and dividend rank: not ranked

AMCOL International (ACO)

Major producer of bentonite, a nonmetallic clay used in many different industries and products.

(888) 444-0058

www.amcol

Initial shares can be purchased directly from the company: $250 minimum.

Optional cash purchases: $25 to $10,000 per transaction

Dividends paid since 1937

S&P earnings and dividend rank: B+

Amerada Hess (AHC)

Oil explorer, producer, refiner, and marketer.

(800) 524-4458

www.hess.com

Optional cash purchases: $50 to $20,000 annually

Dividends paid since 1922

S&P earnings and dividend rank: B

Ameren Corp. (AEE)

Electric utility in Missouri, Illinois, and Iowa.

(800) 255-2237

www.ameren.com

Initial shares can be purchased directly from the company: $250 minimum.

Optional cash purchases: $25 to $120,000 annually

Dividends paid since 1906

S&P earnings and dividend rank: A–

American Electric Power (AEP)

Major electric utility holding company.

(800) 328-6955

www.aep.com

Initial shares can be purchased directly from the company: $250 minimum or automatic monthly investments of at least $25.

Optional cash purchases: $25 to $150,000 annually

Dividends paid since 1909

S&P earnings and dividend rank: B

American Express (AXP)

Provider of travel related, financial advisory, and international banking services.

(800) 842-7629

www.americanexpress.com

Initial shares can be purchased directly from the company: $1,000 minimum or automatic monthly investments of at least $50.

Optional cash purchases: $0 to $120,000 annually

Dividends paid since 1870

S&P earnings and dividend rank: A–

American Greetings (AM)

Leading supplier of greeting cards and gift wrap.

(800) 622-6757

www.americangreetings.com

Optional cash purchases: $100 to $10,000 monthly

Dividends paid since 2004

S&P earnings and dividend rank: B–

American Power Conversion (APCC)

Manufacturer of power protection and management

products and services for computer and electronic applications.

(800) 733-5001

www.apcc.com

Optional cash purchases: $50 to $120,000 annually

Dividends paid since 2003

S&P earnings and dividend rank: B+

American States Water (AWR)

Water utility based in Southern California.

(888) 816-6998

www.aswater.com

Initial shares can be purchased directly from the company: $550 minimum.

Optional cash purchases: $100 to $20,000 monthly

Dividends paid since 1931

S&P earnings and dividend rank: B+

AmerUS Group (AMH)

Provider of life insurance and annuity products.

(8000) 304-9709

www.amerus.co

Initial shares can be purchased directly from the company: $1,000 minimum or automatic monthly investments of at least $100.

Optional cash purchases: $50 to $15,000 monthly

Dividends paid since 1997

S&P earnings and dividend rank: B

AMETEK, Inc. (AME)

Maker of electronic instruments and electric motors.

(877) 854-0864

www.ametek.com

Initial shares can be purchased directly from the company: $250 minimum.

Optional cash purchases: $25 to $10,000 per transaction

Dividends paid since 1942

S&P earnings and dividend rank: A–

AmSouth Bancorp (ASO)

Largest Alabama-based bank; has branches in four southeastern states.

(800) 432-0140

www.amsouth.com

Initial shares can be purchased directly from the company: $1,000 minimum.

Optional cash purchases: $50 to $12,000 annually

Dividends paid since 1943

S&P earnings and dividend rank: A–

Anadarko Petroleum (APC)

Oil and gas exploration and production.

(888) 470-5786

www.anadarko.com

Initial shares can be purchased directly from the company: $1,000 minimum or automatic monthly investments of at least $100 for 10 consecutive months.

Optional cash purchases: $50 to $120,000 monthly

Dividends paid since 1986

S&P earnings and dividend rank: B+

Angelica Corp. (AGL)

Leading maker of uniforms and business career apparel.

(800) 884-4225

www.angelica.com

Optional cash purchases: $10 to $3,000 quarterly

Dividends paid since 1954

S&P earnings and dividend rank: B–

Anheuser-Busch Companies (BUD)

Largest U.S. beer brewer; also has baking and theme park operations.

(888) 213-0964

www.anheuser-busch.com

Optional cash purchases: $25 to $5,000 monthly

Dividends paid since 1932

S&P earnings and quality ranking: A+

Aon Corp. (AOC)

Provider of broad-based insurance products.

(800) 446-2617

www.aon.com

Optional cash purchases: $25 to $1,000 monthly

Dividends paid since 1950

S&P earnings and quality ranking: B+

Apache Corp. (APA)

Independent oil and gas explorer, producer and marketer.

(800) 468-9716

www.apachecorp.com

Optional cash purchases: $50 to $5,000 quarterly

Dividends paid since 1965

S&P earnings and dividend rank: B+

Applied Industrial Technologies (AIT)

Distributor of bearings and power transmission components.

(800) 988-5291

www.appliedindustrial.com

Optional cash purchases: $10 to $1,000 weekly

Dividends paid since 1957

S&P earnings and quality ranking: B+

Aqua America (WTR)

Water utility based in Philadelphia.

(800) 205-8314

www.aquaamerica.com

Initial shares can be purchased directly from the company: $500 minimum or at least $50 for 10 consecutive months.

Optional cash purchases: $50 to $250,000 annually

5 percent discount on reinvested dividends

Dividends paid since 1939

S&P earnings and quality ranking: A–

Arch Chemicals (ARJ)

Maker of specialty chemical products.

(866) 857-2223

www.archchemicals.com

Initial shares can be purchased directly from the company: $500 minimum or automatic monthly investments of at least $50 for 10 consecutive months.

Optional cash purchases: $50 to $10,000 per transaction

Dividends paid since 1999

S&P earnings and dividend rank: not ranked

Arch Coal (ACI)

Coal producer in the central Appalachian region of the United States.

(800) 360-4519

www.archcoal.com

Initial shares can be purchased directly from the company: $250 minimum.

Optional cash purchases: $25 to $10,000 per transaction

Dividends paid since 1997

S&P earnings and dividend rank: not ranked

Archer-Daniels-Midland (ADM)

Processor of agricultural commodities.

(800) 898-8730

www.admworld.com

Optional cash purchases: $10 to $60,000 annually

Dividends paid since 1927

S&P earnings and dividend rank: B+

Archstone-Smith Trust (ASN)

Real estate investment trust.

(800) 982-9293

www.archstonesmith.com

Initial shares can be purchased directly from the company: $200 minimum.

Up to 5 percent discount on reinvested dividends and on optional cash purchases.

Dividends paid since 1970

S&P earnings and dividend rank: not ranked

ArvinMeritor (ARM)

Makes auto parts for original equipment and replacement markets.

(866) 517-4570

www.arvinmeritor.com

Initial shares can be purchased directly from the company: $500 minimum.

Optional cash purchases: $50 to $100,000 annually

Dividends paid since 1997

S&P earnings and quality rank: not ranked

Ashland, Inc. (ASH)

Major petroleum refiner providing motor oil and chemicals.

(800) 622-6757

www.ashland.com

Initial shares can be purchased directly from the company: $500 minimum.

Optional cash purchases: $25 to $500 monthly

Dividends paid since 1936

S&P earnings and dividend rank: B

Associated Banc-Corp. (ASBC)

Commercial bank with operations in Illinois and Wisconsin.

(800) 622-6757

www.associatedbank.com

Optional cash payments: $50 to $50,000 annually

Dividends paid since 1970

S&P earnings and dividend rank: A

Astoria Financial (AF)

New York savings and loan company.

(800) 851-9677

www.astoriafederal.com

Optional cash purchases: $50 to $5,000 quarterly

Dividends paid since 1995

S&P earnings and dividend rank: A–

Atmos Energy Corp. (ATO)

Natural gas utility operating in parts of Kentucky, Louisiana, Texas, Colorado, Kansas, and Missouri.

(800) 543-3038

www.atmosenergy.com

Initial shares can be purchased directly from the company: $1,250 minimum.

Optional cash purchases: $25 to $100,000 annually

Dividends paid since 1984

S&P earnings and dividend rank: B+

AT&T Corp. (T)

Provider of telecommunications services.

(800) 348-8288

www.att.com

Optional cash purchases: $100 to $250,000 annually

Plan fees are above average

Dividends paid since 1881

S&P earnings and dividend rank: B

AveryDennison (AVY)

Leading maker of self-adhesive base materials, labels, and office products.

(877) 498-8861

www.averydennison.com

Initial shares can be purchased directly from the company: $500 minimum or automatic monthly investments of at least $50 for 10 consecutive months.

Optional cash payments: $100 to $150,000 annually

Dividends paid since 1964

S&P earnings and dividend rank: A

Avista Corp. (AVA)

Electric and gas utility in Washington and Idaho.

(800) 222-4931

www.avistacorp.com

Optional cash purchases: up to $100,000 annually

Dividends paid since 1899

S&P earnings and dividend rank: B

Avon Products (AVP)

Direct seller of beauty and related products.

(888) 287-3228

www.avoncompany.com

Optional cash payments: $10 to $5,000 monthly

Dividends paid since 1919

S&P earnings and dividend rank: A

B

Baker Hughes (BHI)

Manufacturer of equipment used in drilling oil and gas wells.

(800) 446-2617

www.bakerhughes.com

Optional cash payments: $10 to $350 monthly

Dividends paid since 1987

S&P earnings and dividend rank: B

Baldor Electric (BEZ)

Major maker of industrial electric motors and drives.

(800) 509-5586

www.baldor.com

Optional cash payments: $50 to $10,000 monthly

Dividends paid since 1938

S&P earnings and dividend rank: A

Ball Corp. (BLL)

Maker of packaging products, as well as provider of aerospace systems.

(800) 446-2617

www.ball.com

Optional cash payments: $25 to $2,000 monthly

5 percent discount on reinvested dividends

Dividends paid since 1958

S&P earnings and dividend rank: B+

Bandag, Inc. (BDG)

Manufacturer of tread rubber used in retreading bus and truck tires.

(800) 730-4001

www.bandag.com

Optional cash payments: $50 to $10,000 quarterly

Dividends paid since 1976

S&P earnings and dividend rank: B

Bank of America (BAC)

Large bank with operations in North Carolina, California, Illinois, and Washington.

(888) 279-3457

www.bankofamerica.com

Initial shares can be purchased directly from the company: $1,000 minimum or automatic monthly investments of at least $50.

Optional cash purchases: $50 to $120,000 annually

Dividends paid since 1903

S&P earnings and dividend rank: A–

Bank of Hawaii (BOH)

Operates largest commercial bank in Hawaii.

(800) 509-5586

www.boh.com

Optional cash payments: $25 to $5,000 quarterly

Dividends paid since 1899

S&P earnings and dividend rank: B+

Bank of New York (BK)

New York commercial banker.

(888) 643-4269

www.bankofny.com

Initial shares can be purchased directly from the company: $1,000 minimum.

Optional cash purchases: $50 to $150,000 annually

Dividends paid since 1785

S&P earnings and dividend rank: A–

Banta Corp. (BN)

Provides printing and graphic arts services.

(800) 937-5449

www.banta.com

Optional cash purchases: $25 to $7,500 quarterly

Dividends paid since 1927

S&P earnings and dividend rank: B

Bard (C.R.) (BCR)

Makes medical, diagnostic, and surgical products; it is the leading maker of urological products.

(800) 446-2617

www.crbard.com

Initial shares can be purchased directly from the company: $250 minimum or automatic monthly investment of at least $25 for 10 consecutive months.

Optional cash payments: $25 minimum; no maximum

Dividends paid since 1960

S&P earnings and dividend rank: B+

Barnes Group (B)

Leading manufacturer of precision mechanical springs.

(800) 288-9541

www.barnesgroupinc.com

Initial shares can be purchased directly from the company: $250 minimum or automatic monthly investments of at least $25 for 10 consecutive months.

Optional cash purchases: $25 to $100,000 annually

Dividends paid since 1934

S&P earnings and dividend rank: B

Bausch & Lomb (BOL)

Maker of health-care products and optical devices.

(800) 288-9541

www.bausch.com

Optional cash payments: $25 to $60,000 monthly

Dividends paid since 1952

S&P earnings and dividend rank: B

Baxter International (BAX)

Major manufacturer of health-care products, mainly for hospitals and laboratories.

(800) 359-8645

www.baxter.com

Optional cash payments: $25 to $25,000 annually

Dividends paid since 1934

S&P earnings and dividend rank: B+

BB&T Corp. (BBT)

Bank holding company with operations in the Carolinas,

Virginia, Maryland, and
Washington, D.C.

(336) 733-3477

www.bbandt.com

*Optional cash payments: $25
to $10,000 monthly*

Dividends paid since 1934

*S&P earnings and dividend
rank: A–*

Beckman Coulter (BEC)

Important maker of laboratory
instruments.

(781) 575-2726

www.beckmancoulter.com

*Optional cash payments: $10
to $60,000 annually*

Dividends paid since 1989

*S&P earnings and dividend
rank: B+*

Becton, Dickinson (BDX)

Manufacturer of medical
supplies and diagnostic
equipment.

(800) 519-3111

*Initial shares can be
purchased directly from the
company: $250 minimum or
automatic monthly
investments of at least $50 for
five consecutive months.*

*Optional cash payments: $50
minimum, no maximum*

Dividends paid since 1926

*S&P earnings and dividend
rank: A*

BellSouth Corp. (BLS)

Second largest telephone
holding company, providing
local service to southeastern
states.

(800) 631-6001

www.bellsouth.com

*Initial shares can be
purchased directly from the
company: $500 minimum or
automatic monthly
investments of at least $50 for
10 consecutive months.*

*Optional cash purchases: $50
to $100,000 annually*

Dividends paid since 1964

*S&P earnings and dividend
rank: A–*

Bemis Co. (BMS)

Maker of consumer and
industrial flexible packaging
products and pressure-sensitive
materials.

(800) 468-9716

www.bemis.com

*Optional cash payments: $25
to $10,000 quarterly*

Dividends paid since 1922

*S&P earnings and dividend
rank: A*

Best Buy (BBY)

Retailer of consumer
electronics, home office
products, entertainment
software, and appliances.

(877) 498-8861

www.bestbuy.com

Initial shares can be purchased directly from the company: $500 minimum or automatic monthly investments of at least $50 for 10 consecutive months.

Optional cash payments: $50 to $250,000 annually

Fees are above-average

Dividends paid since 2003

S&P earnings and dividend rank: B+

Black & Decker (BDK)

Leading manufacturer of power tools and household products.

(800) 433-0140

www.bdk.com

Optional cash payments: $25 to $100,000 annually

Dividends paid since 1937

S&P earnings and dividend rank: B+

Black Hills Corp. (BKH)

Electric utility operating in South Dakota, Wyoming, and Montana.

(800) 468-9716

www.blackhillscorp.com

Initial shares can be purchased directly from the

company: $250 minimum or automatic monthly investments of at least $25 for 10 consecutive months.

Optional cash payments: $25 to $15,000 monthly

Dividends paid since 1942

S&P earnings and dividend rank: B+

Block (H&R) (HRB)

Largest preparer of individual income tax returns.

(888) 213-0968

www.hrblock.com

Optional cash payments: $25 to $5,000 monthly

Dividends paid since 1962

S&P earnings and dividend rank: A–

Blyth Inc. (BTH)

Maker of candle products.

(866) 238-5345

www.blythinc.com

Initial shares can be purchased directly from the company: $250 minimum or automatic monthly investments of at least $50 for five consecutive months.

Optional cash payments: $50 to $125,000 annually

Dividends paid since 2000

S&P earnings and dividend rank: B+

Bob Evans Farms (BOBE)

Operates more than 400 Bob Evans restaurants; produces fresh and fully cooked sausage products.

(800) 272-7675

www.bobevans.com

Initial shares can be purchased directly from the company: $100 minimum.

Optional cash payments: $50 to $20,000 monthly

Dividends paid since 1964

S&P earnings and dividend rank: A–

Boeing Co. (BA)

Leading maker of commercial jets and military aircraft, space systems, and electronic/information systems.

(888) 777-0923

www.boeing.com

Optional cash payments: $50 to $100,000 annually

Fees are above-average

Dividends paid since 1942

S&P earnings and dividend rank: B+

Borders Group (BGP)

Operator of book, music, and movie superstores.

(800) 446-2617

www.bordersgroupinc.com

Initial shares can be purchased directly from the company: $500 minimum or automatic monthly investments of at least $50 for 10 consecutive months.

Optional cash payments: $50 to $250,000 annually

Fees are above-average

Dividends paid since 2004

S&P earnings and dividend rank: B

Borg Warner (BWA)

Manufacturer of engineered systems and components mainly for automotive power train applications.

(800) 851-4229

www.bwauto.com

Initial shares can be purchased directly from the company: $500 minimum or automatic monthly investments of at least $50 for 10 consecutive months.

Optional cash payments: $50 to $120,000 annually

Dividends paid since 1994

S&P earnings and dividend rank: B+

Boston Private Financial Holdings (BPFH)

Provider of banking and investment products to affluent customers in New England and northern California.

(888) 666-1363

www.bostonprivate.com

*Optional cash payments: $50
to $100,000 annually*

Dividends paid since 2000

*S&P earnings and dividend
rank: B+*

Bowater, Inc. (BOW)

Manufacturer of newsprint and
coated paper.

(888) 269-8845

www.bowater.com

*Optional cash payments: $100
to $5,000 monthly*

Dividends paid since 1984

*S&P earnings and dividend
rank: B–*

Bowne & Company (BNE)

Specializes in financial
documentation and
communications services for
corporate compliance and
public financing.

(800) 524-4458

www.bowne.com

*Initial shares can be
purchased directly from the
company: $500 minimum.*

*Optional cash payments: $50
to $100,000 annually*

Dividends paid since 1941

*S&P earnings and dividend
rank: B–*

Brady Corp. (BRC)

Manufacturer of adhesives and
coatings.

(800) 468-9716

www.bradycorp.com

*Optional cash payments: $100
to $10,000 monthly*

Dividends paid since: 1984

*S&P earnings and dividend
rank: B+*

Briggs & Stratton (BGG)

Leading producer of gasoline
engines for outdoor power
equipment.

(800) 365-2759

www.briggsandstratton.com

*Optional cash payments: $25
to $5,000 quarterly*

Dividends paid since 1929

*S&P earnings and dividend
rank: B+*

Bristol-Myers Squibb (BMY)

Major producer of
pharmaceuticals and medical
devices.

(800) 356-2026

www.bms.com

*Optional cash purchases: $105
to $10,025 monthly*

Fees are above-average

Dividends paid since 1900

*S&P earnings and dividend
rank: A–*

Brookline Bancorp (BRKL)

Bank operator in Brookline, Massachusetts.

(888) 750-0060

www.brooklinebank.com

Initial shares can be purchased directly from the company: $250 minimum.

Optional cash payments: $25 to $10,000 per transaction

Dividends paid since 1998

S&P earnings and dividend rank: not ranked

Brown Shoe (BWS)

Maker and retailer of branded footwear.

(800) 446-2617

www.brownshoe.com

Optional cash payments: $25 to $1,000 monthly

Dividends paid since 1923

S&P earnings and dividend rank: B

Brunswick Corp. (BC)

Major manufacturer of pleasure boats and marine engines.

(800) 546-9420

www.brunswick.com

Dividends paid since 1969

S&P earnings and dividend rank: B

Burlington Northern Santa Fe (BNI)

Operator of largest rail system in the United States.

(800) 795-2673

www.bnsf.com

Optional cash payments: $50 to $60,000 annually

Dividends paid since 1940

S&P earnings and dividend rank: A–

C

Cabot Corp. (CBT)

Maker of specialty chemicals, including carbon black; also in oil and gas.

(800) 730-4001

www.cabot-corp.com

Optional cash payments: $10 to $10,000 quarterly

Dividends paid since 1931

S&P earnings and dividend rank: B–

Callaway Golf (ELY)

Designer and manufacturer of golf clubs.

(800) 368-7068

Optional cash payments: $50 to $5,000 monthly

Dividends paid since 1993

S&P earnings and dividend rank: B

Campbell Soup (CPB)

Leading producer of canned soup, frozen dinners, spaghetti, and bakery products.

(800) 446-2617

www.campbellsoupcompany.com

Initial shares can be purchased directly from the company: $500 minimum or automatic monthly investments of at least $50 for 10 consecutive months.

Optional cash payments: $50 to $350,000 annually

Dividends paid since 1902

S&P earnings and dividend rank: B+

Capital Automotive REIT (CARS)

Real estate investment trust that invests in properties used by auto dealerships and other auto-related businesses.

(877) 208-9533

www.capitalautomotive.com

Initial shares can be purchased directly from the company: $100 minimum.

Optional cash payments: $100 to $10,000 monthly

Dividends paid since 1998

S&P earnings and dividend rank: not ranked

Capital One Financial (COF)

Major issuer of VISA and MasterCard credit cards in the United States.

(800) 446-2617

www.capitalone.com

Optional cash payments: $50 to $10,000 monthly

Dividends paid since 1995

S&P earnings and dividend rank: A+

Carlisle Companies (CSL)

Manufacturer of rubber, plastics, and metal products.

(800) 897-9071

www.carlisle.com

Optional cash payments: $10 to $3,000 quarterly

Dividends paid since 1950

S&P earnings and quality rank: A+

Carnival Corp. (CCL)

Operator of major cruise line.

(800) 568-3476

www.carnivalcorp.com

Optional cash purchases: not available

Dividends paid since 1988

S&P earnings and dividend rank: A+

Carpenter Technology (CRS)

Manufacturer of stainless steel, special alloys, and tool steel.

(888) 200-3170

www.cartech.com

Initial shares can be purchased directly from the company: $250 minimum.

Optional cash payments: $25 to $20,000 per transaction

Dividends paid since 1907

S&P earnings and dividend rank: B–

Cascade Natural Gas (CGC)

Natural gas distributor in Washington and Oregon.

(888) 269-8845

www.cngc.com

Initial shares can be purchased directly from the company by residential customers: $250 minimum.

Optional cash purchases: $50 to $20,000 annually

Dividends paid since 1964

S&P earnings and quality rank: B+

Casey's General Stores (CASY)

Operator and franchiser of convenience stores, mainly in small midwestern towns.

(816) 221-0438

www.caseys.com

Optional cash payments: $50 to $10,000 quarterly

Dividends paid since 1990

S&P earnings and dividend rank: A–

Cash America International (CSH)

Acquires and operates pawnshops in the United States, the U.K., and Sweden.

(800) 522-6645

www.cashamerica.com

Initial shares can be purchased directly from the company: $250 minimum or automatic monthly investments of at least $50 for five consecutive months.

Optional cash payments: $50 to $120,000 annually

Dividends paid since 1988

S&P earnings and dividend rank: B

Caterpillar Inc. (CAT)

Major manufacturer of earth-moving equipment and diesel and natural gas engines.

(800) 842-7629

www.cat.com

Initial shares can be purchased directly from the company: $250 minimum or automatic monthly *investments of at least $25 for 10 consecutive months.*

Optional cash payments: $25 minimum

Dividends paid since 1914

S&P earnings and dividend rank: B+

CBRL Group (CBRL)

Operator of restaurants and gift stores.

(800) 568-3476

www.cbrlgroup.com

Optional cash payments: $100 to $500 quarterly

Dividends paid since 1972

S&P earnings and dividend rank: B+

CenterPoint Energy (CNP)

Electric utility serving the Texas Gulf Coast.

(800) 231-6406

www.centerpointenergy.com

Initial shares can be purchased directly from the company: $250 minimum.

Optional cash payments: $50 to $120,000 annually

Dividends paid since 1922

S&P earnings and dividend rank: B

Central Vermont Public Service (CV)

Electric utility operating in Vermont and New Hampshire.

(800) 736-3001

www.cvps.com

Initial shares can be purchased directly from the company: $250 minimum.

Optional cash payments: $100 to $5,000 monthly

Dividends paid since 1944

S&P earnings and dividend rank: B

CenturyTel (CTL)

Telephone holding company with operations in cellular telephone service and nationwide paging systems.

(800) 969-6718

www.centurytel.com

Optional cash payments: $25 to $150,000 annually

Dividends paid since 1974

S&P earnings and dividend rank: A

Chemed Corp. (CHE)

Provides plumbing and pipe-cleaning services, as well as home health-care and major appliance, heating, ventilating, and air-conditioning repair.

(800) 468-9716

www.rotorooterinc.com

Optional cash purchases: $50 to $5,000 monthly

Dividends paid since 1971

S&P earnings and quality rank: B–

Chesapeake Corp. (CSK)

Manufacturer of tissue and packaging products.

(312) 360-5163

www.cskcorp.com

Optional cash payments: $10 to $5,000 quarterly

Dividends paid since 1933

S&P earnings and dividend rank: B–

ChevronTexaco Corp. (CVX)

Major integrated international oil company.

Initial shares can be purchased directly from the company: $250 minimum or automatic monthly investments of at least $50 for five consecutive months.

Optional cash payments: $50 to $100,000 annually

Dividends paid since 1912

S&P earnings and dividend rank: B+

Chittenden Corp. (CHZ)

Operates largest commercial bank in Vermont.

(800) 969-3386

www.chittenden.com

Optional cash payments: $25 to $10,000 quarterly

Dividends paid since 1992

S&P earnings and dividend rank: B+

Chubb Corp. (CB)

Property, casualty, life, and health insurer.

(800) 317-4445

www.chubb.com

Optional cash payments: $10 to $60,000 annually

Dividends paid since 1902

S&P earnings and dividend rank: B+

Church & Dwight (CHD)

Producer of baking soda and sodium bicarbonate-based products under Arm & Hammer brand.

(866) 299-4289

www.churchdwight.com

Optional cash payments: $250 to $5,000 quarterly

Dividends paid since 1901

S&P earnings and dividend rank: A

CIGNA Corp. (CI)

Multiline insurance holding company.

(800) 317-4445

www.cigna.com

Initial shares can be purchased directly from the company: $250 minimum or *automatic monthly investments of at least $25 for 10 consecutive months.*

Optional cash payments: $25 to $100,000 annually

Dividends paid since 1867

S&P earnings and dividend rank: B+

Cincinnati Financial (CINF)

Insurance holding company.

(800) 837-2755

www.cinfin.com

Optional cash payments: $25 to $10,000 monthly

Dividends paid since 1954

S&P earnings and dividend rank: A–

CINergy Corp. (CIN)

Electric and natural gas utility holding company. Owner of shares in Cincinnati Gas & Electric and PSI Energy.

(800) 325-2945

www.cinergy.com

Initial shares may be purchased directly from the company: $250 minimum.

Optional cash payments: $25 to $100,000 annually

Dividends paid since 1853

S&P earnings and quality ranking: B+

Citigroup (C)

Major diversified financial services company.

(877) 936-2737

www.citigroup.com

Optional cash purchases: not available

Dividends paid since 1986

S&P earnings and dividend rank: A+

Citizens Communications (CZN)

Provider of telecommunications, electric, gas, and water services in 18 states.

(800) 757-5755

www.czn.net

Optional cash payments: $100 to $25,000 quarterly

Dividends paid since 2004

S&P earnings and dividend rank: B–

CLACOR, Inc.

Manufacturer of air, fuel, and hydraulic filters, as well as metal and plastic lithographed containers.

(800) 622-6757

www.clarcor.com

Initial shares can be purchased directly from the company: $500 minimum.

Optional cash payments: $500 to $5,000 monthly

Above-average fees

Dividends paid since 1921

S&P earnings and dividend rank: A

Cleco Corp. (CNL)

Electric utility operating in Louisiana.

(781) 575-2723

www.cleco.com

Optional cash payments: $25 to $5,000 monthly

Dividends paid since 1935

S&P earnings and dividend rank: B+

Cleveland-Cliffs (CLF)

Producer and processor of iron ore.

(800) 446-2617

www.cleveland-cliffs.com

Optional cash payments: $20 to $30,000 annually

Dividends paid since 2004

S&P earnings and dividend rank: B–

Clorox Co. (CLX)

Manufacturer of household products.

(781) 575-2726

www.clorox.com

Optional cash payments: $10 to $60,000 annually

Dividends paid since 1968

S&P earnings and dividend ranking: A

CNF Inc. (CNF)

Regional motor carrier specializing in less-than-truckload delivery.

(866) 517-4584

www.cnf.com

Optional cash payments: $25 to $60,000 annually

Above-average fees

Dividends paid since 1995

S&P earnings and dividend rank: B–

Coca-Cola Co. (KO)

World's largest soft drink company.

(888) 265-3747

www.coca-cola.com

Optional cash payments: $10 to $125,000 annually

Dividends paid since 1893

S&P earnings and dividend rank: B+

Coca-Cola Enterprises (CCE)

World's largest bottler of Coca-Cola beverages.

(877) 842-1616

www.cokecce.com

Optional cash payments: $10 to $100,000 annually

Dividends paid since 1986

S&P earnings and dividend rank: B

Colgate-Palmolive (CL)

Well-known maker of household goods.

(800) 756-8700

www.colgate.com

Optional cash payments: $20 to $60,000 annually

Dividends paid since 1895

S&P earnings and dividend rank: A+

Colonial BancGroup (CNB)

Commercial bank based in Alabama.

(888) 843-0622

www.colonialbank.com

Optional cash payments: $10 to $120,000 annually

Dividends paid since 1962

S&P earnings and dividend rank: A–

Colonial Properties Trust (CLP)

Real estate investment trust leasing properties in the southeastern United States.

(800) 730-6001

www.colonialprop.com

Optional cash payments: $200 to $25,000 annually

Dividends paid since 1994

S&P earnings and dividend rank: A–

Comerica Inc. (CMA)

Commercial bank operating in Michigan, Illinois, Texas, Florida, and California.

(800) 468-9716

www.comerica.com

Optional cash payments: $10 to $12,000 annually

Dividends paid since 1936

S&P earnings and dividend rank: A

Commerce Bancorp (CBH)

Bank operator in Philadelphia and southern New Jersey.

(888) 470-5884

www.commerceonline.com

Optional cash payments: $100 to $10,000 monthly

Dividends paid since 1984

S&P earnings and dividend rank: A+

Commercial Federal (CFB)

Operator of banks in Iowa, Kansas, Nebraska, and Colorado.

(800) 468-9716

www.comfedbank.com

Optional cash payments: $50 to $10,000 quarterly

Dividends paid since 1995

S&P earnings and dividend rank: B+

Community Bank System (CBU)

Bank operator in upstate New York.

(800) 278-4353

www.communitybankna.com

Initial shares can be purchased directly from the company: $250 minimum.

Optional cash payments: $25 to $10,000 per transaction

Dividends paid since 1986

S&P earnings and dividend rank: A–

Compass Bancshares (CBSS)

Alabama-based bank with operations in Texas.

(800) 509-4000

www.compassweb.com

Optional cash payments: $25 to $5,000 monthly

Dividends paid since 1939

S&P earnings and dividend rank: A+

Computer Associates (CA)

Designs computer software and systems.

(800) 244-7155

www.ca.com

Optional cash payments: $25 to $3,000 monthly

Above-average fees

Dividends paid since 1990

S&P earnings and dividend rank: B–

ConAgra Foods (CAG)

Major manufacturer of prepared foods and agricultural products.

(800) 214-0349

www.conagra.com

Optional cash payments: $50 to $50,000 annually

Dividends paid since 1976

S&P earnings and dividend rank: A

ConocoPhillips (COP)

Domestic integrated oil company.

(800) 842-7629

www.conocophillips.com

Initial shares can be purchased directly from the company: $250 minimum or automatic monthly investments of at least $25 for 10 consecutive months.

Optional cash payments: $25 to $120,000 annually

Dividends paid since 1934

S&P earnings and dividend rank: B

Consolidated Edison (ED)

Electric utility serving New York City.

(800) 522-5522

www.conedison.com

Optional cash purchases: $100 to $100,000 annually

Dividends paid since 1885

S&P earnings and dividend rank: B+

Constellation Energy Group (CEG)

Electric and gas utility in Maryland.

(800) 258-0499

www.constellationenergy.com

Optional cash payments: $25 to $100,000 annually

Dividends paid since 1910

S&P earnings and dividend rank: B

Cooper Tire & Rubber (CTB)

Maker of tires for autos and trucks, as well as car sealing systems and antivibration products.

(888) 294-8217

Initial shares can be purchased directly from the company: $250 minimum.

Optional cash payments: $100 to $100,000 annually

Dividends paid since 1950

S&P earnings and quality rank: B+

Corn Products International (CPO)

Refiner of corn products.

(866) 517-4574

www.cornproducts.com

Optional cash payments: $100 to $350,000 annually

Above-average fees

Dividends paid since 1998

S&P earnings and dividend rank: B+

Costco Wholesale (COST)

Operator of membership warehouse retail stores.

(800) 249-8982

www.costco.com

Initial shares can be purchased directly from the company: $250 minimum or automatic monthly investments of at least $25 for 10 consecutive months.

Optional cash payments: $25 to $250,000 annually

Above-average fees

Dividends paid since 2004

S&P earnings and dividend rank: A–

Countrywide Financial (CFC)

Major residential mortgage lender.

(800) 524-4458

www.countrywide.com

Optional cash payments: $100 to $3,000 monthly

Dividends paid since 1979

S&P earnings and dividend rank: A–

CPI Corp. (CPY)

Operator of portrait studios through Sears; also owns a photo finishing chain and high-tech copy stores.

(800) 441-9673

www.cpicorp.com

Optional cash payments: $10 to $10,000 quarterly

Dividends paid since 1985

S&P earnings and dividend rank: B–

Crane Co. (CR)

Manufacturer of products for aerospace, fluid handling, construction, and automatic merchandising

(781) 575-2725

www.craneco.com

Optional cash payments: $10 to $5,000 monthly

Dividends paid since 1939

S&P earnings and dividend rank: B

Crompton Corp. (CK)

Maker of specialty chemicals.

(800) 526-0801

www.cromptoncorp.com

Optional cash payments: $30 to $3,000 monthly

Dividends paid since 1933

S&P earnings and dividend rank: B–

CSX Corp. (CSX)

Provider of rail, shipping, and barge services.

(800) 521-5571

www.csx.com

Initial shares can be purchased directly from the company: $500 minimum.

Optional cash payments: $50 to $10,000 monthly

Dividends paid since 1922

S&P earnings and dividend rank: B–

CTS Corp. (CTS)

Maker of electronic components and assemblies.

(866) 326-1180

www.ctscorp.com

Optional cash payments: not available

Above-average fees

Dividends paid since 1930

S&P earnings and dividend rank: B+

CVS Corp. (CVS)

Operator of drugstores in 24 states.

(877) 287-7526

www.cvs.com

Initial shares can be purchased directly from the company: $100 minimum.

Optional cash purchases: $100 to $250,000 annually

Dividends paid since 1916

S&P earnings and dividend rank: B

Curtiss-Wright (CW)

Manufacturer of components and systems for the aerospace, flow-control, and marine industries.

(877) 253-6850

www.curtisswright.com

Initial shares can be purchased directly from the company: $250 minimum.

Optional cash payments: $25 to $10,000 weekly

Above-average fees

Dividends paid since 1974

S&P earnings and dividend rank: A–

D

Dana Corp. (DCN)

Manufacturer of parts for auto industry.

(866) 350-3262

www.dana.com

Optional cash payments: $25 to $2,000 monthly

Dividends paid since 1936

S&P earnings and dividend rank: B–

Darden Restaurants (DRI)

Operator of Red Lobster and Olive Garden restaurants.

(800) 251-8518

www.darden.com

Initial shares can be purchased directly from the company: $1,000 minimum.

Above-average fees

Dividends paid since 1995

S&P earnings and dividend rank: A–

Deere & Co. (DE)

Largest maker of farm equipment; also produces construction machinery and lawn and garden equipment.

(800) 268-7369

www.deere.com

Initial shares can be purchased directly from the company: $500 minimum.

Optional cash payments: $100 to $120,000 annually

Dividends paid since 1937

S&P earnings and dividend rank: B

Delphi Corp. (DPH)

Provider of high tech products for the automotive industry.

(800) 818-6599

www.delphi.com

Initial shares can be purchased directly from the company: $500 minimum.

Optional cash payments: $50 to $120,000 annually

Dividends paid since 1999

S&P earnings and dividend rank: not ranked

Developers Diversified Realty (DDR)

Real estate investment trust (neighborhood shopping centers).

(800) 622-6757

www.ddrc.com

Optional cash payments: $100 to $5,000 quarterly

Dividends paid since 1993

S&P earnings and dividend rank: A

Diebold, Inc. (DBD)

Manufacturer of ATMs and security systems.

(800) 432-0140

www.diebold.com

Initial shares can be purchased directly from the company: $500 minimum.

Optional cash purchases: $50 to $120,000 annually

Dividends paid since 1954

S&P earnings and dividend rank: A

Disney (Walt) (DIS)

Major entertainment company with broadcasting, movie, and theme-park operations.

(800) 948-2222

www.disney.go.com

Initial shares can be purchased directly from the company: $1,000 minimum or automatic monthly investments of at least $100.

Optional cash payments: $100 to $250,000 annually

Dividends paid since 1957

S&P earnings and dividend rank: B

Dollar General (DG)

Operator of chain of discount neighborhood stores.

(888) 266-6785

www.dollargeneral.com

Initial shares can be purchased directly from the company: $50 minimum.

Optional cash purchases: $25 to $7,500 monthly

Dividends paid since 1975

S&P earnings and dividend rank: A+

Dominion Resources (D)

Electric utility operating in North Carolina and Virginia.

(800) 552-4034

www.dom.com

Initial shares can be purchased directly from the company: $350 minimum or automatic monthly investments of at least $40.

Optional cash payments: $40 to $100,000 quarterly

Dividends paid since 1925

S&P earnings and dividend rank: B+

Donaldson Co. (DCI)

Maker of air cleaners and filters for internal combustion engines.

(800) 468-9716

www.donaldson.com

Optional cash payments: $10 to $1,000 monthly

Dividends paid since 1956

S&P earnings and dividend rank: A+

Dover Corp. (DOV)

Diversified maker of elevators, petroleum equipment, and industrial products.

(800) 842-7629

www.dovercorporation.com

Initial shares can be purchased directly from the company: $500 minimum or automatic monthly investments of at least $50 for 10 consecutive months.

Optional cash payments: $50 to $250,000 annually

Dividends paid since 1947

S&P earnings and dividend rank: A–

Dow Chemical (DOW)

Major manufacturer of chemicals, plastics, and metals.

(800) 369-5606

www.dow.com

Optional cash payments: $25 to $120,000 annually

Dividends paid since 1911

S&P earnings and dividend rank: B

Dow Jones & Co. (DJ)

Publisher of the *Wall Street Journal* and *Barron's*.

(800) 842-7629

www.dowjones.com

Initial shares can be purchased directly from the company: $1,000 minimum.

Optional cash payments: $100 to $10,000 monthly

Dividends paid since 1906

S&P earnings and dividend rank: B

DPL Inc. (DPL)

Electric utility operating in Ohio.

(800) 736-3001

www.dplinc.com

Optional cash payments: $25 to $1,000 quarterly

Dividends paid since 1919

S&P earnings and dividend rank: B+

DTE Energy (DTE)

Electric and steam utility operating in southeastern Michigan.

(800) 551-5009

www.dteenergy.com

Initial shares can be purchased directly from the company: $250 minimum.

Optional cash purchases: $50 to $100,000 annually

Dividends paid since 1909

S&P earnings and dividend rank: B+

DuPont (E.I.) de Nemours (DD)

Nation's largest chemical producer.

(888) 983-8766

www.dupont.com

Optional cash purchases: $20 to $5,000 monthly

Dividends paid since 1904

S&P earnings and dividend rank: B

Duke Energy (DUK)

Electric utility operating in the Piedmont region of North and South Carolina.

(800) 488-3853

www.duke-energy.com

Initial shares can be purchased directly from the company: $250 minimum.

Optional cash payments: $50 to $100,000 monthly

Dividends paid since 1988

S&P earnings and dividend rank: B+

Duquesne Light Holdings (DQE)

Electric utility operating in southwestern Pennsylvania.

(800) 247-0400

www.duquesnelight.com

Optional cash payments $10 to $60,000 annually

Dividends paid since 1913

S&P earnings and quality rank: B

E

Eastman Chemical (EMN)

Large maker of chemicals, plastics, and fibers.

(800) 937-5449

www.eastman.com

Initial shares can be purchased directly from the company: $250 minimum.

Optional cash payments: $25 to $10,000 per transaction

Dividends paid since 1994

S&P earnings and dividend rank: B

Eastman Kodak (EK)

Number one maker of photographic products.

(800) 253-6057

www.kodak.com

Initial shares can be purchased directly from the company: $150 minimum or automatic monthly investments of at least $50 for three consecutive months.

Optional cash payments: $50 to $120,000 annually

Dividends paid since 1902

S&P earnings and dividend rank: B–

Ecolab (ECL)

Maker of cleaning, sanitizing, and maintenance products and services.

(781) 575-2724

www.ecolab.com

Optional cash purchases: $10 to $60,000 annually

Dividends paid since 1936

S&P earnings and dividend rank: A

El Paso Corp. (EP)

Operator of large natural gas pipeline system.

(877) 453-1503

www.elpaso.com

Optional cash payments: $50 to $10,000 monthly

Dividends paid since 1992

S&P earnings and dividend rank: not ranked

Electronic Data Systems (EDS)

Major provider of information technology services.

(877) 253-6851

www.eds.com

Initial shares can be purchased directly from the company: $250 minimum.

Optional cash payments: $25 to $10,000 per transaction

Dividends paid since 1984

S&P earnings and dividend rank: B

Emerson Electric (EMR)

Large manufacturer of electrical and electronic products.

(888) 213-0970

www.gotoemerson.com

Initial shares can be purchased directly from the company: $250 minimum or automatic monthly investments of at least $25 for 10 consecutive months.

Optional cash payments: $25 to $250,000 annually

Dividends paid since 1947

Earnings and dividend rank: A

Energen Corp. (EGN)

Central Alabama gas utility.

(888) 764-5603

www.energen.com

Initial shares can be purchased directly from the company: $250 minimum or automatic monthly investments of at least $25.

Optional cash payments: $25 to $250,000 annually

Dividends paid since 1943

S&P earnings and dividend rank: A

Energy East (EAS)

Northeast electric and gas utility.

(800) 542-7480

www.energyeast.com

Initial shares can be purchased directly from the company for $25 minimum by residents of Connecticut, Massachusetts, Maine, and New York.

Optional cash payments: $25 to $100,000 annually

Dividends paid since 1910

S&P earnings and dividend rank: B+

Engelhard Corp. (EC)

Manufacturer of pigments and additives used in the paper, paint, and plastics industries.

(800) 526-0801

www.engelhard.com

Optional cash payments: $10 to $3,000 monthly

Dividends paid since 1981

S&P earnings and dividend rank: B+

Entergy Corp. (ETR)

Owner of five operating utilities in Arkansas, Louisiana, Mississippi, Missouri, and Texas.

(800) 333-4368

www.entergy.com

Initial shares can be purchased directly from the company: $1,000 minimum.

Optional cash purchases: $100 to $3,000 monthly

Dividends paid since 1988

S&P earnings and dividend rank: B+

Entertainment Properties Trust (EPR)

Real estate investment trust.

www.eprkc.com

Initial shares can be purchased directly from the company: $200 minimum.

Optional cash payments: $50 to $100,000 annually

Dividends paid since 1998

S&P earnings and dividend rank: not ranked

Equifax Inc. (EFX)

Provider of information services to businesses for insurance claims and credit evaluation purposes.

(888) 887-2971

www.equifax.com

Initial shares can be purchased directly from the company: $500 minimum.

Optional cash payments: $50 to $100,000 monthly

Dividends paid since 1914

S&P earnings and dividend rank: B+

Equitable Resources (EQT)

Oil and gas explorer and natural gas distributor.

(800) 589-9026

www.eqt.com

Optional cash payments: $25 to $500 monthly

Dividends paid since 1950

S&P earnings and dividend rank: A–

Equity Office Properties Trust (EOP)

Real estate investment trust.

(888) 752-4831

www.equityoffice.com

Initial shares can be purchased directly from the company: $250 minimum or automatic monthly

investments of at least $25 for 10 consecutive months.

Optional cash payments: $25 to $25,000 monthly

Dividends paid since 1997

S&P earnings and dividend rank: not ranked

Essex Property Trust (ESS)

Real estate investment trust that owns and operates multifamily properties and investments.

(312) 360-5354

www.essexproperties.com

Initial shares can be purchased directly from the company: $100 minimum.

Optional cash payments: $100 to $20,000 monthly

Dividends paid since 1994

S&P earnings and dividend rank: A–

Exelon Corp. (EXC)

Electric utility, formed from the merger of PECO Energy and Unicom, operates in northern Illinois and a five-county area surrounding Philadelphia.

(800) 626-8729

www.exeloncorp.dom

Optional cash purchases: $25 to $60,000 annually

Dividends paid since 1902

S&P earnings and dividend rank: B+

ExxonMobil (XOM)

World's leading oil company.

(800) 252-1800

www.exxonmobil.com

Initial shares can be purchased directly from the company: $250 minimum or automatic monthly investments of at least $50 for five consecutive months.

Optional cash payments: $50 to $250,000 annually

Dividends paid since 1882

S&P earnings and dividend rank: A–

F

Federal National Mortgage (Fannie Mae) (FNM)

Largest secondary buyer of real estate mortgages in the United States.

(800) 910-8277

www.fanniemae.com

Initial shares can be purchased directly from the company: $250 minimum or automatic monthly investments of at least $50 for five consecutive months.

Optional cash payments: $25 to $250,000 annually

Dividends paid since 1956

S&P earnings and dividend rank: not ranked

Federal Signal (FSS)

Maker of fire trucks, street cleaning trucks, and signaling equipment.

(800) 446-2617

www.federalsignal.com

Optional cash payments: $100 to $5,000 quarterly

Dividends paid since 1948

S&P earnings and dividend rank: B

Federated Department Stores (FD)

Operator of retail department and specialty stores.

(800) 432-0140

Initial shares can be purchased directly from the company: $500 minimum.

Optional cash payments: $50 to $10,000 per transaction

Dividends paid since 2003

S&P earnings and dividend rank: B

FedEx Corp. (FDX)

Leading provider of express delivery services.

(800) 446-2617

www.fedex.com

Initial shares can be purchased directly from the company: $100 minimum or automatic monthly *investments of at least $50 for 20 months.*

Optional cash payments: $100 to $250,000 annually

Above-average fees

Dividends paid since 2002

S&P earnings and dividend rank: B+

Ferro Corp. (FOE)

Manufacturer of chemical specialties (plastics, coatings, and ceramics).

(800) 622-6757

www.ferro.com

Optional cash payments: $10 to $3,000 monthly

Dividends paid since 1939

S&P earnings and dividend rank: B

Fifth Third Bancorp (FITB)

Bank operating in Ohio, Kentucky, and Indiana.

(888) 294-8285

www.53.com

Initial shares can be purchased directly from the company: $500 minimum.

Optional cash payments: $50 to $5,000 per transaction

Dividends paid since 1952

S&P earnings and dividend rank: A+

First American (FAF)

Offers title insurance and financial and information services related to real estate.

(800) 894-4076

www.firstam.com

Initial shares can be purchased directly from the company: $250 minimum or automatic monthly investments of $50 for five consecutive months.

Optional cash payments: $50 to $5,000 quarterly

Dividends paid since 1909

S&P earnings and dividend rank: B+

First Midwest Bancorp (FMBI)

Commercial banker in Illinois.

(888) 581-9376

www.firstmidwest.com

Optional cash payments: $100 to $5,000 quarterly

Dividends paid since 1983

S&P earnings and dividend rank: A

Foot Locker (FL)

Operator of specialty and shoe stores.

(800) 446-2617

www.footlocker-inc.com

Optional cash payments: $20 to $60,000 annually

Dividends paid since 2003

S&P earnings and dividend rank: B–

Ford Motor (F)

Second largest automaker.

(800) 279-1237

www.ford.com

Initial shares can be purchased directly from the company: $1,000 minimum or automatic monthly investments of at least $100 for 10 consecutive months.

Optional cash payments: $50 to $250,000 annually

Dividends paid since 1983

S&P earnings and dividend rank: B

Fortune Brands (FO)

Maker of hardware and home improvement products.

(800) 225-2719

www.fortunebrands.com

Optional cash payments: $50 to $15,000 quarterly

Dividends paid since 1905

S&P earnings and dividend rank: B

FPL Group (FPL)

Electric utility operating in Florida.

(888) 218-4392

www.fplgroup.com

Optional cash payments: $100 to $100,000 annually

Dividends paid since 1944

S&P earnings and dividend rank: A–

Franklin Resources (BEN)

Provider of mutual fund investment management and services.

(800) 524-4458

www.franklintempleton.com

Optional cash purchases: $100 to $50,000 monthly

Dividends paid since 1981

S&P earnings and dividend rank: A–

Fuller (H.B.)

Manufacturer of adhesives, sealants, paints, coating, and waxes.

(800) 468-9716

Optional cash payments: $10 to $600 monthly

3 percent discount on reinvested dividends

Dividends paid since 1953

S&P earnings and dividend rank: B

G

Gannett Co. (GCI)

Newspaper publisher and broadcaster.

(800) 778-3299

www.gannett.com

Optional cash payments $10 to $5,000 monthly

Dividends paid since 1929

S&P earnings and dividend rank: A

GATX Corp. (GMT)

Railcar leasing and equipment financing.

(800) 851-9677

www.gatx.com

Optional cash payments: $15 to $36,000 annually

Dividends paid since 1919

S&P earnings and dividend rank: A–

General Electric (GE)

Diversified operations in aerospace, appliance, aircraft engines, broadcasting, power systems, and financial services.

(800) 786-2543

www.ge.com

Initial shares can be purchased directly from the company: $250 minimum.

Optional cash purchases: $10 to $10,000 per transaction

Dividends paid since 1899

S&P earnings and dividend rank: A+

General Mills (GIS)

Producer of consumer foods.

(800) 670-4763

www.generalmills.com

Optional cash payments: $10 to $3,000 quarterly

Dividends paid since 1898

S&P earnings and dividend rank: A—

General Motors (GM)

World's largest auto manufacturer.

(800) 331-9922

www.gm.com

Optional cash payments: $25 to $150,000 annually

Dividends paid since 1915

S&P earnings and dividend rank: B

Genuine Parts (GPC)

Maker of automotive and industrial replacement parts and office products.

(800) 568-3476

www.genpt.com

Optional cash payments: $10 to $3,000 quarterly

Dividends paid since 1948

S&P earnings and dividend rank: A

Georgia-Pacific Corp. (GP)

Major manufacturer of plywood, lumber, paper, and pulp.

(800) 519-3111

www.gp.com

Optional cash payments: $25 to $60,000 annually

Dividends paid since 1927

S&P earnings and dividend rank: B–

Glenborough Realty Trust (GLB)

Real estate investment trust (industrial, office, hotel, retail, and multifamily properties).

(800) 525-7686

www.glenborough.com

Initial shares can be purchased directly from the company: $250 minimum.

Optional cash payments: $100 to $10,000 monthly

Dividends paid since 1996

S&P earnings and quality rank: B

Goodrich Corp. (GR)

Producer of specialty chemicals and aerospace products.

(800) 524-4458

www.goodrich.com

Optional cash payments: $25 to $1,000 monthly

Dividends paid since 1939

S&P earnings and dividend rank: B

Granite Construction (GVA)

Heavy construction contractor.

(800) 368-5948

www.graniteconstruction.com

Initial shares can be purchased directly from the company: $3,000 minimum.

Optional cash payments: $100 to $10,000 monthly

Dividends paid since 1990

S&P earnings and dividend rank: A–

Great Plains Energy (GXP)

Electric utility operating in western Missouri and eastern Kansas.

Initial shares can be purchased directly from the company: $500 minimum.

Optional cash payments: $100 to $60,000 annually

Dividends paid since 1921

S&P earnings and dividend rank: B

Greater Bay Bancorp (GBBK)

Bank with operations in San Francisco, Silicon Valley, and Monterey Bay areas of California

(800) 468-9716

www.gbbk.com

Optional cash payments: $50 to $1,000 monthly

Dividends paid since 1996

S&P earnings and dividend rank: A–

Green Mountain Power (GMP)

Electric utility operating in Vermont.

(800) 851-9677

www.gmpvt.com

Plan is open only to residents of Vermont.

Optional cash payments: $50 to $40,000 annually

5 percent discount on reinvested dividends

Dividends paid since 1951

Earnings and dividend rank: B

Guidant Corp. (GDT)

Manufacturer of products used in cardiac rhythm management and coronary artery disease intervention.

(888) 756-3638

www.guidant.com

Initial shares can be purchased directly from the company: $250 minimum or automatic monthly investments of at least $50 for five consecutive months.

Optional cash payments: $50 to $250,000 annually

Dividends paid since 2003

Earnings and dividend rank: B

H

Harland (John H.) (JH)

Provider of products and services to the financial industry.

(800) 519-3111

www.harland.net

Initial shares can be purchased directly from the company: $500 minimum or automatic monthly investments of at least $100 for five consecutive months.

Optional cash payments: $50 to $250,000 annually

Dividends paid since 1932

S&P earnings and dividend rank: B

Harley-Davidson (HDI)

Well-known motorcycle maker.

(866) 360-5339

www.harley-davidson.com

Initial shares can be purchased directly from the company: $500 minimum.

Optional cash payments: $30 to $100,000 annually

Dividends paid since 1993

S&P earnings and quality ranking: A+

Harrah's Entertainment (HET)

Operator of casinos and hotels.

(800) 524-4458

www.harrahs.com

Initial shares can be purchased directly from the company: $200 minimum.

Optional cash payments: $50 to $120,000 annually

Above-average fees

Dividends paid since 2003

Earnings and dividend ranking: B

Harris Corp. (HRS)

Manufacturer of electronic systems, semiconductors, and communication equipment.

(888) 261-6777

www.harris.com

Optional cash purchases: $10 to $5,000 quarterly

Dividends paid since 1941

S&P earnings and dividend rank: B–

Harsco Corp. (HSC)

Industrial manufacturer and services company.

(800) 526-0801

www.harsco.com

Optional cash payments: $10 to $500,000 monthly

Dividends paid since 1939

S&P earnings and dividend rank: B+

Hartford Financial Services Group (HIG)

Multiline insurance company.

(800) 254-2823

www.thehartford.com

Optional cash payments: $50 to $5,000 monthly

Dividends paid since 1996

S&P earnings and dividend rank: B

Hasbro Inc. (HAS)

Manufacturer of toys and games.

(800) 733-5001

www.hasbro.com

Optional cash payments: $25 to $24,000 annually

Dividends paid since 1981

S&P earnings and dividend rank: B

Hawaiian Electric Industries (HE)

Electric utility operating in Hawaii.

(808) 543-5662

www.hei.com

Initial shares can be purchased directly from the company: $250 minimum.

Optional cash payments: $25 to $120,000 annually

Dividends paid since 1901

S&P earnings and dividend rank: B+

Heinz (H.J.) (HNZ)

Major manufacturer of processed foods (ketchup, soups, baby foods).

(800) 253-3399

www.heinz.com

Initial shares can be purchased directly from the company: $250 minimum.

Optional cash payments: $50 to $120,000 annually

Dividends paid since 1911

S&P earnings and dividend rank: B+

Hershey (HSY)

Leading maker of chocolate, confectionery, and pasta products.

(800) 842-7629

www.hersheys.com

Initial shares can be purchased directly from the company: $250 minimum or automatic monthly investments of at least $25 for 10 consecutive months.

Optional cash payments: $25 to $250,000 annually

Dividends paid since 1930

S&P earnings and dividend rank: A–

Hewlett-Packard (HPQ)

Major manufacturer of computer products.

(800) 286-5977

www.hp.com

Optional cash purchases $50 to $100,000 monthly

Dividends paid since 1965

S&P earnings and dividend rank: A–

Hibernia Corp. (HIB)

Bank operator in Louisiana.

(800) 814-0305

www.hibernia.com

Optional cash payments: $100 to $3,000 monthly

Dividends paid since 1993

S&P earnings and dividend rank: A

Highwoods Properties (HP)

Real estate investment trust.

(800) 829-8432

www.highwoods.com

Optional cash purchases: $25 to $10,000 monthly

Dividends paid since 1994

S&P earnings and dividend rank: B+

Hillenbrand Industries (HB)

Major maker of burial caskets and hospital beds.

(800) 716-3607

www.hillenbrand.com

Initial shares can be purchased directly from the company: $250 minimum.

Optional cash purchases: $100 to $50,000 annually

Dividends paid since 1948

S&P earnings and dividend rank: B+

Home Depot (HD)

Operator of home improvement/building materials retail stores.

(877) 437-4273

www.homedepot.com

Initial shares can be purchased directly from the company: $250 minimum.

Optional cash purchases: $25 to $100,000 annually

Dividends paid since 1987

Earnings and dividend rank: A+

Honeywell International (HON)

Manufacturer of automation and control systems for residences, industrial, and space and aviation markets

(800) 647-7147

www.honeywell.com

Optional cash payments: $25 to $120,000 annually

Dividends paid since 1887

S&P earnings and dividend rank: B

Hormel Foods (HRL)

Processor of pork, poultry, and fish food items.

(877) 536-3559

www.hormel.com

Optional cash purchases $25 to $20,000 quarterly

Dividends paid since 1928

S&P earnings and dividend rank: A

Hospitality Properties Trust

Real estate investment trust.

(800) 426-5523

www.hptreit.com

Optional cash purchases: Up to $10,000 quarterly

Dividends paid since 1995

S&P earnings and dividend rank: A–

Hubbell Inc. 'B' (HUB.B)

Manufacturer of electrical wiring devices.

(800) 851-9677

www.hubbell.com

Optional cash payments: $100 to $500 monthly

Dividends paid since 1934

S&P earnings and dividend rank: B+

Hudson United Bancorp (HU)

Commercial bank operating in New Jersey.

(800) 937-5449

www.hudsonunitedbank.com

Optional cash payments: $10 to $200 quarterly

Dividends paid since 1952

Earnings and dividend rank: B+

Huntington Bancshares (HBAN)

Commercial bank operating in Ohio.

(800) 725-0674

www.huntington.com

Optional cash purchases: $200 to $10,000 quarterly

Dividends paid since 1912

S&P earnings and dividend rank: B+

I

Idacorp Inc. (IDA)

Electric utility operating in Idaho and sections of Oregon and Nevada.

(800) 565-7890

www.idacorpinc.com

Initial shares can be purchased directly from the company by automatic investment only: $200 minimum.

Optional cash payments: $10 to $20,000 quarterly

Dividends paid since 1917

S&P earnings and dividend rank: B

IDEX Corp. (IEX)

Illinois Tool Works (ITW)Manufacturer of industrial components and other specialty products and equipment.

(888) 829-7424

www.itw.com

Optional cash purchases: $100 to $10,000 monthly

Dividends paid since 1933

S&P earnings and dividend rank: A+

Imation Corp. (IMN)

Maker of magnetic and optical data storage products.

(800) 432-0140

www.imation.com

Initial shares can be purchased directly from the company: $500 minimum.

Optional cash payments: $50 to $100,000 annually

Dividends paid since 2003

Earnings and dividend rank: B–

Independence Community Bank Corp. (ICBC)

Bank operator in the New York City metropolitan area.

(800) 937-5449

www.icbny.com

Optional cash payments: $100 to $5,000 quarterly

Dividends paid since 1998

Earnings and dividend rank: not ranked

IndyMac Bancorp (NDE)

Bank operator in southern California.

(800) 669-2300

www.indtmacbank.com

Initial shares can be purchased directly from the company: $250 minimum.

Optional cash purchases: $50 to $10,000 monthly

Dividends paid since 2003

Earnings and dividend rank: B+

Intel Corp. (INTC)

Leading manufacturer of semiconductors.

(800) 298-0146

www.intel.com

Optional cash payments: $50 to $15,000 monthly

Dividends paid since 1992

S&P earnings and dividend rank: A

International Business Machines (IBM)

Largest manufacturer of business machines.

(888) 426-6700

www.ibm.com

Initial shares can be purchased directly from the company: $500 minimum or automatic monthly investments of at least $50 for 10 consecutive months.

(888) 426-6700

Optional cash payments: $50 to $250,000 annually

Dividends paid since 1916

S&P earnings and dividend rank: A–

International Flavor & Fragrances (IFF)

Major maker of products used by other manufacturers to improve flavor or fragrance.

(800) 530-8073

www.iff.com

Dividends paid since 1956

S&P earnings and dividend rank: B

International Paper (IP)

Manufacturer of paper and pulpwood products.

(800) 842-7629

www.internationalpaper.com

Initial shares can be purchased directly from the company: $500 minimum.

Optional cash purchases: $50 to $20,000 annually

Dividends paid since 1946

S&P earnings and dividend rank: B–

Intersil Corp. 'A' (ISIL)

Maker of analog, integrated circuits, and wireless networking products and services.

(877) 208-9531

www.intersil.com

Initial shares can be purchased directly from the company: $250 minimum.

Optional cash payments: $25 to $10,000 per transaction

Dividends paid since 2003

S&P earnings and dividend rank: not ranked

Invacare Corp. (IVC)

Manufacturer of wheelchairs and other medical equipment for home health care.

(800) 622-6757

www.invacare.com

Optional cash purchases: $10 to $5,000 per month

Dividends paid since 1994

S&P earnings and dividend rank: B+

Investors Financial Services (IFIN)

Provider of asset administration services for the financial service industry.

(201) 324-0313

www.investorsbnk.com

Initial shares can be purchased directly from the company: $250 minimum.

Optional cash purchases: $100 minimum; no maximum

Dividends paid since 1996

S&P earnings and dividend rank: A–

ITT Industries (ITT)

Diversified company, with interests in defense, automotive, and fluid technology.

(800) 254-2823

www.itt.com

Initial shares can be purchased directly from the company: $500 minimum.

Optional cash payments: $50 to $120,000 annually

Dividends paid since 1996

S&P earnings and dividend rank: B+

J

Jefferson-Pilot (JP)

Insurance holding company, with operations in television and radio communications.

(800) 829-8432

www.jpfinancial.com

Optional cash payments: $20 to $2,000 monthly

Dividends paid since 1913

S&P earnings and dividend rank: A+

Johnson & Johnson (JNJ)

Major manufacturer of health-care and consumer products.

(800) 328-9033

www.jnj.com

Optional cash purchases: $25 to $50,000 annually

Dividends paid since 1944

S&P earnings and dividend rank: A+

Johnson Controls (JCI)

Major maker of automotive systems and building controls.

(877) 602-7397

www.johnsoncontrols.com

Initial shares can be purchased directly from the company: $250 minimum or automatic monthly investments of at least $50 for five consecutive months.

Optional cash payments: $50 to $150,000 quarterly

Dividends paid since 1887

S&P earnings and dividend rank: A+

J.P. Morgan Chase & Co. (JPM)

Commercial banker in New York City and Texas.

(800) 758-4651

www.jpmorganchase.com

Initial shares can be purchased directly from the company: $250 minimum or automatic monthly investments of at least $50 for five consecutive months.

Optional cash purchases: $50 to $250,000 annually

Dividends paid since 1827

S&P earnings and dividend rank: B

K

Kaman Corp. 'A' (KAMNA)

Maker of helicopters and aircraft products.

(800) 227-0291

www.kaman.com

Initial shares can be purchased directly from the company: $250 minimum or automatic monthly investments of $50 for five consecutive months.

Optional cash payments: $50 to $5,000 monthly

Dividends paid since 1972

S&P earnings and dividend rank: B–

Keithley Instruments (KEI)

Major manufacturer of precision electrical measuring instruments.

(800) 622-6757

www.keithley.com

Initial shares can be purchased directly from the company: $250 minimum.

Optional cash payments: $50 to $10,000 monthly

Dividends paid since 1964

S&P earnings and dividend rank: B

Kellogg Co. (K)

Leading maker of cereals and other breakfast items.

(800) 468-9716

www.kelloggcompany.com

Optional cash payments: $25 to $25,000 annually

Dividends paid since 1923

S&P earnings and dividend rank: B+

Kellwood Co. (KWD)

Manufacturer of apparel and camping products.

(800) 278-4353

www.kwdco.com

Initial shares can be purchased directly from the company: $100 minimum.

Optional cash payments: $25 to $3,000 monthly

Dividends paid since 1962

S&P earnings and dividend rank: B+

Kelly Services 'A' (KELYA)

Provider of temporary employees for businesses.

(800) 829-8259

www.kellyservices.com

Initial shares can be purchased directly from the company: $250 minimum or automatic monthly investments of at least $50 for five consecutive months.

Optional cash payments: $25 to $100,000 annually

Dividends paid since 1962

S&P earnings and dividend rank: A–

Kennametal, Inc. (KMT)

Manufacturer of tungsten-based carbide products.

(800) 756-3353

www.kennametal.com

Optional cash payments: $25 to $4,000 quarterly

5 percent discount on reinvested dividends

Dividends paid since 1944

S&P earnings and dividend rank: B

Kerr-McGee (KMG)

Producer of oil, natural gas and industrial chemicals as well as coal.

(800) 786-2556

www.kerr-mcgee.com

Initial shares can be purchased directly from the company: $750 minimum.

Optional cash payments: $10 to $1,000 monthly

Dividends paid since 1941

S&P earnings and dividend rank: B

KeyCorp (KEY)

Commercial bank operating in Ohio, northern United States.

(800) 539-7216

www.keybank.com

Optional cash payments: $10 to $10,000 monthly

Dividends paid since 1963

S&P earnings and dividend rank: A–

KeySpan Corp. (KSE)

Electric and gas utility operating in New York (Long Island and parts of New York City).

(800) 948-1691

www.keyspanenergy.com

Initial shares can be purchased directly from the company: $250 minimum or automatic monthly investments of at least $25 for 10 consecutive months.

Optional cash payments: $25 to $150,000 annually

Dividends paid since 1989

S&P earnings and dividend rank: B

Kilroy Realty (KRC)

Real estate investment trust with properties in southern California.

(888) 816-7506

www.kilroyrealty.com

Initial shares can be purchased directly from the company: $750 minimum.

Optional cash payments: $100 to $5,000 monthly

Dividends paid since 1997

S&P earnings and dividend rank: B+

Kimberly-Clark (KMB)

Manufacturer of facial tissues, disposable diapers, paper towels, and feminine napkins.

(800) 730-4001

www.kimberly-clark.com

Optional cash payments: $25 to $3,000 quarterly

Dividends paid since 1935

S&P earnings and dividend rank: A

Kinder Morgan (KMI)

Natural gas company.

(800) 847-4351

www.kindermorgan.com

Initial shares can be purchased directly from the company: $250 minimum or automatic monthly investments of at least $25 for 10 consecutive months.

Optional cash payments: $25 minimum; no maximum

Dividends paid since 1937

Earnings and dividend rank: B

Knight Ridder Inc. (KRI)

Major newspaper publisher.

(800) 851-9677

www.kri.com

Optional cash purchases: $25 to $10,000 monthly

Dividends paid since 1941

S&P earnings and dividend rank: A–

L

Laclede Group (LG)

Natural gas utility operating in St. Louis.

(800) 884-4225

www.thelacledegroup.com

Optional cash payments: $100 to $30,000 annually

Dividends paid since 1946

S&P earnings and dividend rank: B+

Lancaster Colony (LANC)

Manufacturer of automotive and specialty food products, as well as glassware and candles.

(800) 278-4353

www.lancastercolony.com

Optional cash payments: $50 to $20,000 annually

Dividends paid since 1963

S&P earnings and dividend rank: A

Lance, Inc. (LNCE)

Maker of bakery items and snack foods.

(800) 829-8432

www.lance.com

Optional cash payments: $10 to $100 monthly

Dividends paid since 1945

S&P earnings and dividend rank: B

La-Z-Boy (LZB)

Maker of reclining chairs and upholstered furniture.

(734) 241-4414

www.lazyboy.com

Optional cash payments: $25 to $1,000 monthly

Dividends paid since 1963

S&P earnings and dividend rank: A–

Lear Corp. (LEA)

Manufacturer of automotive interior systems.

(800) 524-4458

www.lear.com

Initial shares can be purchased directly from the company: $250 minimum.

Optional cash payments: $50 to $150,000 annually

Dividends paid since 2004

S&P earnings and dividend rank: B+

Lehman Brothers Holdings (LEH)

Offers investment banking services.

(800) 824-5707

www.lehman.com

Initial shares can be purchased directly from the company: $500 minimum.

Optional cash purchases: $50 to $175,000 annually

Dividends paid since 1994

S&P earnings and dividend rank: A

Lexington Corporate Properties Trust (LXP)

Real estate investment trust (warehouses, manufacturing facilities, office buildings).

Optional cash purchases: Not available

5 percent discount on reinvested dividends

Dividends paid since 1994

S&P earnings and dividend rank: A–

Libbey Inc. (LBY)

Major manufacturer of glass tableware.

(800) 524-4458

www.libbey.com

Initial shares can be purchased directly from the company: $100 minimum.

Optional cash payments: $20 to $25,000 annually

Dividends paid since 1993

S&P earnings and quality rank: B

Liberty Property Trust (LRY)

Real estate investment trust (suburban industrial and office properties).

(800) 944-2214

www.libertyproperty.com

Initial shares can be purchased directly from the company: $1,000 minimum.

Optional cash payments: $250 to $10,000 monthly

3 percent discount on reinvested dividends

Dividends paid since 1994

S&P earnings and dividend rank: A–

Lilly (Eli) (LLY)

Major manufacturer of prescription drugs.

(800) 833-8699

www.lilly.com

Initial shares can be purchased directly from the company: $1,000 minimum.

Optional cash payments: $50 to $150,000 annually

Dividends paid since 1885

S&P earnings and dividend rank: B+

Limited Brands (LTD)

Operator of women's apparel stores.

(800) 829-8432

www.limited.com

Optional cash payments: $30 to $6,000 quarterly

Dividends paid since 1970

S&P earnings and dividend rank: B+

Lincoln National Corp. (LNC)

Multiline insurance holding company.

(800) 949-0197

www.lfg.com

Initial shares can be purchased directly from the company: $500 minimum.

Optional cash payments: $100 to $250,000 annually

Dividends paid since 1920

S&P earnings and dividend rank: B+

Liz Claiborne (LIZ)

Maker of women's designer apparel.

(866) 828-8170

www.lizclaiborne.com

Initial shares can be purchased directly from the company: $500 minimum.

Optional cash purchases: $100 to $10,000 per transaction

Dividends paid since 1984

S&P earnings and dividend rank: A

Lockheed Martin (LMT)

Major defense and space contractor.

(800) 446-2617

www.lockheedmartin.com

Initial shares can be purchased directly from the

company: $250 minimum or automatic monthly investments of at least $50.

Optional cash payments: $50 minimum; no maximum

Dividends paid since 1995

S&P earnings and dividend rank: B–

Longs Drug Stores (LDG)

Operator of a drugstore chain in the western United States.

(800) 468-9716

www.longs.com

Initial shares can be purchased directly from the company: $500 minimum or automatic monthly investments of at least $50 for 10 consecutive months.

Optional cash payments: $25 to $5,000 quarterly

Dividends paid since 1961

S&P earnings and dividend rank: B+

Louisiana-Pacific (LPX)

Manufacturer of lumber, particle board, plywood, and pulp.

(781) 575-2726

www.lpcorp.com

Optional cash payments: $25 to $12,000 annually

Dividends paid since 2004

Earnings and dividend rank: B–

Lowe's Companies (LOW)

Retailer of lumber, building materials, home decorations, and hardware.

(877) 282-1174

www.lowes.com

Initial shares can be purchased directly from the company: $250 minimum.

Optional cash payments: $25 to $250,000 annually

Dividends paid since 1961

S&P earnings and dividend rank: A+

Lubrizol Corp. (LZ)

Manufacturer of specialty chemicals.

(877) 573-3998

www.lubrizol.com

Initial shares can be purchased directly from the company: $250 minimum or automatic monthly investments of at least $25 for 10 consecutive months.

Optional cash payments: $25 to $10,000 per transaction

Dividends paid since 1935

S&P earnings and dividend rank: B

Lyondell Chemical (LYO)

Producer of petrochemicals and refiner of petroleum products.

(877) 749-4981

www.lyondell.com

Optional cash payments: $25 to $10,000 quarterly

Dividends paid since 1989

S&P earnings and dividend rank: B–

M

MacDermid Inc. (MRD)

Maker of specialty chemicals and equipment for electronic and metal markets.

(877) 268-5209

www.macdermid.com

Optional cash payments: $50 minimum; no maximum

Dividends paid since 1946

S&P earnings and dividend rank: A–

Mack-Cali Realty (CLI)

Real estate investment trust (properties in the Northwest and Southwest).

(800) 317-4445

Initial shares can be purchased directly from the company: $2,000 minimum.

Optional cash payment: $100 to $5,000 monthly

Dividends paid since 1994

S&P earnings and dividend ranking: B+

Manitowoc Company (MTW)

Manufacturer of heavy lift cranes and operator of shipyard.

(800) 519-3111

www.manitowoc.com

Optional cash payments: $10 to $60,000 annually

Dividends paid since 1945

S&P earnings and dividend rank: B

Manpower Inc. (MAN)

World's largest temporary employment services company.

(800) 851-9677

www.manpower.com

Optional cash payments: $25 to $10,000 annually

Dividends paid since 1994

S&P earnings and dividend rank: B+

Marathon Oil (MRO)

Producer of oil and gas.

(800) 884-5426

www.marathon.com

Initial shares can be purchased directly from the company: $500 minimum.

Optional cash payments: $50 to $10,000 monthly

Up to 3 percent discount on reinvested dividends and optional cash payments

Dividends paid since 1991

S&P earnings and dividend rank: B+

Marcus Corp. (MCS)

Operator of hotels, resorts, motels, theaters, and restaurants.

(800) 246-5761

www.marcuscorp.com

Optional cash purchases: $100 to $1,500 monthly

Dividends paid since 1983

S&P earnings and dividend rank: B

Marsh & McLennan (MMC)

Operator of insurance brokerage; also in investment services and consulting.

(800) 457-8968

www.marshmac.com

Initial shares can be purchased directly from the company: $500 minimum.

Optional cash purchases: $50 to $250,000 annually

Above-average fees

Dividends paid since 1923

S&P earnings and dividend rank: A–

Marshall & Ilsley (MI)

Commercial bank in Wisconsin.

(800) 529-3163

www.micorp.com

Optional cash payments: $25 to $20,000 annually

Dividends paid since 1936

S&P earnings and dividend rank: A

Masco Cop. (MAS)

Maker of building and home improvement products.

(800) 524-4458

www.masco.com

Optional cash payments: $50 to $5,000 monthly

Dividends paid since 1944

S&P earnings and dividend rank: A–

Massey Energy (MEE)

Major coal producer.

(804) 788-1800

www.masseyenrgyco.com

Initial shares can be purchased directly from the company: $250 minimum or automatic monthly investments of at least $50 for five consecutive months.

Optional cash payments: $50 to $100,000 annually

Dividends paid since 2001

S&P earnings and dividend rank: not ranked

Mattel Inc. (MAT)

Leading toy company.

(888) 909-9922

www.mattel.com

Initial shares can be purchased directly from the

company: $500 minimum or automatic monthly investments of at least $100 for five consecutive months.

Optional cash payments: $100 to $100,000 annually

Dividends paid since 1990

Earnings and dividend rank: B+

May Department Stores (MAY)

Large department store chain.

(800) 524-4458

www.mayco.com

Optional cash payments: $25 minimum; no maximum

Dividends paid since 1911

S&P earnings and dividend rank: B+

Maytag Corp. (MYG)

Manufacturer of major home appliances.

(888) 237-0935

www.maytagcorp.com

Optional cash purchases: $25 to $5,000 monthly

Dividends paid since 1946

S&P earnings and dividend rank: B

McCormick & Co. (MKC)

Manufacturer of spices, flavorings, and seasonings.

(800) 468-9716

www.mccomick.com

Initial shares can be purchased directly from the company: $250 minimum.

Optional cash payments: $50 to $50,000 per transaction

Dividends paid since 1925

S&P earnings and dividend rank: A+

McDonald's Corp. (MCD)

Leading franchiser of fast-food restaurants.

(800) 621-7825

www.mcdonalds.com

Initial shares can be purchased directly from the company: $500 minimum or automatic monthly investments of at least $50.

Optional cash payments: $50 to $250,000 annually

Dividends paid since 1976

S&P earnings and dividend rank: A

McGraw-Hill Companies (MHP)

Publisher of educational and professional books and magazines; also offers financial information (Standard & Poor's) and has television interests.

(888) 201-5538

www.mcgraw-hill.com

Initial shares can be purchased directly from the

company: $500 minimum or automatic monthly investments of at least $100.

Optional cash payments: $100 to $10,000 monthly

Dividends paid since 1937

S&P earnings and dividend rank: not ranked

McKesson Corp. (MCK)

Distributor of drugs and toiletries.

(866) 216-3060

www.mckesson.com

Optional cash payments: $10 to $10,000 monthly

Dividends paid since 1995

S&P earnings and dividend rank: B

MDU Resources Group (MDU)

Gas and electric utility; also producer of oil, gas, and coal.

(800) 813-3324

www.mdu.com

Initial shares can be purchased directly from the company: $250 minimum or automatic monthly investments of at least $25 for 10 months.

Optional cash payments: $25 to $10,000 monthly

Dividends paid since 1937

S&P earnings and dividend rank: A

Medtronic (MDT)

Maker of cardiac pacemakers and other cardiac devices.

(888) 648-8154

www.medtronic.com

Initial shares can be purchased directly from the company: $250 minimum or automatic monthly investments of at least $25 for 10 consecutive months.

Dividends paid since 1977

S&P earnings and dividend rank: A–

Mellon Financial (MEL)

Major bank operating in Delaware, Maryland, New Jersey, Pennsylvania, and Canada.

Initial shares can be purchased directly from the company: $500 minimum or automatic monthly investments of at least $100 for five consecutive months.

Optional cash payments: $100 to $100,000 annually

Dividends paid since 1895

S&P earnings and dividend rank: A–

Mercantile Bankshares (MRBK)

Bank operating in Maryland.

(800) 524-4458

www.mercantile.net

Optional cash payments: $25 to $5,000 quarterly

Dividends paid since 1909

S&P earnings and dividend rank: A

Merck & Co. (MRK)

Manufacturer of pharmaceuticals and specialty chemicals.

(800) 831-8248

www.merck.com

Initial shares can be purchased directly from the company: $350 minimum or automatic monthly investments of at least $50.

Optional cash payments: $50 to $50,000 annually

Dividends paid since 1936

S&P earnings and dividend rank: A+

Meredith Corp. (MDP)

Publisher of magazines and books with interest in TV stations.

(800) 468-9716

Optional cash payments: Not available

Dividends paid since 1930

S&P earnings and dividend rank: A–

Merrill Lynch (MER)

Major financial services company.

(888) 460-7641

www.ml.com

Optional cash payments: not available

Dividends paid since 1961

S&P earnings and dividend rank: A–

Michaels Stores (MIK)

Retailer of arts and crafts merchandise.

(800) 577-4676

www.michaels.com

Initial shares can be purchased directly from the company: $500 minimum.

Optional cash payments: $100 to $2,500 monthly

Dividends paid since 2003

S&P earnings and dividend rank: B

Microsoft Corp. (MSFT)

Major software company.

(800) 842-7629

www.microsoft.com

Initial shares can be purchased directly from the company: $1,000 minimum or automatic monthly investments of at least $50 per month.

Optional cash purchases: $50 to $50,000 annually

Dividends paid since 2003

S&P earnings and dividend rank: B+

Miller (Herman) (MLHR)

Manufacturer of office furniture.

(800) 446-2617

www.hermanmiller.com

Optional cash purchases: $25 to $60,000 annually

Above-average fees

Dividends paid since 1945

Earnings and dividend rank: B+

Modinie Manufacturing (MOD)

Manufacturer of auto parts and heating and air-conditioning equipment.

(800) 813-3324

www.modine.com

Initial shares can be purchased directly from the company: $500 minimum.

Optional cash payments: $10 to $5,000 monthly

Dividends paid since 1959

S&P earnings and dividend rank: A–

Molex Inc. (MOLX)

Maker of connectors and switches for autos, computers, and other equipment.

(800) 286-9178

www.molex.com

Initial shares can be purchased directly from the

company: $500 minimum or automatic monthly investments of at least $100 for five consecutive months.

Optional cash payments: $100 to $100,000 annually

Dividends paid since 1976

S&P earnings and dividend rank: A–

Monsanto Co. (MON)

Manufacturer of agricultural products.

(888) 725-9529

www.monsanto.com

Initial shares can be purchased directly from the company: $250 minimum or automatic monthly investments of at least $25 for 10 consecutive months.

Optional cash payments: $25 to $250,000 annually

Dividends paid since 2001

S&P earnings and dividend rank: not ranked

Motorola Inc. (MOT)

Maker of communications equipment and semiconductors.

(800) 403-7831

www.motorola.com

Initial shares can be purchased directly from the company: $500 minimum or automatic monthly investments of at least $40 for 10 consecutive months.

Optional cash payments: $50 to $250,000 annually

Dividends paid since 1942

S&P earnings and dividend rank: B+

MTS Systems (MTSC)

Manufacturer of testing and simulation systems.

(800) 468-9716

www.mts.com

Optional cash payments: $50 to $25,000 monthly

Above-average fees

Dividends paid since 1967

S&P earnings and dividend rank: B+

Mylan Laboratories (MYL)

Major manufacturer of generic pharmaceuticals.

(800) 937-5449

www.mylan.com

Optional cash purchases: $50 to $5,000 quarterly

Dividends paid since 1983

S&P earnings and dividend rank: A–

N

National City Corp. (NCC)

Bank operating in Ohio, Kentucky, and Indiana.

(800) 622-6757

www.nationalcity.com

Optional cash payments: $20 to $25,000 monthly

Dividends paid since 1936

S&P earnings and dividend rank: A

National Fuel Gas (NFG)

Natural gas company.

(800) 648-8166

www.natfuel.com

Initial shares can be purchased directly from the company: $1,000 minimum.

Optional cash payments: $100 to $120,000 annually

Dividends paid since 1903

S&P earnings and dividend rank: B+

Nature's Sunshine Products (NATR)

Manufacturer and direct seller of nutritional and herbal products.

(801) 342-4300

www.naturessunshile.com

Optional cash payments: $20 to $20,000 annually

Dividends paid since 1988

S&P earnings and dividend rank: B+

Neiman-Marcus Group 'A' (NMG.A)

Operator of specialty retail stores.

(800) 842-7629

www.neimanmarcus.com

Initial shares can be purchased directly from the company: $250 minimum or automatic monthly investments of at least $25 for 10 consecutive months.

Optional cash payments: $25 minimum; no maximum

Dividends paid since 2004

S&P earnings and dividend rank: B

New Jersey Resources (NJR)

Gas utility operating in New Jersey.

(800) 817-3955

Initial shares can be purchased directly from the company: $25 minimum.

Optional cash payments: $25 to $60,000 annually

Dividends paid since 1951

S&P earnings and dividend rank: A

New Plan Excel Realty Trust (NXL)

Real estate investment trust (neighborhood shopping centers).

(800) 730-6001

www.newplan.com

Optional cash payments: $100 to $20,000 quarterly

5 percent discount on reinvested dividends

Dividends paid since 1942

S&P earnings and dividend rank: A

New York Community Bancorp (NYB)

Bank operator in New York (Queens), New Jersey, and Connecticut.

(800) 368-5948

www.qcsb.com

Optional cash purchases: $100 to $25,000 quarterly

Dividends paid since 1994

S&P earnings and dividend rank: A–

New York Times ('A')

Newspaper and magazine publisher; also operates radio and television stations.

(800) 317-4445

www.nyto.com

Optional cash payments: $10 to $3,000 quarterly

Dividends paid since 1958

S&P earnings and dividend rank: A–

Newell Rubbermaid (NWL)

Manufacturer of consumer housewares and hardware.

(800) 432-0140

www.newellco.com

Initial shares can be purchased directly from the company: $250 minimum or automatic monthly investments of at least $25 for 10 consecutive months.

Optional cash payments: $25 to $100,000 annually

Dividends paid since 1946

S&P earnings and dividend rank: B

NICOR Inc. (GAS)

Natural gas utility holding company.

(888) 642-6748

www.nicorinc.com

Optional cash payments: $50 to $5,000 monthly

Dividends paid since 1954

S&P earnings and dividend rank: B

Nike Inc. ('B')

Manufacturer of athletic footwear and apparel.

(800) 756-8200

www.nike.com

Initial shares can be purchased directly from the company: $500 minimum or automatic monthly investments of at least $50.

Optional cash payments: $50 to $250,000 annually

Dividends paid since 1984

S&P earnings and dividend rank: A

NiSource Inc. (NI)

Electric and gas utility based in Indiana.

(877) 547-5990

www.nisource

Optional cash payments: $25 to $5,000 quarterly

Dividends paid since 1987

Earnings and dividend rank: B

Nordson Corp. (NDSN)

Manufacturer of industrial application equipment.

(800) 622-6757

www.nordson.com

Optional cash payments: $10 to $4,000 quarterly

Dividends paid since 1969

S&P earnings and dividend rank: B

Norfolk Southern (NSC)

Major railroad operator and motor carrier.

(866) 272-9472

www.nscorp.com

Optional cash payments: $10 to $1,000 monthly

Dividends paid since 1901

S&P earnings and dividend rank: B

North Fork Bancorp (NFB)

New York-based bank operator (mainly on Long Island).

(800) 317-4445

www.northforkbank.com

Optional cash purchases: $200 to $15,000 monthly

Fees are above-average

Dividends paid since 1994

S&P earnings and dividend rank: A

Northeast Utilities (NU)

Electric utility operating in Massachusetts, Connecticut, and New Hampshire.

(800) 999-7269

www.nu.com

Initial shares can be purchased directly from the company: $250 minimum.

Optional cash payments: $100 to $10,000 monthly

Dividends paid since 1999

S&P earnings and dividend rank: B

Northrop Grumman (NOC)

Manufacturer of military aircraft and other defense products.

(800) 756-8200

www.northgrum.com

Optional cash payments: $100 to $1,000 monthly

Dividends paid since 1951

S&P earnings and dividend rank: B+

Northwest Natural Gas (NWN)

Gas utility operating in Oregon and Washington.

(888) 777-0321

www.nng.com

Optional cash payments: up to $50,000 annually

Dividends paid since 1952

S&P earnings and dividend rank: B+

NSTAR (NST)

Electric and gas utility operating in Boston.

(800) 338-8446

www.nstaronline.com

Initial shares can be purchased directly from the company: $500 minimum.

Optional cash payments: $50 to $250,000 annually

Dividends paid since 1879

S&P earnings and dividend rank: B+

Nucor Corp. (NUE)

Major maker of steel joists and steel products.

(800) 829-8432

www.nucor.com

Optional cash payments: $10 to $3,000 quarterly

Dividends paid since 1973

Earnings and dividend rank: B

O

OGE Energy (OGE)

Electric utility operating in Oklahoma and Arkansas.

(888) 216-8114

www.oge.com

Initial shares can be purchased directly from the company: $250 minimum.

Optional cash payments: $25 to $100,000 annually

Dividends paid since 1908

S&P earnings and dividend rank: A–

Old Republic International (ORI)

Insurance company based in Chicago.

(781) 575-2724

www.oldrepublic.com

Optional cash payments: $100 to $5,000 quarterly

Dividends paid since 1942

S&P earnings and dividend rank: A–

Olin Corp. (OLN)

Manufacturer of specialty chemicals, metals, and defense products.

(800) 306-8594

www.olin.com

Optional cash payments: $50 to $50,000 annually

Above-average fees

Dividends paid since 1926

S&P earnings and divided rank: B–

Omnicare Inc. (OCR)

Provider of longtime care pharmacy services.

(800) 317-4445

www.omnicare.com

Optional cash payments: $10 to $10,000 annually

Dividends paid since 1989

S&P earnings and dividend rank: A–

Omnicom Group (OMC)

Major international advertising agency.

(800) 842-7629

www.omnicomgroup.com

Initial shares can be purchased directly from the company: $250 minimum or automatic monthly investments of at least $75.

Optional cash payments: $75 to $120,000 annually

Dividends paid since 1986

S&P earnings and dividend rank: A+

ONEOK (OKE)

Natural gas utility operating in Oklahoma and Kansas, as well as oil and gas producer.

(866) 235-0232

www.oneok.com

Initial shares can be purchased directly from the company: $250 minimum.

Optional cash payments: $25 to $10,000 per transaction

Dividends paid since 1939

S&P earnings and dividend rank: A–

Owens & Minor (OMI)

Distributor of medical and pharmaceuticals supplies.

(800) 633-4236

www.owens-minor.com

Optional cash payments: $50 to $5,000 annually

Dividends paid since 1926

S&P earnings and dividend rank: A–

P

Pall Corp. (PLL)

Manufacturer of filtration products.

(800) 633-4236

www.pall.com

Optional cash payments: $100 to $5,000 monthly

Dividends paid since 1974

S&P earnings and dividend rank: B

Parker-Hannifin (PH)

Maker of fluid power systems.

(800) 633-4236

www.parker.com

Optional cash payments: $10 to $5,000 monthly

Dividends paid since 1949

S&P earnings and dividend rank: A–

Paychex (PAYX)

Provider of computer payroll services.

(877) 814-9688

www.paychex.com

Initial shares can be purchased directly from the company: $250 minimum.

Optional cash payments: $100 to $10,000 monthly

Dividends paid since 1988

S&P earnings and dividend rank: A+

Penney (J.C.) (JCP)

Major department store retailer.

(800) 842-9470

www.jcpenney.com

Initial shares can be purchased directly from the company: $250 minimum.

Optional cash payments: $25 to $10,000 monthly

Dividends paid since 1922

S&P earnings and dividend rank: B–

Pentair Inc. (PNR)

Manufacturer of industrial equipment.

(800) 468-9716

www.pentair.com

Optional cash payments: $10 to $3,000 quarterly

Dividends paid since 1976

S&P earnings and dividend rank: A–

Peoples Energy (PGL)

Gas utility operating in Chicago.

(800) 901-8878

www.peoplesenergy.com

Initial shares can be purchased directly from the company: $250 minimum.

Optional cash purchases: $25 to $100,000 annually

Dividends paid since 1937

S&P earnings and dividend rank: B

Pep Boys—Manny, Mo, Jack (PBY)

Retailer chain (automotive parts and accessories).

(800) 278-4353

www.pepboys.com

Optional cash purchases: $100 to $10,000 quarterly

Dividends paid since 1950

S&P earnings and dividend rank: B

Pepco Holdings (POM)

Electric utility operating in Washington, D.C., Maryland, and Virginia.

(800) 527-3726

www.pepcoholdings.com

Optional cash payments: $25 to $200,000 annually

Dividends paid since 1904

S&P earnings and dividend rank: B

Pepsi Bottling Group (PBG)

PBG, 38 percent owned by PepsiCo, is the largest bottler of Pepsi-Cola drinks.

(800) 432-01240

www.pbg.com

Initial shares can be purchased directly from the company: $500 minimum or automatic monthly investments of at least $50 for 10 consecutive months.

Optional cash payments: $50 to $5,000 monthly

Dividends paid since 1999

S&P earnings and dividend rank: not ranked

PepsiAmericas (PAS)

Producer and distributor of Pepsi-Cola drinks.

(877) 602-1611

www.pepsiamericas.com

Initial shares can be purchased directly from the company: $250 minimum.

Optional cash payments: $50 to $120,000 annually

Dividends paid since 1959

Earnings and dividend rank: B–

PepsiCo (PEP)

Producer of soft drinks and snack foods (Frito-Lay brand).

(800) 226-0083

www.pepsico.com

Optional cash payments: $25 to $5,000 monthly

Dividends paid since 1952

S&P earnings and dividend rank: A+

PerkinElmer (PKI)

Manufacturer of scientific analytical instruments.

(800) 842-7629

www.perkinelmer.com

Initial shares can be purchased directly from the company: $250 minimum or automatic monthly investments of at least $25 for 10 consecutive months.

Optional cash payments: $25 to $25,000 annually

Dividends paid since 1965

S&P earnings and dividend rank: B

Pfizer (PFE)

Major manufacturer of pharmaceuticals, health-care, and animal health-care products.

(800) 733-9393

www.pfizer.com

Initial shares can be purchased directly from the company: $500 minimum.

Optional cash payments: $50 to $120,000 annually

Dividends paid since 1901

S&P earnings and dividend rank: A

PG&E (PCG)

Gas and electric utility operating in California.

(800) 367-7731

www.pgecorp.com

Initial shares can be purchased directly from the company: $250 minimum or automatic monthly investments of at least $50 for five consecutive months.

Optional cash payments: $50 to $100,000 annually

Dividends paid since 2005

S&P earnings and dividend rank: B

Phelps Dodge (PD)

Largest U.S. copper producer.

(800) 842-7629

www.phelpsdodge.com

Initial shares can; be purchased directly from the company: $1,000 minimum or automatic monthly

investments of at least $100 for 10 consecutive months.

Optional cash payments: $100 to $10,000 per month

Dividends paid since 2004

S&P earnings and dividend rank: B–

Piedmont Natural Gas (PNY)

Provider of natural gas to the Piedmont area of North and South Carolina.

(800) 937-5449

www.piedmontng.com

Initial shares can be purchased directly from the company: $250 minimum.

Optional cash payments: $25 to $120,000 annually

5 percent discount on reinvested dividends

Dividends paid since 1956

S&P earnings and dividend rank: A–

Pier 1 Imports (PIR)

Large specialty retailer of imported home furnishings.

(888) 884-8086

www.pier1.com

Initial shares can be purchased directly from the company: $500 minimum.

Optional cash payments: $50 to $5,000 monthly

Dividends paid since 1986

S&P earnings and dividend rank: A–

Pinnacle West Capital (PNW)

Electric utility operating in Arizona.

(800) 457-2983

Initial shares can be purchased directly from the company: $50 minimum.

Optional cash payments: $50 to $150,000 annually

Dividends paid since 1993

S&P earnings and dividend rank: A

Pitney Bowes (PBI)

Major manufacturer of postage meters and mailing systems.

(800) 648-8170

www.pb.com

Optional cash payments: $100 to $3,000 quarterly

Dividends paid since 1934

S&P earnings and dividend rank: A–

PNC Financial Services Group (PNC)

Bank operating in Pennsylvania, Indiana, Kentucky, Ohio, New Jersey, and Delaware.

(800) 982-7652

www.pnc.com

Optional cash payments: $50 to $5,000 monthly

Dividends paid since 1865

S&P earnings and dividend rank: B+

Polaris Industries (PII)

Manufacturer of snowmobiles, motorcycles, and ATVs.

(800) 468-9716

www.polarisindustries.com

Optional cash payments: $25 to $5,000 monthly

Dividends paid since 1987

S&P earnings and dividend rank: A–

Potlatch Corp. (PCH)

Manufacturer of lumber, plywood, paper, and paperboard.

(312) 360-5390

www.potlatchcorp.com

Optional cash payments: $25 to $100 monthly

Dividends paid since 1939

S&P earnings and dividend rank: A

PPG Industries (PPG)

Manufacturer of glass, coatings, resins, fiber, and chemicals.

(800) 648-8160

www.ppg.com

Initial shares can be purchased directly from the company: $500 minimum.

Optional cash payments: $100 to $10,000 monthly

Dividends paid since 1899

S&P earnings and dividend rank: B

PPL Corp. (PPL)

Electric utility operating in east-central Pennsylvania.

(800) 345-3085

www.pplweb.com

Optional cash payments: up to $80,000 annually

Dividends paid since 1946

S&P earnings and dividend rank: B

Praxair (PX)

Major manufacturer of industrial gases.

(800) 524-4458

Optional cash payments: $50 to $24,000 annually

Dividends paid since 1992

Earnings and dividend rank: A

Procter & Gamble (PG)

Giant manufacturer of household items, personal care products, and consumer foods.

(800) 764-7483

www.pg.com

Initial shares can be purchased directly from the company: $250 minimum.

Optional cash purchases: $50 to $25,000 monthly

Dividends paid since 1891

S&P earnings and dividend rank: A

Progress Energy (PGN)

Electric utility operating in North and South Carolina.

(800) 663-4236

www.progress-energy.com

Initial shares can be purchased directly from the company: $250 minimum.

Optional cash payments: $50 to $25,000 monthly

Dividends paid since 1937

S&P earnings and dividend rank: A–

ProLogis (PLD)

Real estate investment trust (industrial distribution facilities).

(800) 956-3378

www.prologis.com

Initial shares can be purchased directly from the company: $200 minimum.

Optional cash payments: $200 to $10,000 monthly

2 percent discount on reinvested dividends and on optional cash payments

Dividends paid since 1994

S&P earnings and dividend rank: B+

Protective Life Corp. (PL)

Provider of different types of insurance.

(800) 524-4458

www.protective.com

Optional cash payments: $25 to $6,000 quarterly

Dividends paid since 1926

S&P earnings and dividend rank: A

Provident Bankshares (PBKS)

Commercial banker operating in Maryland.

(866) 820-0125

www.providentbankmd.com

Initial shares can be purchased directly from the company: $250 minimum or automatic monthly investments of at least $50 for five consecutive months.

Optional cash payments: $50 to $10,000 quarterly

Dividends paid since 1988

S&P earnings and dividend rank: A

Public Enterprise Services (PEG)

(800) 242-0813

www.pseg.com

Initial shares can be purchased directly from the company: $250 minimum or automatic monthly investments of at least $50.

Optional cash payments: $50 to $125,000 annually

Dividends paid since 1907

S&P earnings and dividend rank: B+

Puget Energy (PSD)

Electric utility operating in Washington State.

(800) 997-8438

www.pse.com

Initial shares can be purchased directly from the company: $250 minimum or automatic monthly investments of at least $50 for five consecutive months.

Optional cash payments: $50 to $10,000 monthly

Dividends paid since 1943

S&P earnings and dividend rank: B

Q

Quaker Chemical Corporation (KWR)

Manufacturer of specialty chemical products.

(800) 278-4353

www.quakerchem.com

Optional cash purchases: $300 to $24,000 annually

Dividends paid since 1972

S&P earnings and dividend rank: B+

QUALCOMM (QCOM)

Manufacturer of digital wireless telecommunications products.

(312) 588-4157

www.qualcomm.com

Initial shares can be purchased directly from the company: $500 minimum.

Optional cash payments: $50 minimum

Dividends paid since 2003

S&P earnings and dividend rank: B

Quanex Corp. (NX)

Manufacturer of steel bars and aluminum flat-rolled products.

(800) 468-9716

www.quanex.com

Initial shares can be purchased directly from the company: $250 minimum.

Optional cash payments: $50 to $10,000 quarterly

Dividends paid since 1988

S&P earnings and dividend rank: B

Questar Corp. (STR)

Natural gas company; also in commercial real estate and microwave communications.

Initial shares can be purchased directly from the

company: $250 minimum or automatic monthly investments of at least $50 for five consecutive months

Optional cash payments: $50 to $100,000 annually

Dividends paid since 1935

S&P earnings and dividend rank: A–

R

RadioShack Corp. (RSH)

Consumer electronics retailer.

(888) 218-4374

Initial shares can be purchased directly from the company: $250 minimum.

Optional cash payments: $50 to $150,000 annually

Dividends paid since 1987

S&P earnings and dividend rank: B+

Rayonier (RYN)

Real estate investment trust. produces and markets specialty pulp, timber, and wood products; owns 2.2 million acres of timberland in the United States and New Zealand.

(800) 659-0158

www.rayonier.com

Optional cash payments: $50 to $20,000 annually

Dividends paid since 1994

S&P earnings and dividend rank: B+

Raytheon Co. (RTN)

Defense electronics, commercial aircraft, and appliances.

(800) 360-4519

www.raytheon.com

Optional cash payments: $25 to $25,000 quarterly

Above-average fees

Dividends paid since 1964

S&P earnings and dividend rank: B–

Reader's Digest Association (RDA)

Publisher and marketer of magazines, books, and home entertainment products.

(800) 242-4653

www.rd.com

Initial shares can be purchased directly from the company: $1,000 minimum.

Optional cash payments: $100 to $10,000 monthly

Dividends paid since 1990

S&P earnings and dividend rank: B–

Regency Centers (REG)

Real estate investment trust (neighborhood shopping centers).

(800) 829-8432

www.regencyrealty.com

Optional cash payments: $50 to $10,000 quarterly

Dividends paid since 1994

S&P earnings and dividend rank: A–

Regions Financial (RF)

Commercial banker operating primarily in Alabama and northwestern Florida.

(800) 524-2879

www.regions.com

Initial shares can be purchased directly from the company: $1,000 minimum.

Optional cash payments: $100 to $15,000 annually

Dividends paid since 1968

S&P earnings and dividend rank: A–

Republic Bancorp (RBNC)

Large bank operator in Michigan, Ohio, and Indiana.

(800) 426-5523

www.republicbancorp.com

Optional cash payments: $10 to $5,000 monthly

Dividends paid since 1992

S&P earnings and dividend rank: A–

Reynolds American (RAI)

Producer of cigarettes.

(800) 524-4458

www.reynoldsamerican.com

Initial shares can be purchased directly from the

company: $500 minimum or automatic monthly investments of at least $50 for 10 consecutive months.

Optional cash payments: $50 to $250,000 annually

Dividends paid since 1999

S&P earnings and divided rank: not ranked

RLI Corp. (RLI)

Insurance company providing specialty property and casualty coverage and contact lens insurance; also distributes contact lenses and provides office automation systems for eye care practitioners.

(800) 468-9716

www.rlicorp.com

Optional cash payments: $25 to $2,000 monthly

Dividends paid since 1976

S&P earnings and dividend rank: A

Rockwell Automation (ROK)

Manufacturer of components and systems for use in communication and aviation applications.

(800) 204-7800

www.rockwell.com

Initial shares can be purchased directly from the company: $1,000 minimum or automatic monthly

investments of at least $100 for 10 consecutive months.

Optional cash payments: $100 to $100,000 annually

Dividends paid since 1948

S&P earnings and dividend rank: B+

Rockwell Collins (COL)

Manufacturer of aviation electronics and mobile communications products.

(888) 253-4522

www.rockwellcollins.com

Initial shares can be purchased directly from the company: $1,000 minimum or automatic monthly investments of at least $100 for 10 consecutive months.

Optional cash payments: $100 to $100,000 annually

Dividends paid since 2001

S&P earnings and dividend rank: not ranked

Rohm & Haas (ROH)

Manufacturer of specialty chemicals and plastics.

(800) 633-4236

www.rohmhaas.com

Optional cash payments: $50 to $100,000 annually

Dividends paid since 1927

S&P earnings and dividend rank: A

Rollins Inc. (ROL)

Operations in pest controls, protective services, and lawn care.

(800) 568-3476

www.rollinscorp.com

Optional cash payments: not available

Dividends paid since 1961

S&P earnings and dividend rank: B+

RPM International (RPM)

Manufacturer of protective coatings and fabrics.

(800) 988-5238

www.rpminc.com

Optional cash payments: $25 to $5,000 monthly

Dividends paid since 1969

S&P earnings and dividend rank: A

Ruddick Corp. (RDK)

Operator of supermarkets and manufacturer of thread and yarn.

(800) 633-4236

www.ruddickcorp.com

Optional cash payments: $20 to $3,000 monthly

Dividends paid since 1976

S&P earnings and dividend rank: A–

Russell Corp. (RML)

Manufacturer of leisure apparel, athletic uniforms, and knit shirts.

(800) 568-3476

www.russellcorp.com

Optional cash payments: $50 to $2,000 monthly

Dividends paid since 1963

S&P earnings and dividend rank: B–

Ryder System (R)

Equipment leasing and transportation services.

(781) 575-3170

www.ryder.com

Optional cash payments: $25 to $60,000 annually

Dividends paid since 1976

S&P earnings and dividend rank: B

Ryerson Tull (RT)

Steel processor and distributor.

(800) 524-4458

www.ryersontull.com

Initial shares can be purchased directly from the company: $500 minimum or automatic monthly investments of at least $25 monthly.

Optional cash payments: $25 to $120,000 annually

Dividends paid since 1995

S&P earnings and dividend rank: B–

S

Sanderson Farms (SAFM)

Large producer, processor, and distributor of fresh and frozen chicken and other prepared food items.

(800) 756-3353

www.sandersonfarms.com

Initial shares can be purchased directly from the company: $500 minimum.

Optional cash payments: $50 to $10,000 monthly

Above-average fees

Dividends paid since 1987

S&P earnings and dividend rank: B+

Sara Lee Corp. (SLE)

Producer of packaged bakery, meats, and coffee products, and has operations in food service.

(888) 422-9881

www.saralee.com

Initial shares can be purchased directly from the company: $500 annually.

Optional cash purchases: $100 to $120,000 annually

Dividends paid since 1946

S&P earnings and dividend rank: A–

SBC Communications (SBC)

Provider of telecommunications services in Arkansas, Kansas, Missouri, Oklahoma, and Texas.

(800) 351-7221

www.sbc.com

Initial shares can be purchased directly from the company: $500 minimum.

Optional cash payments: $50 to $120,000 annually

Dividends paid since 1984

S&P earnings and dividend rank: B+

SCANA Corp. (SCG)

Electric and gas utility operating in South Carolina.

(800) 763-5891

www.scana.com

Initial shares can be purchased directly from the company: $250 minimum.

Optional cash payments: $25 to $100,000 annually

Dividends paid since 1946

S&P earnings and dividend rank: B

Schering-Plough (SGP)

Major manufacturer of pharmaceuticals and consumer products.

(877) 429-1240

www.sch-plough.com

Optional cash payments: $25 to $36,000 annually

Dividends paid since 1952

S&P earnings and dividend rank: A–

Schwab (Charles) (SCH)

Large discount brokerage company.

(800) 468-9716

www.schwab.com

Optional cash payments: $10 to $5,000 monthly

Dividends paid since 1989

S&P earnings and dividend rank: B+

Scientific-Atlanta (SFA)

Maker of electronic communications products.

(800) 524-4458

www.scientificatlanta.com

Optional cash payments: $25 to $40,000 annually

Dividends paid since 1996

S&P earnings and dividend rank: A–

Selective Insurance Group (SIGI)

Property-casualty insurer.

(800) 446-2617

www.selective.com

Optional cash payments: $100 to $1,000 quarterly

Dividends paid since 1929

S&P earnings and dividend rank: B+

Sempra Energy (SRE)

Electric and gas utility operating in California.

(800) 821-2550

www.sempra.com

Initial shares can be purchased directly from the company: $500 minimum or automatic monthly investments of at least $50 for 10 consecutive months.

Optional cash payments: $25 to $150,000 annually

Dividends paid since 1998

S&P earnings and dividend rank: B

Sensient Technologies (SXT)

Maker of food flavorings and colors as well as seasonings.

(800) 468-9716

www.sensient-tech.com

Optional cash payments: $25 to $1,500 monthly

Dividends paid since 1934

S&P earnings and dividend rank: A–

Sherwin-Williams (SHW)

Manufacturer of paints and varnishes.

(800) 432-0140

www.sherwin-williams.com

Optional cash payments: $10 to $2,000 monthly

Dividends paid since 1979

S&P earnings and dividend rank: A

Simon Property Group (SPG)

Real estate investment trust (regional malls).

(888) 213-0965

www.simon.com

Optional cash purchases: not available

Dividends paid since 1994

S&P earnings and dividend rank: B+

Smith (A.O.) (AOS)

Manufacturer of truck frames and components and electric motors.

(800) 637-7549

www.aosmith.com

Optional cash purchases: $25 to $5,000 quarterly

Dividends paid since 1983

S&P earnings and dividend rank: B–

Smucker (J.M.) (SJM)

Major producer of jellies, preserves, soups, and other items.

(800) 456-1169

www.smucker.com

Initial shares can be purchased directly from the company: $250 minimum.

Optional cash purchases: $25 to $50,000 annually

Dividends paid since 1949

S&P earnings and dividend rank: A–

Snap-On (SNA)

Manufacturer of hand tools, power tools, and shop equipment.

(800) 446-2617

www.snapon.com

Initial shares can be purchased directly from the company: $500 minimum or automatic monthly investments of at least $100 for five consecutive months.

Optional cash payments: $100 to $150,000 annually

Dividends paid since 1939

S&P earnings and dividend rank: B

Sonoco Products (SON)

Manufacturer of paper packaging products.

(800) 633-4236

www.sonoco.com

Initial shares can be purchased directly from the company: $250 minimum or automatic monthly investments of at least $50 for five consecutive months.

Optional cash payments: $50 to $120,000 annually

Dividends paid since 1925

S&P earnings and dividend rank: B+

South Financial Group (TSFG)

Bank holding company operating in South Carolina.

(800) 368-5948

www.thesouthgroup.com

Optional cash payments: $25 to $10,000 monthly

5 percent discount on reinvested dividends

Dividends paid since 1994

S&P earnings and dividend rank: B+

Southern Co. (SO)

Electric utility operating in the Southeast.

(800) 554-7626

www.southernco.com

Initial shares can be purchased directly from the company: $250 minimum.

Optional cash purchases: $25 to $150,000 annually

Dividends paid since 1948

S&P earnings and dividend rank: A–

Southwest Gas (SWX)

Natural gas utility operating in Arizona, Nevada, and California.

(800) 331-1119

www.swgas.com

Initial shares can be purchased directly from the company by residents of Arizona, California, and Nevada: $300 minimum.

Optional cash purchases: $25 to $100,000 annually

Dividends paid since 1956

S&P earnings and dividend rank: B+

Sovereign Bancorp (SOV)

Bank operating in eastern Pennsylvania, Delaware, and New Jersey.

(800) 685-4524

www.sovereignbank.com

Optional cash purchases: $50 to $5,000 quarterly

Dividends paid since 1987

S&P earnings and dividend rank: B+

Sovran Self Storage (SSS)

Real estate investment trust (self-storage properties.)

(800) 278-4353

www.sovranss.com

Initial shares can be purchased directly from the company: $100 minimum.

Optional cash purchases: $100 to $10,000 monthly

2 percent discount on reinvested dividends and on optional cash payments

Dividends paid since 1995

S&P earnings and dividend rank: B+

Sprint Group (FON)

Diversified telecommunications system; one of the largest long distance carriers.

(800) 259-3755

www.sprint.com

Optional cash payments: $25 to $5,000 quarterly

Dividends paid since 1939

S&P earnings and dividend rank: B

St. Paul Travelers Cos. (STA)

Property-liability insurer.

(888) 326-5102

www.stpaultravelers.com

Optional cash payments: $25 to $50,000 annually

Dividends paid since 2003

S&P earnings and dividend rank: not ranked

Standard Register (SR)

Manufacturer of business forms and equipment.

(800) 633-4236

www.stdreg.com

Optional cash payments: $25 to $60,000 annually

Dividends paid since 1927

S&P earnings and dividend rank: B–

Stanley Works (SWK)

Manufacturer of hand tools and hardware.

(800) 543-6757

www.stanleyworks.com

Initial shares can be purchased directly from the company: $250 minimum.

Optional cash payments: $100 to $150,000 annually

Dividends paid since 1877

S&P earnings and dividend rank: B+

Staples Inc. (SPLS)

Retailer of office supplies.

(888) 875-9002

www.staples.com

Initial shares can be purchased directly from the company: $250 minimum or automatic monthly investments of at least $25 for 10 consecutive months.

Optional cash payments: $25 to $250,000 annually

Dividends paid since 2004

Earnings and dividend rank: B+

State Street Corp. (STTX)

Bank operating in Massachusetts, and a major mutual fund custodian.

(877) 639-7788

www.statestreet.com

Optional cash purchases: $100 to $25,000 monthly

Above-average fees

Dividends paid since 1910

S&P earnings and dividend rank: B

Stride Rite (SRR)

Manufacturer and retailer of footwear for children and adults.

(800) 442-2001

www.striderite.com

Optional cash payments: $10 to $1,000 monthly

Dividends paid since 1955

S&P earnings and dividend rank: B+

SunTrust Banks (STI)

Commercial banker operating in Georgia, Florida, and Tennessee.

(800) 568-3476

www.suntrust.com

Optional cash payments: $10 to $60,000 annually

Dividends paid since 1985

S&P earnings and dividend rank: A+

Superior Industries International (SUP)

Manufacturer of custom automotive accessories.

(800) 851-9677

www.superiorindustries.com

Optional cash payments: $50 to $5,000 quarterly

Dividends paid since 1985

S&P earnings and dividend rank: B+

Supervalu In. (SVU)

Major food wholesaler and manager of retail supermarkets and general merchandise stores.

(877) 536-3555

www.supervalu.com

Optional cash payments: $10 to $3,000 quarterly

Dividends paid since 1936

S&P earnings and dividend rank: A–

Susquehanna Bancshares (SUSQ)

Commercial banker operating in Pennsylvania, New Jersey, and Maryland.

(800) 524-4458

www.susqpatriotbank.com

Initial shares can be purchased directly from the company: $250 minimum.

Optional cash payments: $50 to $25,000 annually

Dividends paid since 1982

S&P earnings and dividend rank: A–

Synovus Financial (SNV)

Georgia-based bank operating in the Southeast.

(800) 503-8903

www.synovus.com

Initial shares can be purchased directly from the company: $250 minimum.

Optional cash payments: $50 to $250,000 annually

Dividends paid since 1930

S&P earnings and dividend rank: A+

Sysco Corp. (SYY)

Major wholesale food distributor.

(800) 730-4001

www.sysco.com

Optional cash payments: $100 to $10,000 monthly

Dividends paid since 1970

S&P earnings and dividend rank: A+

T

Target Corp. (TGT)

Operator of discount department stores.

(800) 317-4445

www.target.com

Optional shares can be purchased directly from the company: $500 minimum or automatic monthly investments of at least $50 for 10 consecutive months.

Optional cash payments: $50 to $100,000 annually

Dividends paid since 1965

S&P earnings and dividend rank: A+

TCF Financial (TCB)

Bank operating in Minnesota, Illinois, Michigan, and Wisconsin.

(800) 730-4001

www.tcfbank.com

Optional cash payments: $25 to $25,000 quarterly

Dividends paid since 1988

S&P earnings and dividend rank: A

TECO Energy (TE)

Holding company for Tampa Electric.

(800) 652-9222

www.tecoenergy.com

Optional cash payments: $25 to $100,000 annually

Dividends paid since 1900

S&P earnings and dividend rank: B–

Tektronix Inc. (TEK)

Manufacturer of electronic equipment.

(800) 411-7025

www.tektronix.com

Initial shares can be purchased directly from the company: $500 maximum.

Optional cash payments: $100 to $10,000 monthly

Dividends paid since 2003

S&P earnings and dividend rank: B–

Teleflex Inc. (TFX)

Manufacturer of industrial products and surgical devices.

(877) 842-1572

www.teleflex.com

Initial shares can be purchased directly from the company: $250 minimum.

Optional cash payments: $25 to $10,000 monthly

Dividends paid since 1977

S&P earnings and dividend rank: A

Telephone & Data Systems (TDS)

Offers telecommunications in 29 states.

(877) 337-1575

www.teldta.com

Optional cash payments: $10 to $5,000 quarterly

5 percent discount on reinvested dividends

Dividends paid since 1974

S&P earnings and dividend rank: B

Temple-Inland (TIN)

Manufacturer of containers, paperboard, pulp, and building materials.

(781) 575-2725

www.templeinland.com

Optional cash payments: $25 to $1,000 quarterly

Dividends paid since 1984

S&P earnings and dividend rank: B

Textron Inc. (TXT)

Diversified company with interests in aerospace, commercial products, and financial services.

(800) 829-8432

www.textron.com

Optional cash payments: $25 to $12,000 annually

Dividends paid since 1942

S&P earnings and dividend rank: B+

Thomas Industries (TII)

Manufacturer of lighting products, compressors, and vacuum pumps.

(800) 627-6757

www.thomasind.com

Optional cash payments: $25 to $3,000 monthly

Dividends paid since 1955

S&P earnings and dividend rank: A

Tidewater Inc. (TDW)

Provider of services for offshore oil drilling.

(781) 575-3170

www.tdw.com

Optional cash payments: $25 to $5,000 quarterly

Dividends paid since 1997

S&P earnings and dividend rank: B

Tiffany & Co. (TIF)

Retailer of fine jewelry and other luxury items.

(888) 778-1307

www.tiffany.com

Initial shares can be purchased directly from the company: $250 minimum or

automatic monthly investments of at least $25 for 10 consecutive months.

Optional cash payments: $25 to $100,000 annually

Dividends paid since 1988

S&P earnings and dividend rank: A

Timken Co. (TKR)

Major manufacturer of bearings and alloy steels.

(800) 622-6757

www.timken.com

Initial shares can be purchased directly from the company: $1,000 minimum or automatic monthly investments of at least $100 for 10 consecutive months.

Optional cash payments: $100 to $250,000 annually

Dividends paid since 1922

S&P earnings and dividend rank: B–

Torchmark Corp. (TMK)

Offers insurance and financial services.

(800) 446-2617

www.torchmarkcorp.com

Optional cash payments: $100 to $3,000 quarterly

Dividends paid since 1933

S&P earnings and dividend rank: A

Tredegar Corp. (TG)

Manufacturer of plastic films and aluminum extrusions, with energy interests.

(600) 622-6757

www.tredegar.com

Optional cash purchases: $25 to $4,000 monthly

Dividends paid since 1989

S&P earnings and dividend rank: B

Tribune Co. (TRB)

Newspaper publisher, broadcaster, and cable TV operator.

(800) 446-2617

www.tribune.com

Initial shares can be purchased directly from the company: $500 minimum or automatic monthly investments of at least $50 for 10 consecutive months.

Optional cash payments: $50 to $120,000 annually

Dividends paid since 1902

S&P earnings and dividend rank: B+

TrustCo Bank Corp. (TRST)

Bank operator in upstate New York.

(518) 381-3601

www.trustcobank.com

Initial shares can be purchased directly from the company: $50 minimum.

Optional cash payments: $25 minimum; no maximum

Dividends paid since 1982

S&P earnings and dividend rank: A+

TXU Corp. (TXU)

Electric utility operating in Texas.

(800) 828-0812

www.txucorp.com

Initial shares can be purchased directly from the company: $500 minimum.

Optional cash payments: $25 to $250,000 annually

Dividends paid since 1946

S&P earnings and dividend rank: B

Tyco International (TYC)

Diversified company offering fire protection and electronic security systems, flow-control products, electronic products, and disposable medical products.

(800) 842-7629

www.tycoint.com

Initial shares can be purchased directly from the company: $2,500 minimum.

Optional cash purchases: $50 minimum; no maximum

Dividends paid since 1975

S&P earnings and dividend rank: B–

Tyson Foods 'A' (TSN)

World's largest producer of poultry products.

(800) 317-4445

www.tysonfoods.com

Initial shares can be purchased directly from the company: $250 minimum or automatic monthly investments of $25.

Optional cash payments: $50 minimum, no maximum; $25 minimum with automatic debits from bank or checking accounts

Dividends paid since 1976

S&P earnings and dividend rank: B

U

UGI Corp. (UGI)

Gas and electric utility operating in Pennsylvania.

(800) 756-3353

www.ugicorp.com

Optional cash payments: $25 to $3,000 quarterly

Dividends paid since 1885

S&P earnings and dividend rank: A

UIL Holdings (UIL)

Electric utility operating in Connecticut.

(877) 681-8024

www.uil.com

Initial shares can be purchased directly from the company: $250 minimum or automatic monthly investments of at least $25 for 10 consecutive months.

Optional cash payments: $25 to $10,000 per transaction

Dividends paid since 1900

S&P earnings and dividend rank: B+

UST Inc.

Major producer of smokeless tobacco, cigars, pipes, and wine.

(800) 730-4001

www.ustinc.com

Optional cash payments: $10 to $10,000 monthly

Dividends paid since 1912

S&P earnings and dividend rank: A–

U.S. Bancorp (USB)

Commercial banker operating in Wisconsin, Illinois, Minnesota, and Arizona.

(800) 842-7629

www.usbank.com

Initial shares can be purchased directly from the

company: *$250 minimum or automatic monthly investments of at least $50 for five consecutive months.*

Optional cash payments: $25 to $250,000 annually

Dividends paid since 1863

S&P earnings and dividend rank: B+

Umpqua Holdings (UMPQ)

Bank operating in Oregon.

(503) 435-2491

www.unpquabank.com

Initial shares can be purchased directly from the company: $250 minimum or automatic monthly investments of at least $25 for 10 consecutive months.

Optional cash payments: $25 to $250,000 annually

Dividends paid since 1998

S&P earnings and dividend rank: not ranked

Union Pacific (UNP)

Rail operator, motor carrier, with interests in oil, gas, and mining.

(800) 317-2512

www.up.com

Optional cash payments: $10 to $60,000 annually

Dividends paid since 1900

S&P earnings and dividend rank: B

United Bankshares (UBSI)

Bank holding company based in West Virginia.

(800) 526-0801

www.ubsi.wv.com

Optional cash payments: $25 to $10,000 quarterly

Dividends paid since 1994

S&P earnings and dividend rank: B+

United Dominion Realty Trust (UDR)

Real estate investment trust (apartments in the Southeast).

(800) 780-2691

www.udrt.com

Optional cash payments: $50 to $25,000 quarterly

Dividends paid since 1973

S&P earnings and dividend rank: B–

United Parcel 'B' (UPS)

Express deliverer of packages.

(888) 663-8325

www.ups.com

Initial shares can be purchased directly from the company: $250 minimum or automatic monthly investments of at least $100 for three consecutive months.

Optional cash payments: $100 to $120,000 annually

Dividends paid since 2000

S&P earnings and dividend rank: not ranked

United Technologies (UTX)

Major supplier of aerospace and climate control products and services.

(800) 519-3111

www.utc.com

Optional cash payments: $100 to $120,000 annually

Dividends paid since 1936

S&P earnings and dividend rank: A+

Unitrin Inc. (UTR)

Insurance holding company.

(800) 829-8432

www.unitrin.com

Initial shares can be purchased directly from the company: $500 minimum or automatic monthly investments of at least $50 for 10 consecutive months.

Optional cash payments: $50 to $100,000 annually

Dividends paid since 1990

S&P earnings and dividend rank: B

Universal Corp. (UVV)

Producer of leaf tobacco and building products.

(800) 468-9716

www.universalcorp.com

Optional cash payments: $10 to $1,000 monthly

Dividends paid since 1927

S&P earnings and dividend rank: A

Unocal Corp. (UCL)

Independent oil and gas explorer and producer.

(800) 252-2233

www.unocal.com

Optional cash payments: $50 to $10,000 monthly

Dividends paid since 1916

S&P earnings and dividend rank: B+

UnumProvident Corp. (UNM)

Insurance provider.

(800) 446-2617

www.unum.com

Optional cash payments: $100 to $60,000 annually

Above-average fees

Dividends paid since 1925

S&P earnings and dividend rank: B–

V

Valspar Corp. (VAL)

Manufacturer of paints and coatings.

(800) 842-7629

www.valspar.com

Initial shares can be purchased directly from the company: $1,000 minimum.

Optional cash payments: $100 to $10,000 monthly

Above-average fees

Dividends paid since 1964

S&P earnings and dividend rank: A–

Vectren Corp. (VVC)

Electric and gas utility operating in Indiana.

(800) 622-6757

www.vectren.com

Optional cash payments: $25 to $50,000 annually

Dividends paid since 1946

S&P earnings and dividend rank: B+

Verizon Communications (VZ)

Full-service telecommunications provider.

(800) 631-2355

www.verizon.com

Initial shares can be purchased directly from the company: $1,000 minimum or automatic monthly investments of at least $100 for 10 consecutive months.

Optional cash payments: $50 to $200,000 annually

Dividends paid since 1984

S&P earnings and dividend rank: B

VF Corp. (VFC)

Manufacturer of sportswear and intimate apparel.

(781) 575-2725

www.vfc.com

Optional cash payments: $10 to $3,000 quarterly

Dividends paid since 1941

S&P earnings and dividend rank: A–

Viacom Inc. 'B' (VIA.B)

Large media company that owns CBS, MTV, Showtime, BET, and other cable channels; also has publishing and movie operations.

(800) 507-7799

www.viacom.com

Initial shares can be purchased directly from the company: $250 minimum.

Optional cash payments: $50 to $120,000 annually

Above-average fees

Dividends paid since 2003

S&P earnings and dividend rank: B–

Vulcan Materials (VMC)

Manufacturer of construction materials and chemicals.

(866) 886-9902

www.vulcanmaterials.com

Initial shares can be purchased directly from the company: $250 minimum.

Optional cash payments: $10 to $60,000 annually

Dividends paid since 1934

S&P earnings and dividend rank: A

W

Wachovia Corp. (WB)

Bank operating in North Carolina, South Carolina, and Georgia.

(800) 347-1246

www.wachovia.com

Optional cash payments: $20 to $15,000 monthly

Dividends paid since 1914

S&P earnings and dividend rank: A–

Wal-Mart Stores (WMT)

Largest retailer in the United States.

(800) 438-6278

www.walmart.com

Initial shares can be purchased directly from the company: $250 minimum or automatic monthly investments of at least $25.

Optional cash payments: $50 to $150,000 annually

Dividends paid since 1973

S&P earnings and dividend rank: A+

Washington Mutual (WM)

Northwest-based bank.

(800) 234-5835

www.wamu.com

Initial shares can be purchased directly from the company: $500 minimum or automatic monthly investments of at least $50 for 10 consecutive months.

Optional cash payments: $50 to $100,000 annually

Dividends paid since 1986

S&P earnings and dividend rank: A

Waste Management (WMI)

Provider of waste management services.

(800) 286-9178

www.wm.com

Initial shares can be purchased directly from the company: $500 minimum or automatic monthly investments of at least $100 for five consecutive months.

Optional cash payments: $50 to $100,000 annually

Dividends paid since 1998

S&P earnings and dividend rank: B

Wausau-Mosinee Paper Corp. (WPP)

Producer of writing and specialty papers.

(800) 509-5586

www.wausaumosinee.com

Optional cash payments: $25 to $5,000 quarterly

Dividends paid since 1960

S&P earnings and dividend rank: B

Webster Financial (WBS)

Savings bank based in Waterbury, Connecticut.

(800) 278-4353

www.websterbank.com

Optional cash payments: $100 to $10,000 quarterly

Dividends paid since 1987

S&P earnings and dividend rank: A

Weingarten10 Realty Investors (WRI)

Real estate investment trust (shopping centers).

(800) 550-4689

www.weingarten.com

Initial shares can be purchased directly from the company: $250 minimum or automatic monthly investments of at least $25 for 10 consecutive months.

Optional cash payments: $25 to $25,000 monthly

Dividends paid since 1958

S&P earnings and dividend rank: A–

Wells Fargo (WFC)

California-based bank.

(877) 840-0942

www.wellsfargo.com

Initial shares can be purchased directly from the company: $250 minimum or automatic monthly investments of at least $25 for 10 consecutive months.

Optional cash payments: $25 to $10,000 monthly

Dividends paid since 1939

S&P earnings and dividend rank: A

Wendy's International (WEN)

Operator of Wendy's and Tim Hortons fast-food restaurants.

(877) 581-8121

www.wendys-invest.com

Initial shares can be purchased directly from the company: $250 minimum or automatic monthly investments of at least $25 for 10 consecutive months.

Optional cash payments: $25 to $10,000 per transaction

Dividends paid since 1976

S&P earnings and dividend rank: A–

Westar Energy (WR)

Electric and gas utility operating in Kansas and Oklahoma.

(900) 527-2495

www.wstnres.com

Initial shares can be purchased directly from the company: $250 minimum.

Optional cash payments: $50 to $10,000 monthly

Up to 3 percent discount of reinvested dividends and optional cash payments

Dividends paid since 1924

S&P earnings and dividend rank: B

Weyerhaeuser Co. (WY)

Timber and forest products company.

(800) 561-4405

www.weyerhaeuser.com

Optional cash payments: $100 to $25,000 quarterly

Dividends paid since 1933

S&P earnings and dividend rank: B

WGL Holdings (WGL)

Gas utility operating in Washington, D.C., Virginia, and Maryland.

(800) 330-5682

www.wglholdings.com

Optional cash payments: $25 to $20,000 quarterly

Dividends paid since 1852

S&P earnings and dividend rank: B+

Whirlpool Corp. (WHR)

Major manufacturer of household appliances.

(800) 446-2617

www.whirlpoolcorp.com

Initial shares can be purchased directly from the company: $250 minimum or automatic monthly investments of at least $50 for five consecutive months.

Optional cash payments: $50 to $250,000 annually

Dividends paid since 1929

S&P earnings and dividend rank: B

Whitney Holding Corp. (WTNY)

Louisiana-based bank operating in Mississippi, Alabama, and Florida.

(877) 777-0800

www.whitneybank.com

Optional cash payments: $50 to $5,000 quarterly

Dividends paid since 1993

S&P earnings and dividend rank: B+

Wilmington Trust (WL)

Commercial bank based in Delaware.

(800) 999-9867

www.wilmingtontrust.com

Optional cash payments: $10 to $5,000 quarterly

Dividends paid since 1914

S&P earnings and dividend rank: A+

Wisconsin Energy Corp. (WEC)

Gas and electric utility serving Wisconsin and Michigan.

(800) 558-9663

www.wisconsinenergy.com

Initial shares can be purchased directly from the company: $250 minimum.

Optional cash payments: $25 to $100,000 annually

Dividends paid since 1939

S&P earnings and dividend rank: B

Woodward Governor (WGOV)

Manufacturer of fuel control systems and components for aircraft and industrial engines.

(877) 253-6843

www.woodward.com

Initial shares can be purchased directly from the company: $250 minimum or

automatic monthly investments of at least $25 for 10 consecutive months.

Optional cash payments: $25 to $10,000 per transaction

Dividends paid since 1940

S&P earnings and dividend rank: B+

Worthington Industries (WOR)

Manufacturer of processed steel and plastics.

(800) 622-6757

www.worthingtonindustries.com

Optional cash payments: $50 to $5,000 monthly

Dividends paid since 1968

S&P earnings and dividend rank: B

WPS Resources (WPS)

Gas and electric utility based in Wisconsin.

(800) 236-1551

www.wpsr.com

Initial shares can be purchased directly from the company: $100 minimum.

Optional cash payments: $25 to $100,000 annually

Dividends paid since 1940

S&P earnings and dividend rank: B+

Wrigley (William) Jr. (WWY)

World's largest producer of chewing gum.

(800) 446-2617

www.wrigley.com

Optional cash payments: $50 to $5,000 monthly

Dividends paid since 1913

S&P earnings and dividend rank: A+

Wyeth(WYE)

Manufacturer of pharmaceuticals, medical supplies, and food and agricultural products.

(800) 565-2067

www.wyeth.com

Initial shares can be purchased directly from the company: $500 minimum or automatic monthly investments of at least $50.

Optional cash payments: $50 to $120,000 annually

Dividends paid since 1919

S&P earnings and dividend rank: B

X-Y-Z

Xcel Energy (XEL)

Electric and gas utility operating in 12 western and midwestern states.

(877) 778-6786

www.xcelenergy.com

Optional cash payments: $50 to $100,000 annually

Dividends paid since 1910

S&P earnings and dividend rank: B

XTO Energy (XTO)

Oil and gas developer and producer.

(800) 938-6387

www.crosstimbers.com

Initial shares can be purchased directly from the company: $500 minimum or automatic monthly investments of at least $50 for 10 consecutive months.

Optional cash payments: $50 to $120,000 annually

Dividends paid since 1993

S&P earnings and dividend rank: B+

York International (YRK)

Manufacturer of heating, ventilating, air-conditioning, and refrigeration products.

(800) 524-4458

www.york.com

Initial shares can be purchased directly from the company: $1,000 minimum or automatic monthly investments of at least $100.

Optional cash payments: $100 to $120,000 annually

Dividends paid since 1991

S&P earnings and dividend rank: B

Yum Brands (YUM)

Owner and franchiser of KFC, Pizza Hut, and Taco Bell restaurants.

(888) 439-4986

www.yum.com

Initial shares can be purchased directly from the company: $250 minimum.

Optional cash payments: $25 to $250,000 annually

Dividends paid since 2004

S&P earnings and dividend rank: not ranked

Zions Bancorp (ZION)

Banker operating in Utah, Colorado, Nevada, and Arizona.

(801) 524-4787

www.zionsbancorporation.com

Optional cash purchases: $10 to $5,000 quarterly

Dividends paid since 1966

S&P earnings and dividend rank: A

DRIP Companies in S&P 1500 with Five-Year (2000–2005) Annual Dividend Growth Rate of at Least 6 Percent

Company	Ticker	S&P Quality Rank	Rate (%)
CBRL Group	CBRL	B+	164.43
Waste Management	WMI	B	145.24
Kinder Morgan	KMI	B	86.19
XTO Energy	XTO	B+	76.23
PepsiAmericas Inc.	PAS	B–	52.48
Pepsi Bottling Group	PBG	NR	47.88
Harley-Davidson	HDI	A+	47.29
Countrywide Financial	CFC	A–	45.47
M.D.C. Holdings	MDC	A+	41.97

Sanderson Farms	SAFM	B+	40.29
New York Community Bancorp	NYB	A–	36.26
Tyco International	TYC	B–	34.59
Independence Community Bank	ICBC	NR	33.15
Brookline Bancorp	BRKL	NR	32.94
Mattel, Inc.	MAT	B+	32.26
Cash Amer. International	CSH	B	32.06
Intel Corp.	INTC	A	31.85
Citigroup Inc.	C	A+	31.16
Anadarko Petroleum	APC	B+	30.97
Lehman Brothers Holdings	LEH	A	30.15
First American	FAF	B+	27.03
Lowe's Cos.	LOW	A+	26.82
Pier 1 Imports	PIR	A–	26.52
Equitable Resources	EQT	A–	25.46
McDonald's Corp.	MCD	A	25.36
Mylan Labs	MYL	A–	25.23
Ball Corp.	BLL	B+	24.73
Dime Community Bancshares	DCOM	NR	24.72
MacDermid, Inc.	MRD	A–	23.89
Rayonier Inc.	RYN	B+	23.46
Exelon Corp.	EXC	B+	23.36
Apache Corp.	APA	B+	22.91
AFLAC Inc.	AFL	A	22.88
Harris Corp.	HRS	B–	22.38
Legg Mason Inc.	LM	A	22.07
Baxter International	BAX	B+	21.90
Washington Mutual	WM	A	21.43
Casey's Genl Stores	CASY	A–	21.41
Home Depot	HD	A+	21.23
Investors Financial Svcs.	IFIN	A–	21.18
Wal-Mart Stores	WMT	A+	21.02
Sysco Corp.	SYY	A+	20.89
News Corp. 'A'	NWS.A	NR	20.78

Lockheed Martin	LMT	B–	20.62
Polaris Industries	PII	A–	19.99
Rollins Inc.	ROL	B+	19.49
Wendy's International	WEN	A–	19.16
Praxair Inc.	PX	A	19.05
Black & Decker Corp.	BDK	B+	19.00
Wells Fargo	WFC	A	18.57
Astoria Financial	AF	A–	18.27
Schwab (Charles) Corp.	SCH	B+	17.20
AMETEK, Inc.	AME	A–	17.17
State Street Corp.	STT	A	16.86
Commercial Federal	CFB	B+	16.69
RLI Corp.	RLI	A	16.67
Republic Bancorp	RBNC	A–	16.65
NIKE, Inc. 'B'	NKE	A	16.54
Johnson & Johnson	JNJ	A+	16.26
Owens & Minor	OMI	A–	16.25
United Technologies	UTX	A+	16.22
Tiffany & Co.	TIF	A	16.04
Pfizer, Inc.	PFE	A	15.97
Fifth Third Bancorp	FITB	A+	15.93
Limited Brands	LTD	B+	15.90
Medtronic, Inc.	MDT	B+	15.46
TCF Financial	TCB	A	15.20
Bank of Hawaii	BOH	B+	14.97
Borg Warner	BWA	B+	14.82
Old Republic International	ORI	A–	14.71
Johnson Controls	JCI	A+	14.61
Vintage Petroleum	VPI	B–	14.47
Becton, Dickinson	BDX	A	14.45
U.S. Bancorp	USB	B+	14.43
Bank of America	BAC	A–	14.31
Miller (Herman)	MLHR	B+	14.31
Manpower Inc.	MAN	B+	14.31

Green Mountain Power	GMP	B	14.15
Nucor Corp.	NUE	B	13.93
Meredith Corp	MDP	A–	13.90
Allstate Corp	ALL	B+	13.88
Anchor Bancorp Wisc	ABCW	A	13.74
Archer-Daniels-Midland	ADM	B+	13.70
First Midwest Bancorp	FMBI	A	13.70
North Fork Bancorp	NFB	A	13.33
Waddell & Reed Financial 'A'	WDR	NR	13.24
Colgate-Palmolive	CL	A+	13.18
Greater Bay Bancorp	GBBK	A–	13.11
First Bancorp	FBP	A	13.09
Vital Signs	VITL	B+	13.03
Marshall & Ilsley	MI	A	12.98
Entergy Corp.	ETR	B+	12.86
Target Corp.	TGT	A+	12.85
Everest Re Group	RE	A	12.81
PPL Corp.	PPL	B	12.79
Smucker (J.M.)	SJM	A	12.70
PepsiCo Inc.	PEP	A+	12.67
ONEOK Inc.	OKE	A–	12.47
Avon Products	AVP	A	12.45
Paychex Inc.	PAYX	A+	12.31
Commerce Bancorp	CBH	A+	12.28
Zions Bancorp	ZION	A	12.14
Cincinnati Financial	CINF	A–	12.04
Donaldson Co.	DCI	A+	11.91
Harland (John H.)	JH	B	11.87
Temple-Inland	TIN	B	11.86
Beckman Coulter	BEC	B+	11.75
Block (H&R)	HRB	A–	11.72
Northeast Utilities	NU	B	11.71
Synovus Financial	SNV	A+	11.70
Amerada Hess	AHC	B	11.68

Automatic Data Processing	ADP	A+	11.59
ConocoPhillips	COP	B	11.59
Marriott International 'A'	MAR	B+	11.54
BellSouth Corp.	BLS	A–	11.50
Knight Ridder Inc.	KRI	A–	11.50
Jefferson-Pilot	JP	A+	11.49
Superior Industries Int'l	SUP	B+	11.19
Hasbro Inc.	HAS	B	11.17
McCormick & Co.	MKC	A+	11.17
Kimberly-Clark	KMB	A	11.13
Air Products & Chemicals	APD	B+	11.07
Hershey Co.	HSY	A–	11.02
Hibernia Corp. 'A'	HIB	A	10.94
T.Rowe Price Group	TROW	A	10.90
Teleflex Inc.	TFX	A	10.87
Coca-Cola Co.	KO	B+	10.76
Provident Bankshares	PBKS	A	10.76
Procter & Gamble	PG	A	10.63
BB&T Corp.	BBT	A–	10.45
Computer Assoc. Int'l	CA	B–	10.41
Reader's Digest Assn.	RDA	B–	10.41
Burlington Northn Santa Fe	BNI	A–	10.31
South Financial Group	TSFG	B+	10.31
Darden Restaurants	DRI	A	10.30
Franklin Resources	BEN	A–	10.29
Compass Bancshares	CBSS	A+	10.25
Westamerica Bancorporation	WABC	A	10.21
Hudson United Bancorp	HU	B+	10.20
Union Pacific	UNP	B	10.15
Webster Financial	WBS	A	10.13
Regions Financial	RF	A–	10.08
Whitney Holding	WTNY	B+	9.82
Boeing Co.	BA	B+	9.80
Nature's Sunshine Products	NATR	B+	9.74

Anheuser-Busch Cos.	BUD	A+	9.59
Carnival Corp.	CCL	A+	9.57
Masco Corp.	MAS	A–	9.57
Tribune Co.	TRB	B+	9.57
Lancaster Colony	LANC	A	9.56
Walgreen Co.	WAG	A+	9.49
Dollar General	DG	A+	9.45
General Electric	GE	A+	9.28
Wrigley, (Wm) Jr	WWY	A+	9.17
American Express	AXP	A–	9.07
Int'l Business Machines	IBM	A–	9.07
Pentair, Inc.	PNR	A–	8.93
Protective Life Corp.	PL	A	8.48
Bemis Co.	BMS	A	8.46
Altria Group	MO	A+	8.29
Sovereign Bancorp	SOV	B+	8.23
Mercantile Bankshares	MRBK	A	8.22
Ingersoll-Rand 'A'	IR	A	8.20
Sara Lee Corp.	SLE	A–	8.20
Whirlpool Corp.	WHR	B	8.15
Illinois Tool Works	ITW	A+	8.06
Abbott Laboratories	ABT	A	8.05
SunTrust Banks	STI	A+	8.01
Umpqua Holdings	UMPQ	NR	8.01
Lilly (Eli)	LLY	B+	7.98
Fortune Brands	FO	B	7.86
New York Times 'A'	NYT	A–	7.85
Granite Construction	GVA	A–	7.82
Rohm & Haas	ROH	A	7.74
Sherwin-Williams	SHW	A	7.71
Libbey Inc.	LBY	B	7.68
Aqua America	WTR	A–	7.56
Cabot Corp.	CBT	B–	7.54
Curtiss-Wright	CW	A–	7.52

Entertainment Properties Trust	EPR	NR	7.30
Hillenbrand Industries	HB	B+	7.30
3M Co.	MMM	A–	7.29
Molex Inc.	MOLX	A–	7.27
Ecolab Inc.	ECL	A	7.24
Clorox Co.	CLX	A	7.23
Arch Coal	ACI	NR	7.17
Caterpillar Inc.	CAT	B+	7.16
Community Bank System	CBU	A–	7.11
Simon Property Group	SPG	B+	7.10
Eaton Corp.	ETN	B+	7.02
McGraw-Hill Companies	MHP	NR	6.98
Comerica Inc.	CMA	A	6.83
Bob Evans Farms	BOBE	A–	6.82
York International	YRK	B	6.80
Colonial BancGroup	CNB	A–	6.72
Deere & Co.	DE	B	6.71
Applied Indus. Technologies	AIT	B+	6.69
AmSouth Bancorp	ASO	A–	6.58
Corn Products Int'l	CPO	B+	6.58
SCANA Corp.	SCG	B	6.55
Avery Dennison Corp.	AVY	A	6.54
Universal Corp.	UVV	A	6.39
Essex Property Trust	ESS	A–	6.35
Archstone-Smith Trust	ASN	NR	6.20
Wilmington Trust Corp.	WL	A+	6.19
SBC Communications	SBC	B+	6.18
Vulcan Materials	VMC	A–	6.15
Chevron Corp.	CVX	B+	6.12
Albemarle Corp.	ALB	B+	6.03
ConAgra Foods	CAG	A	6.03

100 Companies with Largest Market Values in S&P 500 Index

		Ticker	Percentage	Cum. Pct.
1	General Electric	GE	3.37	3.37
2	ExxonMobil	XOM	3.36	6.73
3	Microsoft Corp.	MSFT	2.29	9.03
4	Citigroup Inc.	C	2.21	11.23
5	Pfizer Inc.	PFE	1.88	13.12
6	Johnson & Johnson	JNJ	1.77	14.89
7	Bank of America	BAC	1.68	16.58
8	Wal-Mart Stores	WMT	1.48	18.06
9	Intel Corp.	INTC	1.48	19.53
10	American Int'l Group	AIG	1.38	20.92
11	Altria Group	MO	1.23	22.15
12	Procter & Gamble	PG	1.20	23.35
13	JPMorgan Chase & Co.	JPM	1.14	24.49
14	Cisco Systems	CSCO	1.12	25.61
15	Int'l Business Machines	IBM	1.10	26.71
16	Chevron Corp.	CVX	1.08	27.79
17	Wells Fargo	WFC	0.95	28.74
18	Dell Inc.	DELL	0.88	29.62

19	Verizon Communications	VZ	0.88	30.50
20	Coca-Cola Co.	KO	0.87	31.36
21	PepsiCo Inc.	PEP	0.83	32.19
22	Home Depot	HD	0.77	32.96
23	ConocoPhillips	COP	0.74	33.70
24	SBC Communications	SBC	0.72	34.42
25	Time Warner Inc.	TWX	0.72	35.14
26	Wachovia Corp. (New)	WB	0.72	35.85
27	United Parcel Service	UPS	0.71	36.56
28	Abbott Laboratories	ABT	0.70	37.26
29	Amgen	AMGN	0.69	37.95
30	Hewlett-Packard	HPQ	0.62	38.57
31	Merck & Co.	MRK	0.62	39.19
32	Comcast Corp.	CMCSA	0.62	39.81
33	United Health Group	UNH	0.61	40.42
34	Lilly (Eli) & Co.	LLY	0.58	41.00
35	Medtronic Inc.	MDT	0.58	41.57
36	American Express	AXP	0.57	42.15
37	Wyeth	WYE	0.55	42.69
38	Tyco International	TYC	0.54	43.24
39	Oracle Corp.	ORCL	0.54	43.77
40	Morgan Stanley	MWD	0.53	44.30
41	Federal Nat'l Mortgage	FNM	0.52	44.82
42	3M Co.	MMM	0.51	45.33
43	Boeing Co.	BA	0.50	45.83
44	Qualcomm Inc.	QCOM	0.50	46.33
45	U.S. Bancorp	USB	0.49	46.82
46	United Technologies	UTX	0.48	47.30
47	Merrill Lynch	MER	0.48	47.78
48	Viacom Inc.	VIA.B	0.47	48.25
49	Disney (Walt) Co.	DIS	0.47	48.72
50	Gillette Co.	G	0.46	49.19
51	Bristol-Myers Squibb	BMY	0.45	49.64
52	BellSouth	BLS	0.45	50.08

53	Target Corp.	TGT	0.44	50.52
54	Walgreen Co.	WAG	0.43	50.96
55	News Corp.	NWS.A	0.43	51.38
56	Texas Instruments	TXN	0.43	51.81
57	Yahoo Inc.	YHOO	0.42	52.23
58	Goldman Sachs Group	GS	0.41	52.64
59	Federal Home Loan Mtg.	FRE	0.41	53.06
60	Lowe's Cos.	LOW	0.41	53.47
61	Motorola Inc.	MOT	0.41	53.88
62	Schlumberger Ltd.	SLB	0.41	54.29
63	DuPont (E.I.)	DD	0.39	54.69
64	Dow Chemical	DOW	0.39	55.08
65	WellPoint Inc.	WLP	0.39	55.47
66	eBay Inc.	EBAY	0.37	55.84
67	Allstate Corp.	ALL	0.37	56.21
68	Sprint Corp.	FON	0.34	56.55
69	Nextel Communications	NXTL	0.33	56.88
70	Washington Mutual	WM	0.33	57.21
71	Anheuser-Busch	BUD	0.33	57.53
72	McDonald's Corp.	MCD	0.32	57.86
73	Exelon Corp.	EXC	0.32	58.17
74	Prudential Financial	PRU	0.31	58.49
75	MBNA Corp.	KRB	0.30	58.79
76	MetLife Inc.	MET	0.30	59.09
77	EMC Corp.	EMC	0.30	59.40
78	Caterpillar Inc.	CAT	0.30	59.70
79	First Data	FDC	0.29	59.98
80	Honeywell Int'l Inc.	HON	0.29	60.27
81	Occidental Petroleum	OXY	0.28	60.55
82	Apple Computer	AAPL	0.28	60.83
83	Kimberly-Clark	KMB	0.27	61.10
84	Carnival Corp.	CCL	0.26	61.37
85	Schering-Plough	SGP	0.26	61.63
86	Duke Energy	DUK	0.25	61.88

87	Lehman Bros.	LEH	0.25	62.13
88	St. Paul Travelers Cos.	STA	0.24	62.38
89	Applied Materials	AMAT	0.24	62.62
90	Lockheed Martin	LMT	0.24	62.86
91	Colgate-Palmolive	CL	0.24	63.10
92	Emerson Electric	EMR	0.24	63.34
93	Southern Co.	SO	0.24	63.58
94	Dominion Resources	D	0.23	63.81
95	Cardinal Health	CAH	0.23	64.03
96	SunTrust Banks	STI	0.23	64.26
97	Automatic Data Process.	ADP	0.22	64.48
98	FedEx Corp.	FDX	0.22	64.71
99	Halliburton Co.	HAL	0.22	64.93
100	Corning Inc.	GLW	0.22	65.15

Index

About the Author

Formerly the managing editor of Standard & Poor's investment advisory newsletter, *The Outlook*, Joseph Tigue retired in early 2003 after nearly 25 years with the company. He is coauthor of *The Dividend Rich Investor*, which was picked as one of the best books of its kind in print by *The New York Review of Books*. He is also the author of *The Standard & Poor's Guide to Long-Term Investing*.

Tigue has been widely quoted on the stock market in newspapers around the nation and has frequently appeared on television, including CNBC, CNN, PBS, and NBC. He is a graduate of New York University. He was born in Pittston, PA, and raised in Waterbury CT. He and his wife of 45 years live on Long Island. They are the proud parents of three daughters and are blessed with three grandchildren.